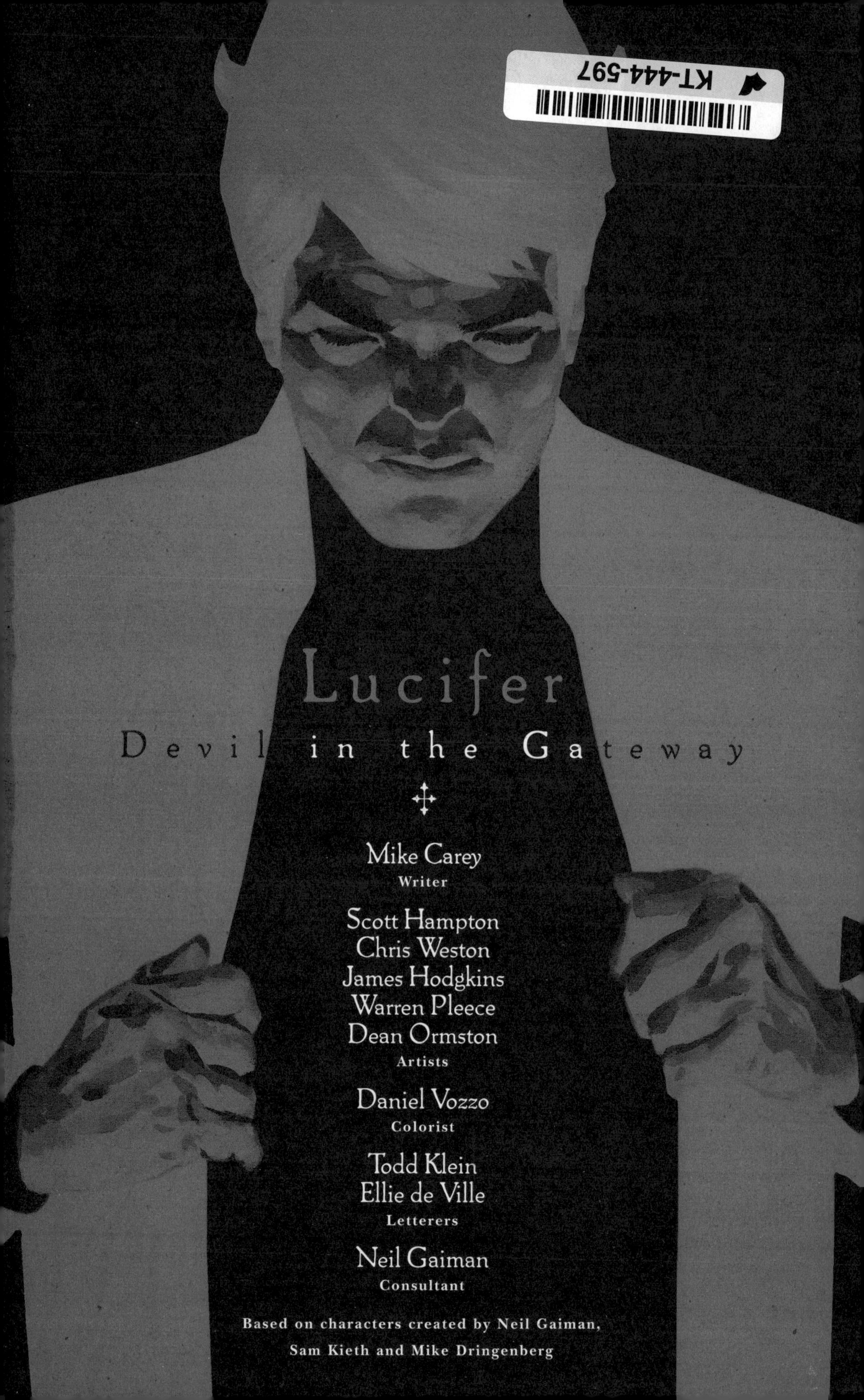

Lucifer

Devil in the Gateway

Mike Carey
Writer

Scott Hampton
Chris Weston
James Hodgkins
Warren Pleece
Dean Ormston
Artists

Daniel Vozzo
Colorist

Todd Klein
Ellie de Ville
Letterers

Neil Gaiman
Consultant

Based on characters created by Neil Gaiman, Sam Kieth and Mike Dringenberg

LUCIFER: DEVIL IN THE GATEWAY

Published by DC Comics. Cover, foreword and compilation
copyright © 2001 DC Comics. All Rights Reserved.

Originally published in single magazine form as
THE SANDMAN PRESENTS: LUCIFER 1-3 and
LUCIFER 1-4. Copyright © 1999, 2000 DC Comics.
All Rights Reserved.

DC Comics, 1700 Broadway, New York, NY 10019
A Warner Bros. Entertainment Company
Printed in Canada. Third Printing.
ISBN: 1-56389-733-4

Collection cover composited from covers for LUCIFER 2 and 4,
originally painted by Duncan Fegredo

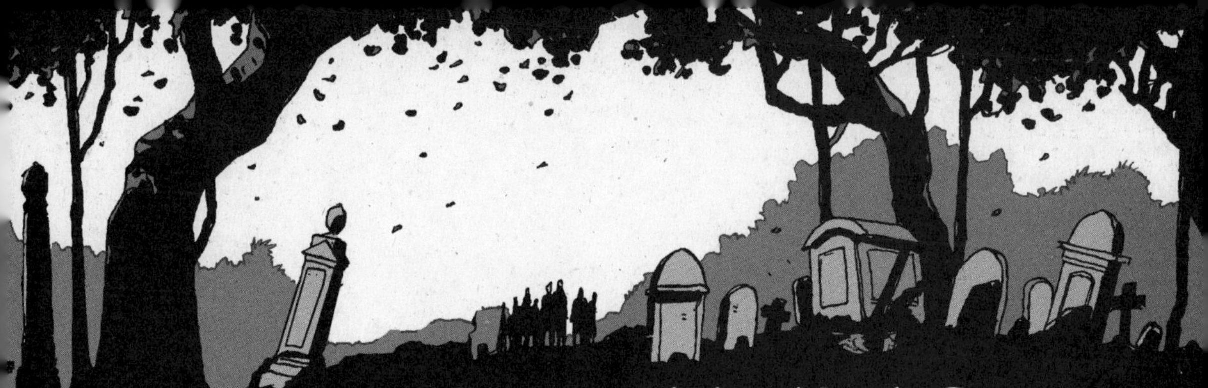

Foreword by Neil Gaiman

Writing Lucifer was never hard, not in the way that some other writing was hard. His stories, and his alone, would turn up in my head with beginnings, and middles, and ends. Of all the hundreds of characters in THE SANDMAN, he, above all, had his own agenda from the moment he first came on stage.

I took him, or went with him, on his journey from ruler of Hell in THE SANDMAN #4 (there was a nominal triumvirate in charge at the time, imposed by DC's head office, but you always knew which member of the triumvirate called the shots); to his resignation in the "Season of Mists" story — during the course of which he closed Hell, quit, kissed Mazikeen goodbye, and had his wings cut off; and from there to a nightclub called Lux, where he played cocktail piano and watched everyone else's problems with amused disdain.

He might only have been a supporting character in the SANDMAN story, but there was no doubt in my mind that he was a star.

Lucifer needed his own comic. It seemed obvious, at least to me. He was arrogant, funny, manipulative, cold, brilliant, powerful, and the former Lord of Hell, who resigned because he was done. Heaven wouldn't trust him, Hell would hate him, but anyone who needed a dirty job done would approach Lucifer to do it. (That would have been my approach, anyway.)

Sometime in 1991 I had a meeting in a hotel room with a writer who wanted to write something for VERTIGO. He asked me if there was any character I'd suggest pitching to the powers that be at VERTIGO as a spinoff series.

"Lucifer," I said.

He looked doubtful. I tried to reassure him by explaining what kind of comic it could be, invoking everything from the Kabala to Hannibal Heyes and Kid Curry in *Alias Smith and Jones* ("I sure wish the governor would let a few more people in on our secret!"), and at the end of our conversation he looked no less doubtful than he had looked at the start.

"Anybody else?" he said.

It was a question I slowly grew used to as the decade continued. "Who'd make a good spinoff character?"

"Lucifer," I'd say.

And, like the writer in the hotel room, they'd say, "Anyone else?" I think they were mostly worried that a comic starring the Devil (even a Devil who had got bored, and tired, and resigned) might lead somebody to burn down the DC offices. This was particularly true when they were located at 666 Fifth Avenue.

And anyway, to tell good Lucifer stories, we would need a good writer.

In this case, a writer named Mike Carey. Who got it, without needing it to be explained. Mike Carey's Lucifer is even more manipulative, charming and dangerous than I could have hoped. The supporting cast are real people, living and dead, in a real world. Carey's stories are elegantly told, solidly written (for my money, he's easily one of the half-dozen best writers of mainstream comics, and climbing), and they are good comics. Which, like the people in them, are going somewhere.

His collaborators are doing an excellent job of picturing Mike's world.

I still expect the success of Lucifer to prompt someone with more convictions than sense to attempt to burn down the DC offices. Until they do, I shall keep reading.

— Neil Gaiman
The Ice Hotel, Québec
February 2001

The Morningstar Option

Mike Carey
Writer

Scott Hampton
Artist

Todd Klein
Letterer

Jennifer Lee
Assistant Editor

Alisa Kwitney
Editor

Neil Gaiman
Consultant

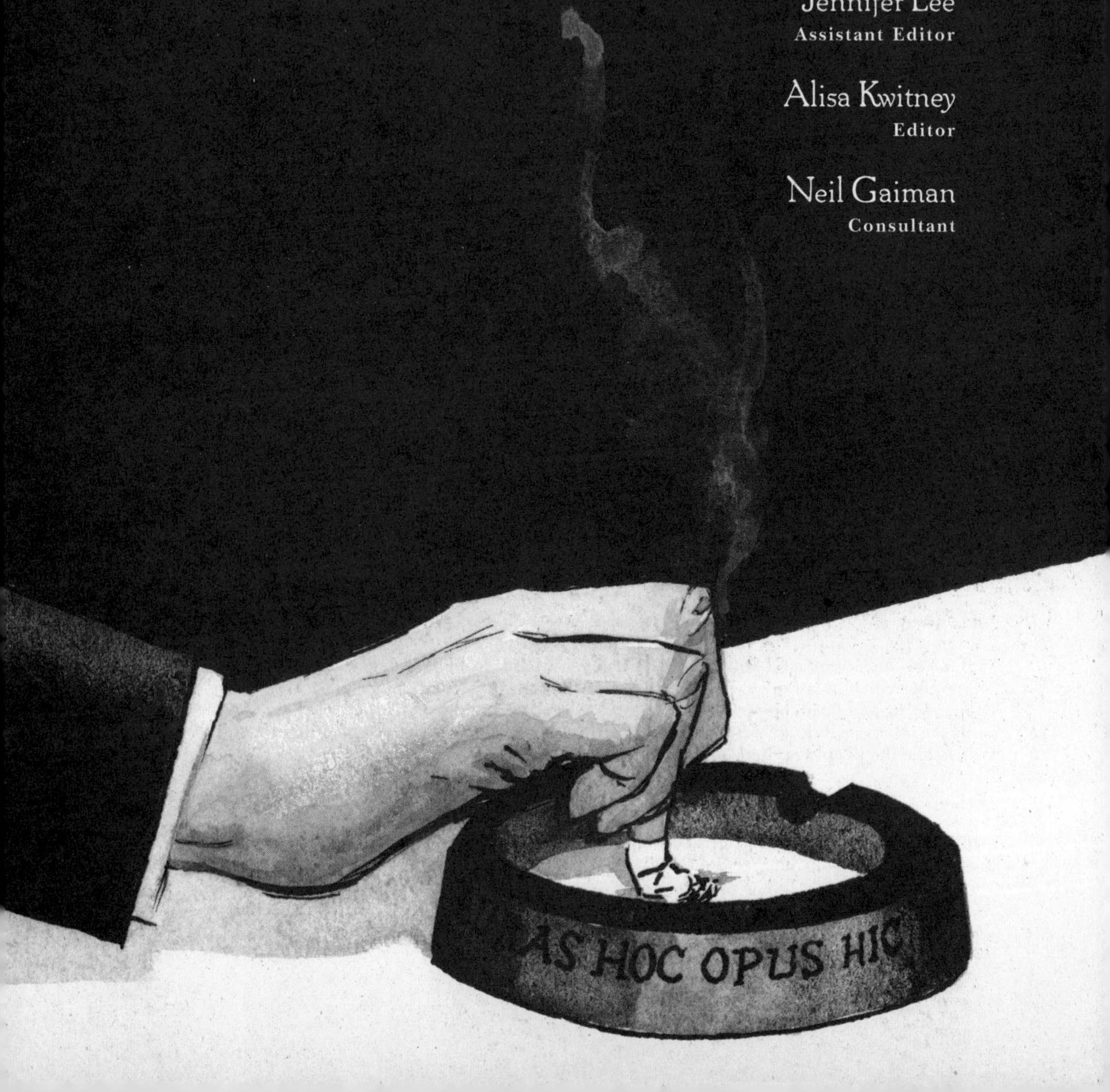
HOC OPUS

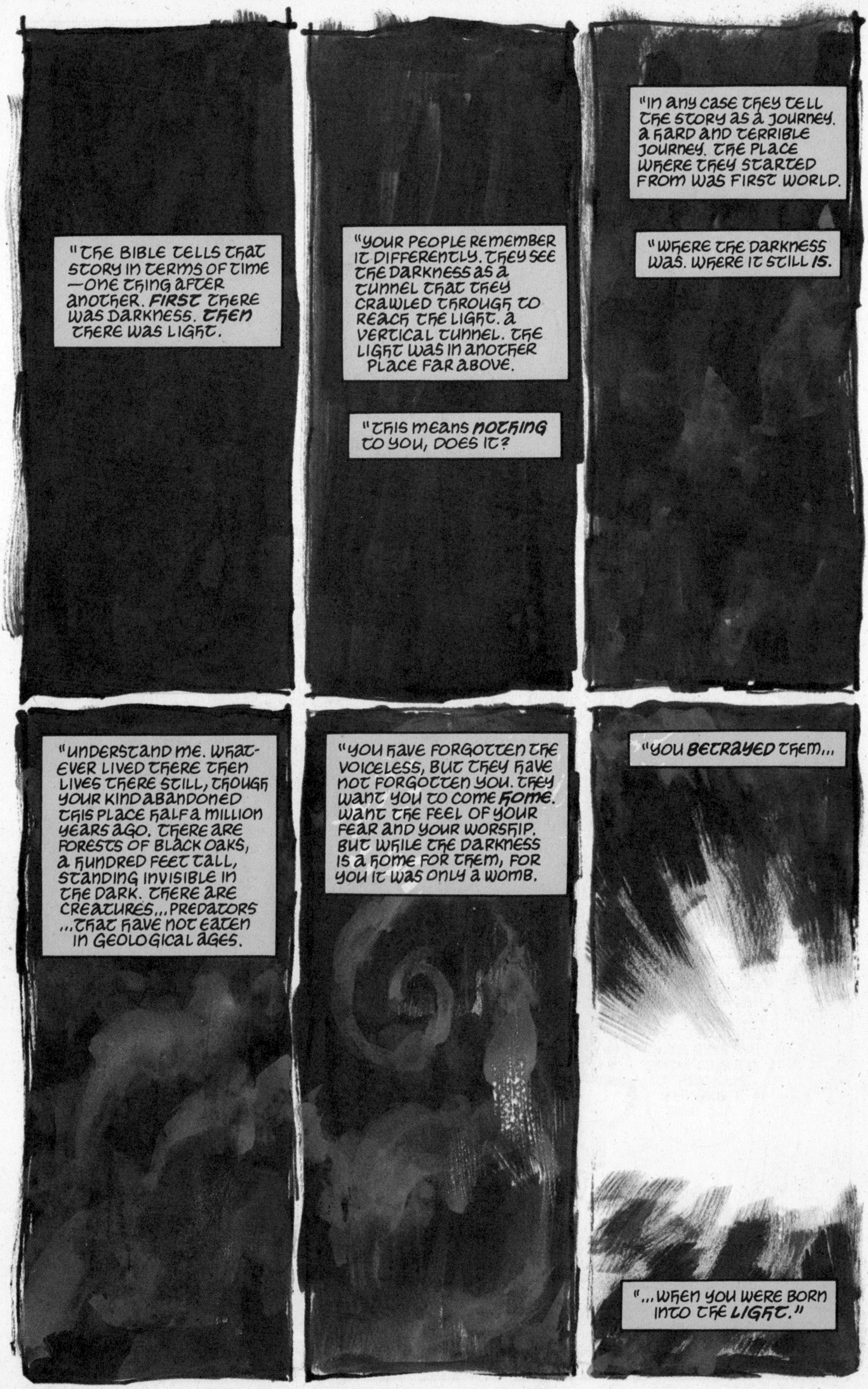
"THE BIBLE TELLS THAT STORY IN TERMS OF TIME —ONE THING AFTER ANOTHER. FIRST THERE WAS DARKNESS. THEN THERE WAS LIGHT.
"YOUR PEOPLE REMEMBER IT DIFFERENTLY. THEY SEE THE DARKNESS AS A TUNNEL THAT THEY CRAWLED THROUGH TO REACH THE LIGHT. A VERTICAL TUNNEL. THE LIGHT WAS IN ANOTHER PLACE FAR ABOVE.
"THIS MEANS NOTHING TO YOU, DOES IT?
"IN ANY CASE THEY TELL THE STORY AS A JOURNEY. A HARD AND TERRIBLE JOURNEY. THE PLACE WHERE THEY STARTED FROM WAS FIRST WORLD.
"WHERE THE DARKNESS WAS. WHERE IT STILL IS.
"UNDERSTAND ME. WHATEVER LIVED THERE THEN LIVES THERE STILL, THOUGH YOUR KIND ABANDONED THIS PLACE HALF A MILLION YEARS AGO. THERE ARE FORESTS OF BLACK OAKS, A HUNDRED FEET TALL, STANDING INVISIBLE IN THE DARK. THERE ARE CREATURES... PREDATORS ...THAT HAVE NOT EATEN IN GEOLOGICAL AGES.
"YOU HAVE FORGOTTEN THE VOICELESS, BUT THEY HAVE NOT FORGOTTEN YOU. THEY WANT YOU TO COME HOME. WANT THE FEEL OF YOUR FEAR AND YOUR WORSHIP. BUT WHILE THE DARKNESS IS A HOME FOR THEM, FOR YOU IT WAS ONLY A WOMB.
"YOU BETRAYED THEM...
"...WHEN YOU WERE BORN INTO THE LIGHT."

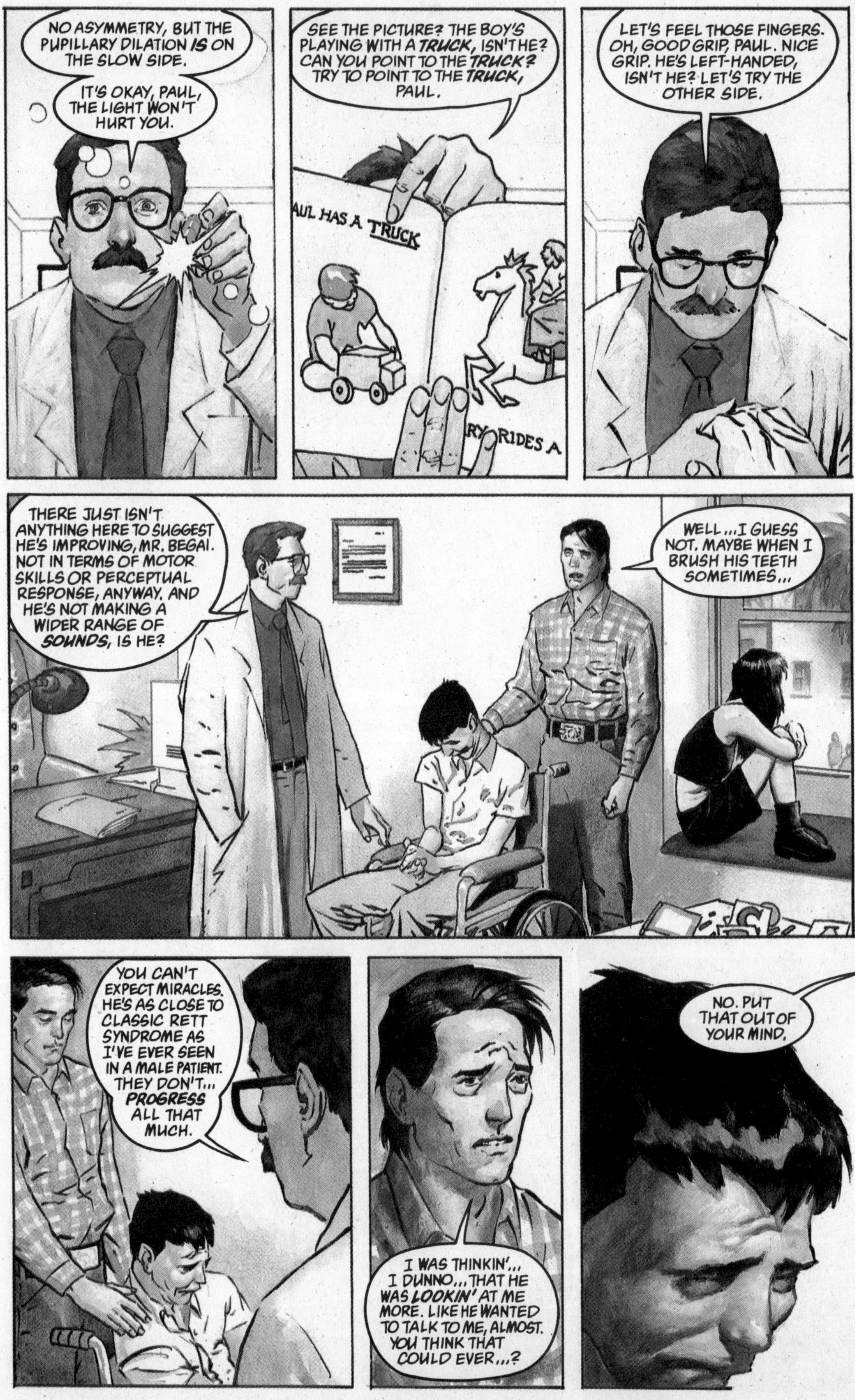
NO ASYMMETRY, BUT THE PUPILLARY DILATION IS ON THE SLOW SIDE.
IT'S OKAY, PAUL, THE LIGHT WON'T HURT YOU.
SEE THE PICTURE? THE BOY'S PLAYING WITH A TRUCK, ISN'T HE? CAN YOU POINT TO THE TRUCK? TRY TO POINT TO THE TRUCK, PAUL.
AUL HAS A TRUCK
RY RIDES A
LET'S FEEL THOSE FINGERS. OH, GOOD GRIP, PAUL. NICE GRIP. HE'S LEFT-HANDED, ISN'T HE? LET'S TRY THE OTHER SIDE.
THERE JUST ISN'T ANYTHING HERE TO SUGGEST HE'S IMPROVING, MR. BEGAI. NOT IN TERMS OF MOTOR SKILLS OR PERCEPTUAL RESPONSE, ANYWAY. AND HE'S NOT MAKING A WIDER RANGE OF SOUNDS, IS HE?
WELL... I GUESS NOT. MAYBE WHEN I BRUSH HIS TEETH SOMETIMES...
YOU CAN'T EXPECT MIRACLES. HE'S AS CLOSE TO CLASSIC RETT SYNDROME AS I'VE EVER SEEN IN A MALE PATIENT. THEY DON'T... PROGRESS ALL THAT MUCH.
I WAS THINKIN'... I DUNNO... THAT HE WAS LOOKIN' AT ME MORE. LIKE HE WANTED TO TALK TO ME, ALMOST. YOU THINK THAT COULD EVER...?
NO. PUT THAT OUT OF YOUR MIND.

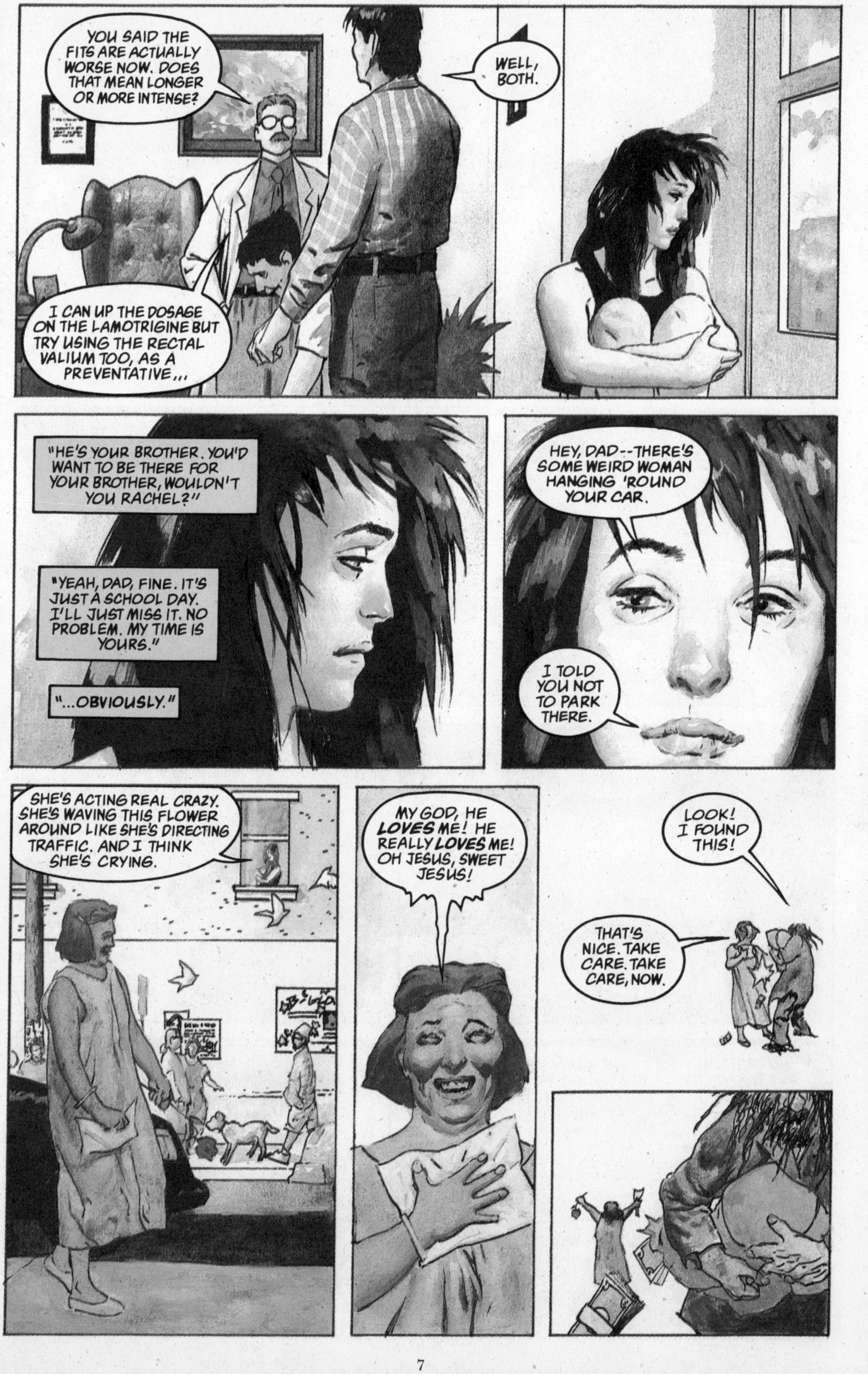
YOU SAID THE FITS ARE ACTUALLY WORSE NOW. DOES THAT MEAN LONGER OR MORE INTENSE?
WELL, BOTH.
I CAN UP THE DOSAGE ON THE LAMOTRIGINE BUT TRY USING THE RECTAL VALIUM TOO, AS A PREVENTATIVE...
"HE'S YOUR BROTHER. YOU'D WANT TO BE THERE FOR YOUR BROTHER, WOULDN'T YOU RACHEL?"
"YEAH, DAD, FINE. IT'S JUST A SCHOOL DAY. I'LL JUST MISS IT. NO PROBLEM. MY TIME IS YOURS."
"...OBVIOUSLY."
HEY, DAD--THERE'S SOME WEIRD WOMAN HANGING 'ROUND YOUR CAR.
I TOLD YOU NOT TO PARK THERE.
SHE'S ACTING REAL CRAZY. SHE'S WAVING THIS FLOWER AROUND LIKE SHE'S DIRECTING TRAFFIC. AND I THINK SHE'S CRYING.
MY GOD, HE **LOVES** ME! HE REALLY **LOVES** ME! OH JESUS, SWEET JESUS!
LOOK! I FOUND THIS!
THAT'S NICE. TAKE CARE. TAKE CARE, NOW.

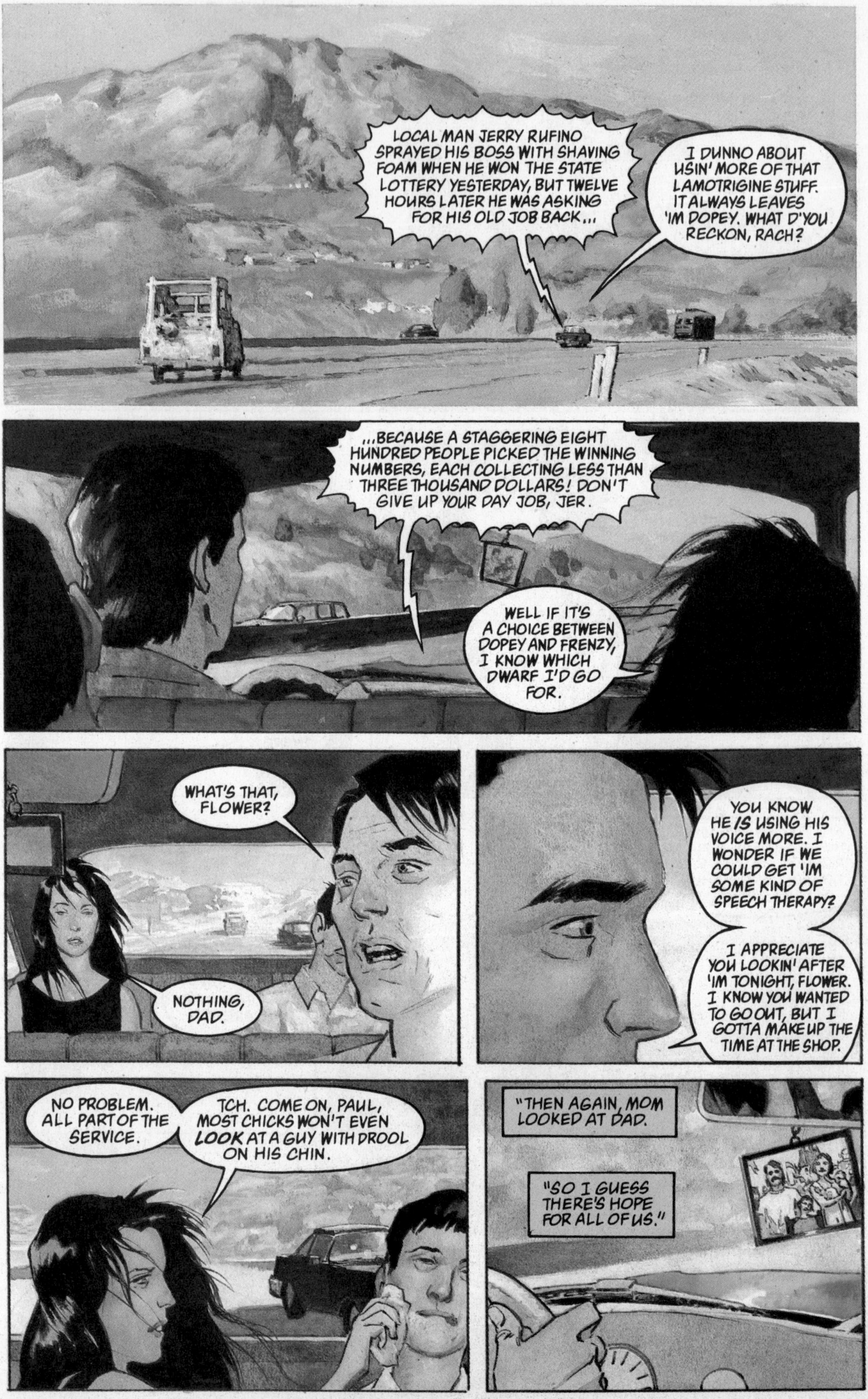
LOCAL MAN JERRY RUFINO SPRAYED HIS BOSS WITH SHAVING FOAM WHEN HE WON THE STATE LOTTERY YESTERDAY, BUT TWELVE HOURS LATER HE WAS ASKING FOR HIS OLD JOB BACK...
I DUNNO ABOUT USIN' MORE OF THAT LAMOTRIGINE STUFF. IT ALWAYS LEAVES 'IM DOPEY. WHAT D'YOU RECKON, RACH?
...BECAUSE A STAGGERING EIGHT HUNDRED PEOPLE PICKED THE WINNING NUMBERS, EACH COLLECTING LESS THAN THREE THOUSAND DOLLARS! DON'T GIVE UP YOUR DAY JOB, JER.
WELL IF IT'S A CHOICE BETWEEN DOPEY AND FRENZY, I KNOW WHICH DWARF I'D GO FOR.
WHAT'S THAT, FLOWER?
NOTHING, DAD.
YOU KNOW HE *IS* USING HIS VOICE MORE. I WONDER IF WE COULD GET 'IM SOME KIND OF SPEECH THERAPY?
I APPRECIATE YOU LOOKIN' AFTER 'IM TONIGHT, FLOWER. I KNOW YOU WANTED TO GO OUT, BUT I GOTTA MAKE UP THE TIME AT THE SHOP.
NO PROBLEM. ALL PART OF THE SERVICE.
TCH. COME ON, PAUL, MOST CHICKS WON'T EVEN *LOOK* AT A GUY WITH DROOL ON HIS CHIN.
"THEN AGAIN, MOM LOOKED AT DAD.
"SO I GUESS THERE'S HOPE FOR ALL OF US."

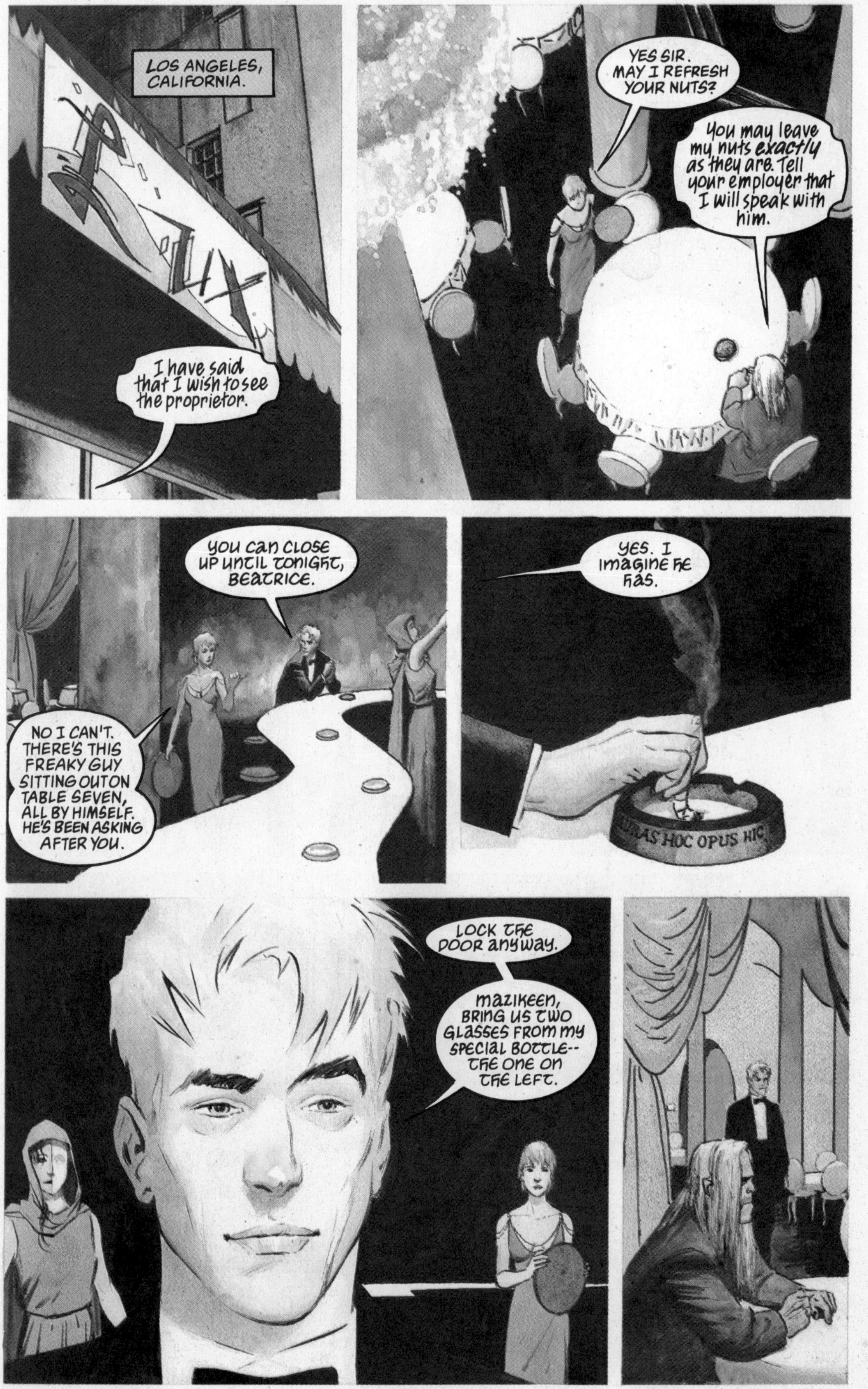
LOS ANGELES, CALIFORNIA.
I have said that I wish to see the proprietor.
YES SIR. MAY I REFRESH YOUR NUTS?
You may leave my nuts exactly as they are. Tell your employer that I will speak with him.
YOU CAN CLOSE UP UNTIL TONIGHT, BEATRICE.
NO I CAN'T. THERE'S THIS FREAKY GUY SITTING OUT ON TABLE SEVEN, ALL BY HIMSELF. HE'S BEEN ASKING AFTER YOU.
YES. I IMAGINE HE HAS.
...URAS HOC OPUS HIC...
LOCK THE DOOR ANYWAY.
MAZIKEEN, BRING US TWO GLASSES FROM MY SPECIAL BOTTLE-- THE ONE ON THE LEFT.

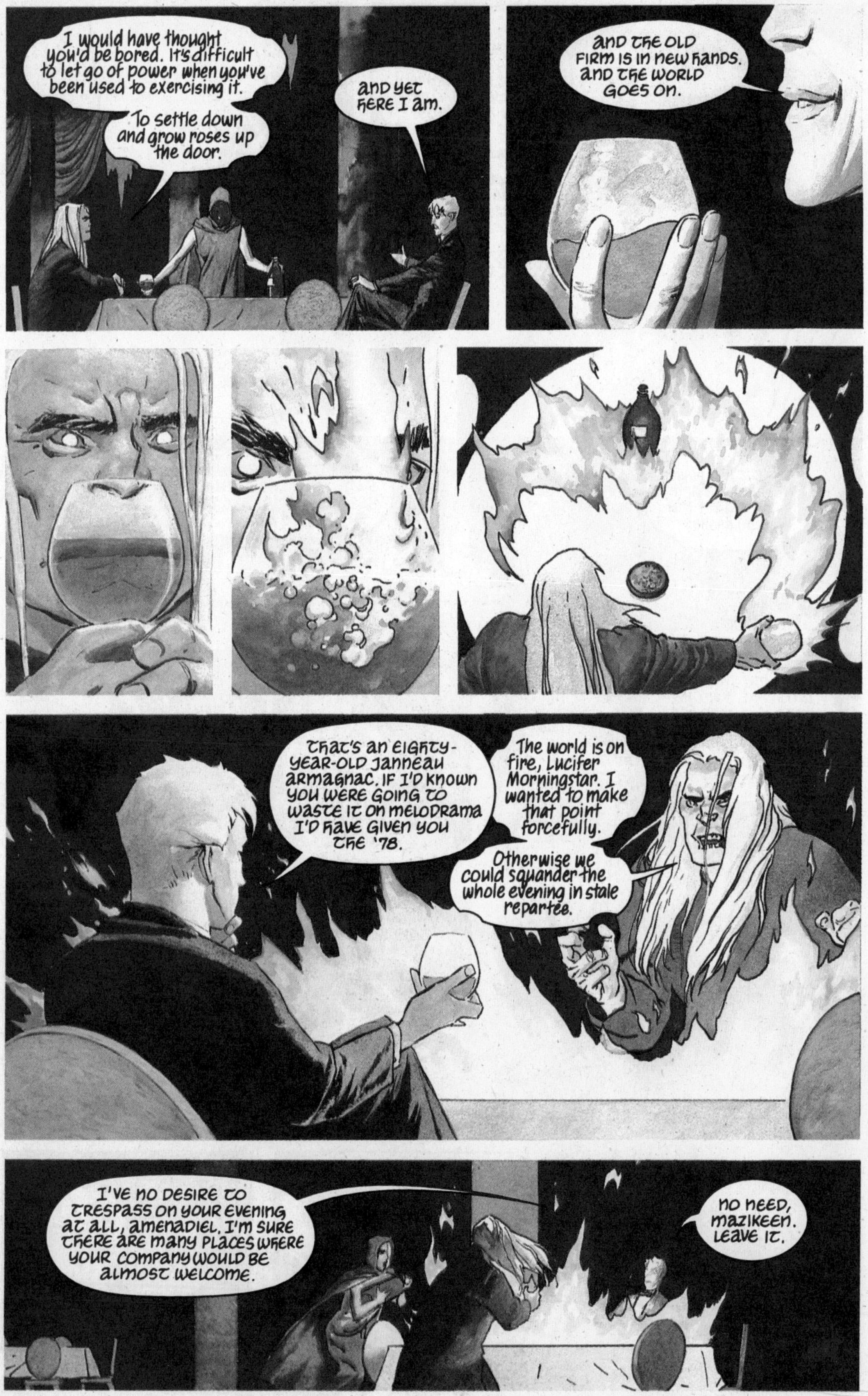
I would have thought you'd be bored. It's difficult to let go of power when you've been used to exercising it.
To settle down and grow roses up the door.
and yet here I am.
and the old firm is in new hands. and the world goes on.
That's an eighty-year-old Janneau armagnac. If I'd known you were going to waste it on melodrama I'd have given you the '78.
The world is on fire, Lucifer Morningstar. I wanted to make that point forcefully.
Otherwise we could squander the whole evening in stale repartee.
I've no desire to trespass on your evening at all, Amenadiel. I'm sure there are many places where your company would be almost welcome.
no need, Mazikeen. leave it.

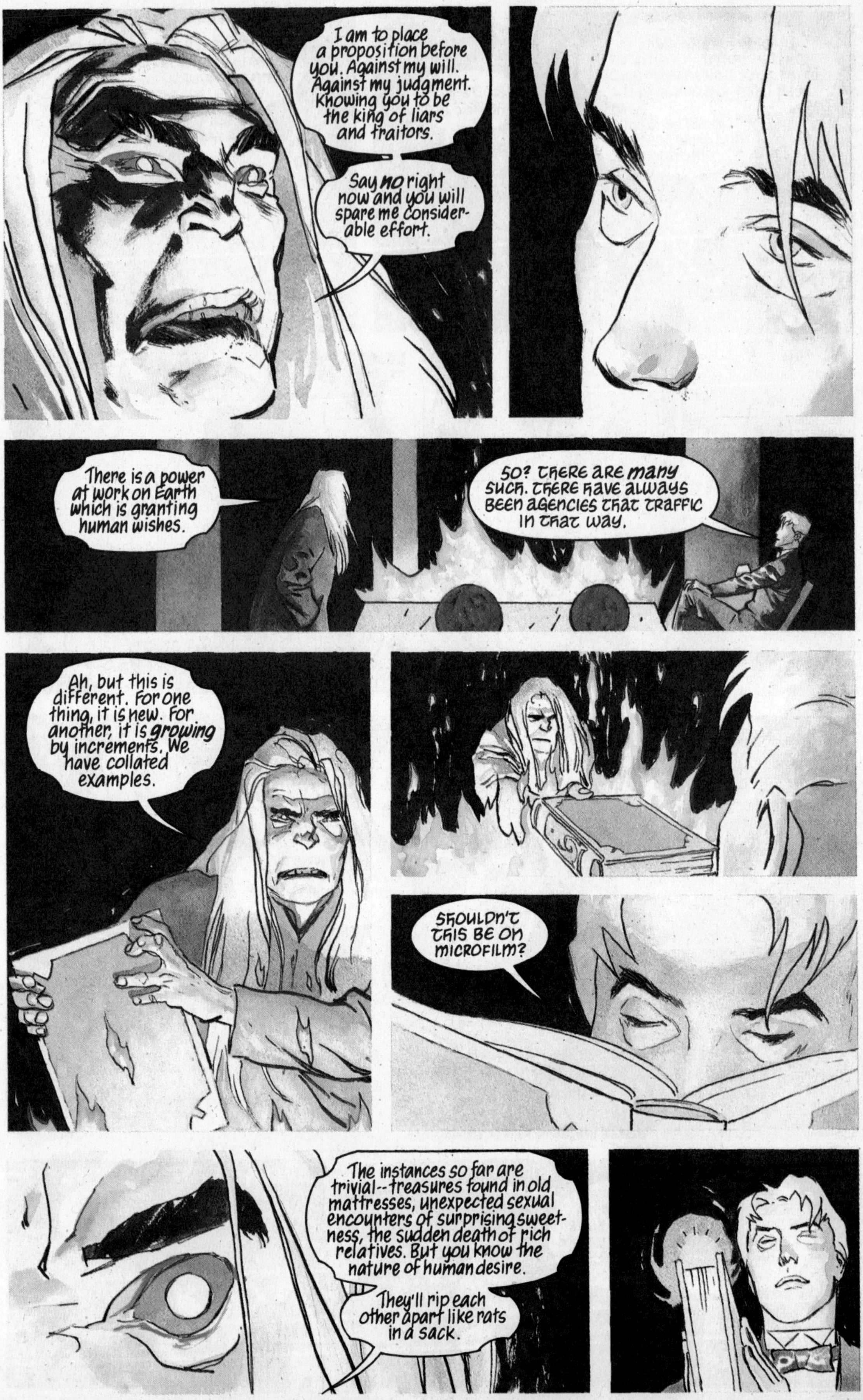
I am to place a proposition before you. Against my will. Against my judgment. Knowing you to be the king of liars and traitors.
Say NO right now and you will spare me considerable effort.
There is a power at work on Earth which is granting human wishes.
SO? THERE ARE MANY SUCH. THERE HAVE ALWAYS BEEN AGENCIES THAT TRAFFIC IN THAT WAY.
Ah, but this is different. For one thing, it is new. For another, it is growing by increments. We have collated examples.
SHOULDN'T THIS BE ON MICROFILM?
The instances so far are trivial--treasures found in old mattresses, unexpected sexual encounters of surprising sweetness, the sudden death of rich relatives. But you know the nature of human desire.
They'll rip each other apart like rats in a sack.

WHY ME?

Because heaven wishes neither to intervene directly in this nor to stand by and let it happen.

You represent a third option. I am told that you will name your price.

That I MAY name my PRICE OR that I WILL name it?

Will.

YOU'D THINK PART OF OMNISCIENCE WOULD BE KNOWING WHEN TO STOP.

BUT STILL...

LIVING HERE AMONG THEM-- WATCHING THEM LIVE AND DIE AND BUILD AND BREAK--YOU CAN'T HELP BUT THINK ABOUT HOW IMPERMANENT EVERYTHING IS IN THIS UNIVERSE. NOTHING REALLY WORKMAN-LIKE. NOTHING MADE TO LAST.

A LETTER OF PASSAGE.

Your pardon?

SAY THAT MY PRICE IS A LETTER OF PASSAGE.

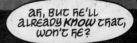

AH, BUT HE'LL ALREADY KNOW THAT, WON'T HE?

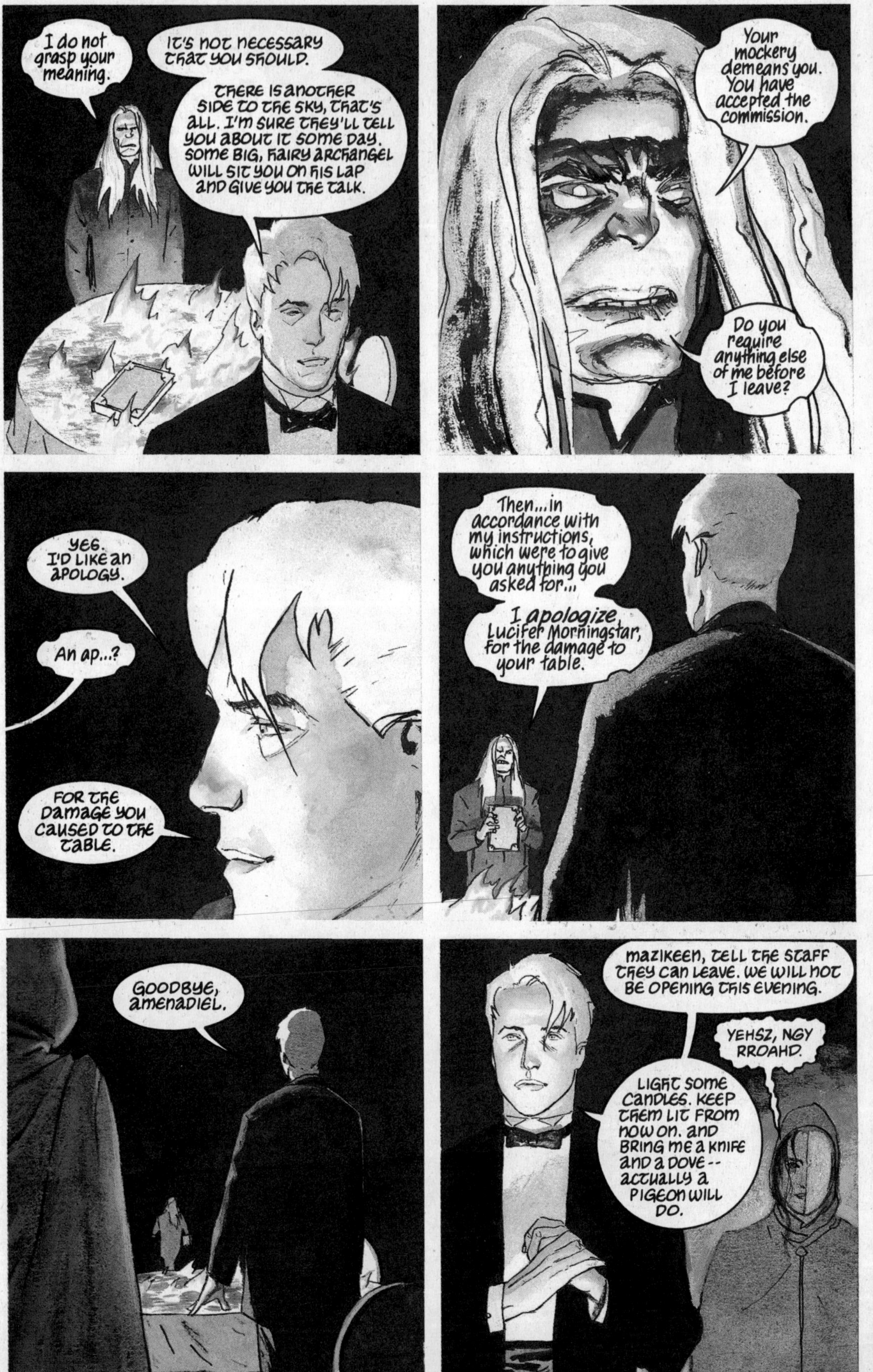
I do not grasp your meaning.
IT'S NOT NECESSARY THAT YOU SHOULD.
THERE IS ANOTHER SIDE TO THE SKY, THAT'S ALL. I'M SURE THEY'LL TELL YOU ABOUT IT SOME DAY. SOME BIG, HAIRY ARCHANGEL WILL SIT YOU ON HIS LAP AND GIVE YOU THE TALK.
Your mockery demeans you. You have accepted the commission.
Do you require anything else of me before I leave?
YES. I'D LIKE AN APOLOGY.
An ap...?
FOR THE DAMAGE YOU CAUSED TO THE TABLE.
Then... in accordance with my instructions, which were to give you anything you asked for...
I *apologize*, Lucifer Morningstar, for the damage to your table.
GOODBYE, AMENADIEL.
MAZIKEEN, TELL THE STAFF THEY CAN LEAVE. WE WILL NOT BE OPENING THIS EVENING.
YEHSZ, NGY RROAHD.
LIGHT SOME CANDLES. KEEP THEM LIT FROM NOW ON. AND BRING ME A KNIFE AND A DOVE -- ACTUALLY A PIGEON WILL DO.

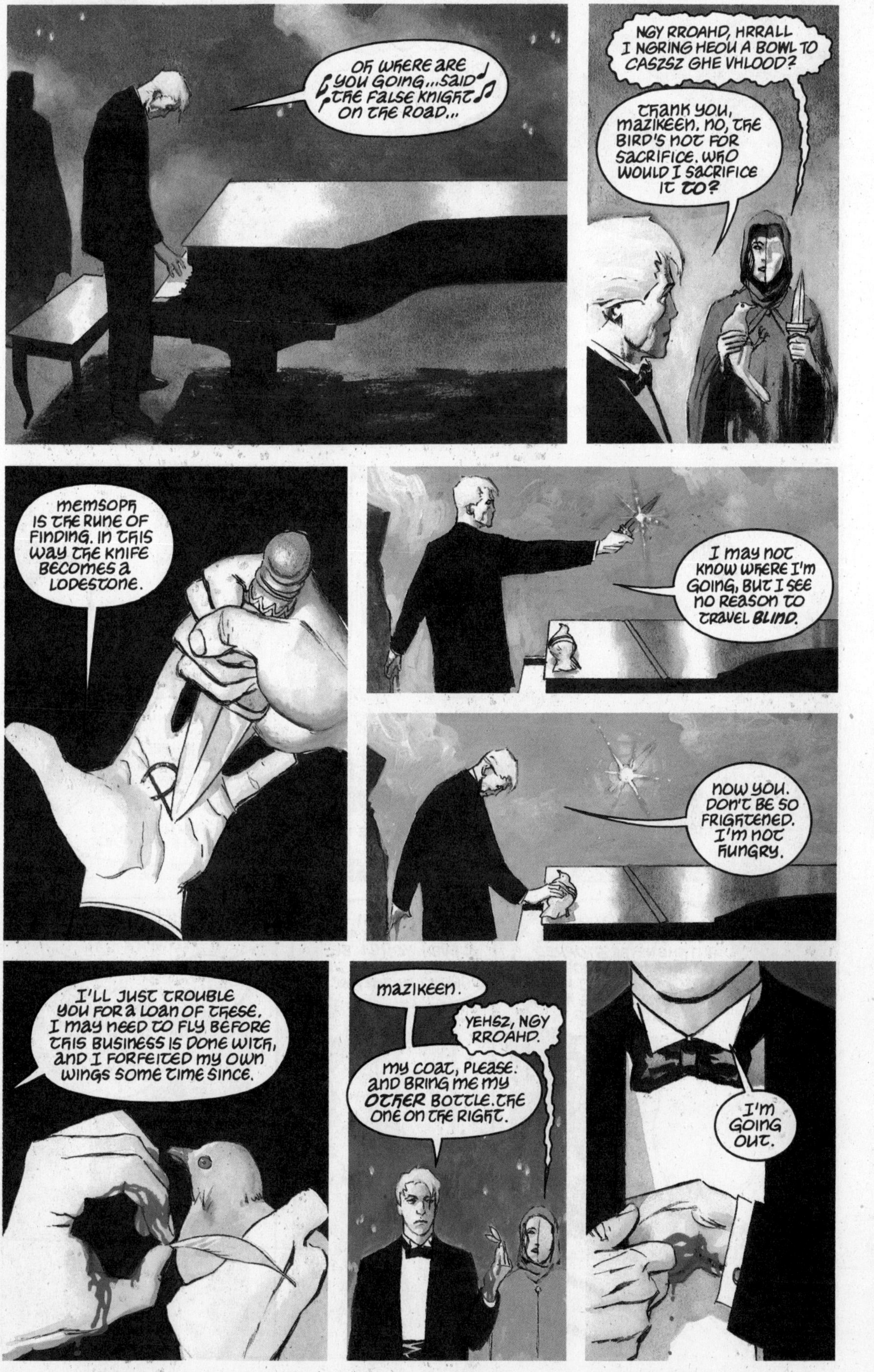
OH WHERE ARE YOU GOING...SAID THE FALSE KNIGHT ON THE ROAD...
NGY RROAHD, HRRALL I NGRING HEOU A BOWL TO CASZSZ GHE VHLOOD?
THANK YOU, MAZIKEEN. NO, THE BIRD'S NOT FOR SACRIFICE. WHO WOULD I SACRIFICE IT TO?
MEMSOPH IS THE RUNE OF FINDING. IN THIS WAY THE KNIFE BECOMES A LODESTONE.
I MAY NOT KNOW WHERE I'M GOING, BUT I SEE NO REASON TO TRAVEL BLIND.
NOW YOU. DON'T BE SO FRIGHTENED. I'M NOT HUNGRY.
I'LL JUST TROUBLE YOU FOR A LOAN OF THESE. I MAY NEED TO FLY BEFORE THIS BUSINESS IS DONE WITH, AND I FORFEITED MY OWN WINGS SOME TIME SINCE.
MAZIKEEN.
YEHSZ, NGY RROAHD.
MY COAT, PLEASE. AND BRING ME MY OTHER BOTTLE. THE ONE ON THE RIGHT.
I'M GOING OUT.

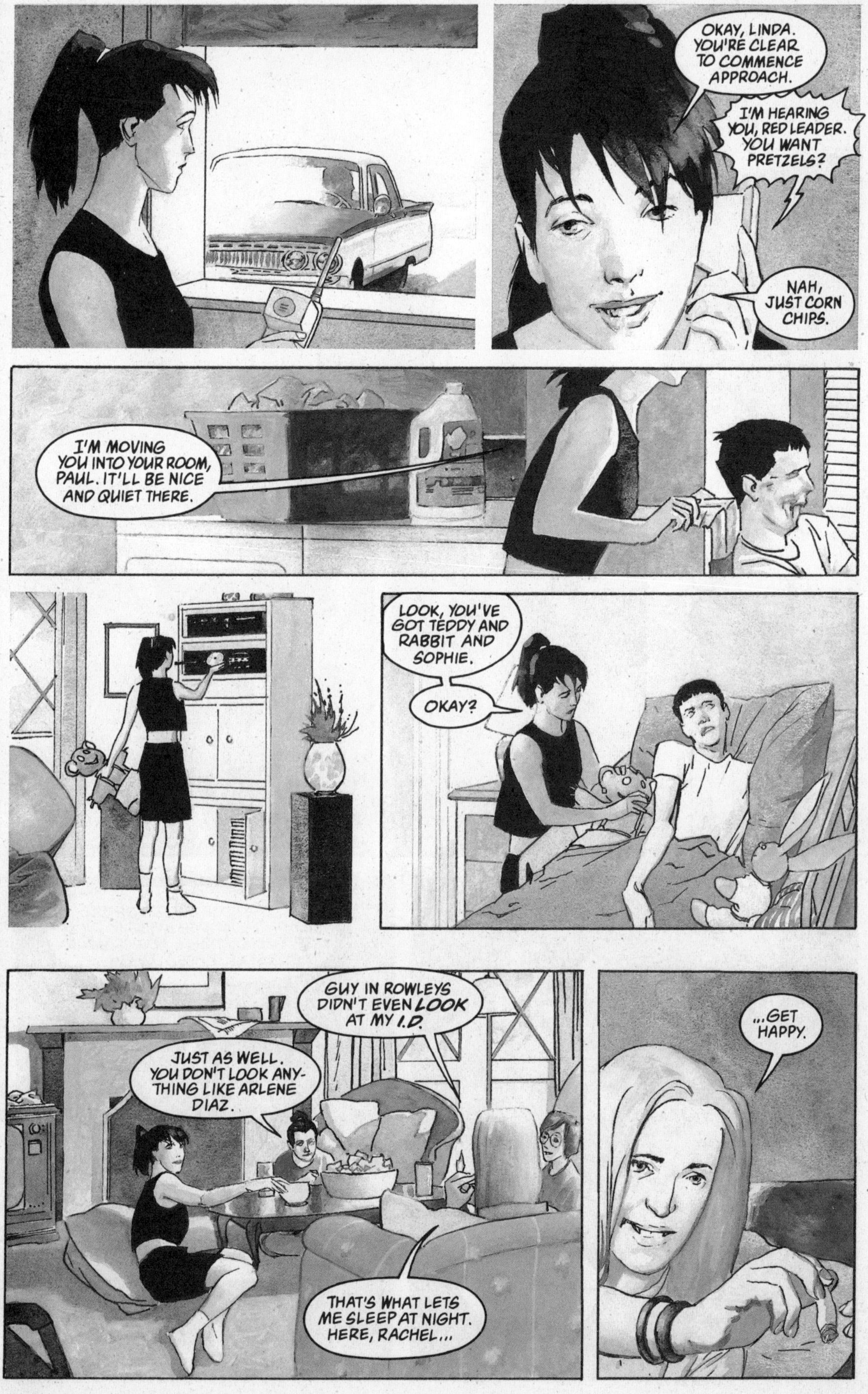
OKAY, LINDA. YOU'RE CLEAR TO COMMENCE APPROACH.
I'M HEARING YOU, RED LEADER. YOU WANT PRETZELS?
NAH, JUST CORN CHIPS.
I'M MOVING YOU INTO YOUR ROOM, PAUL. IT'LL BE NICE AND QUIET THERE.
LOOK, YOU'VE GOT TEDDY AND RABBIT AND SOPHIE.
OKAY?
GUY IN ROWLEYS DIDN'T EVEN LOOK AT MY I.D.
JUST AS WELL. YOU DON'T LOOK ANYTHING LIKE ARLENE DIAZ.
THAT'S WHAT LETS ME SLEEP AT NIGHT. HERE, RACHEL...
...GET HAPPY.

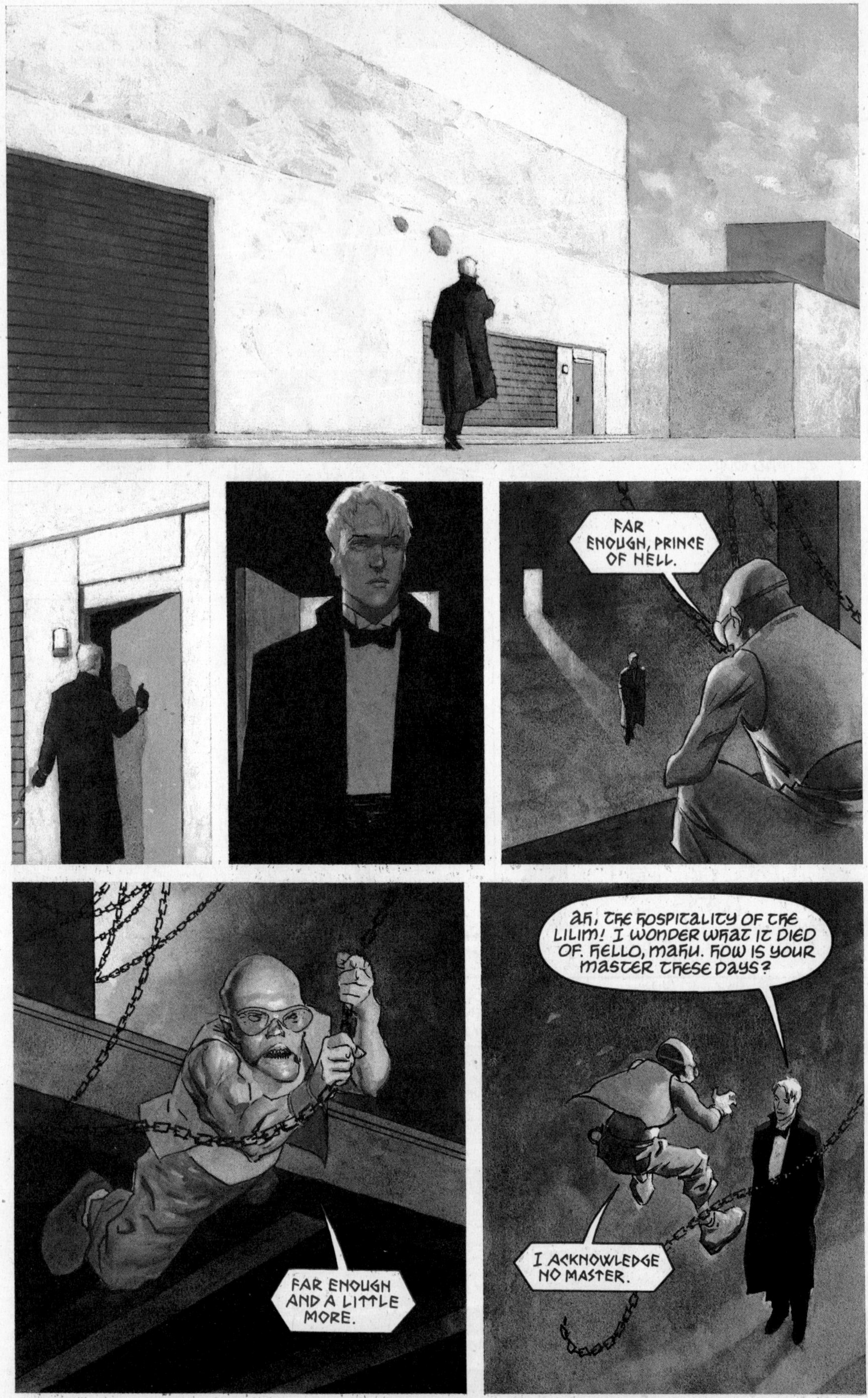

FAR ENOUGH, PRINCE OF HELL.
FAR ENOUGH AND A LITTLE MORE.
AH, THE HOSPITALITY OF THE LILIM! I WONDER WHAT IT DIED OF. HELLO, MAHU. HOW IS YOUR MASTER THESE DAYS?
I ACKNOWLEDGE NO MASTER.

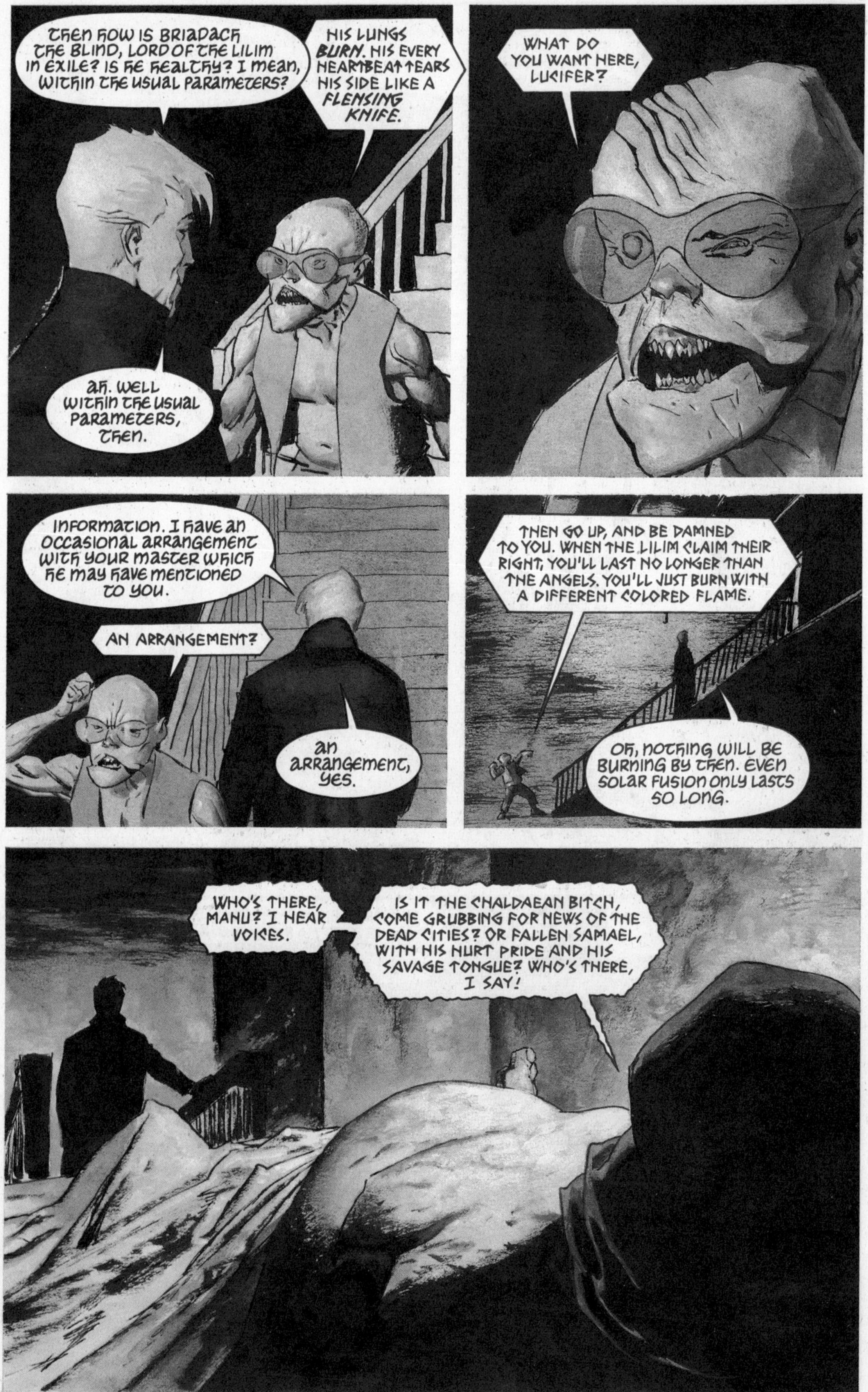

THEN HOW IS BRIADACH THE BLIND, LORD OF THE LILIM IN EXILE? IS HE HEALTHY? I MEAN, WITHIN THE USUAL PARAMETERS?
HIS LUNGS BURN. HIS EVERY HEARTBEAT TEARS HIS SIDE LIKE A FLENSING KNIFE.
AH. WELL WITHIN THE USUAL PARAMETERS, THEN.
WHAT DO YOU WANT HERE, LUCIFER?
INFORMATION. I HAVE AN OCCASIONAL ARRANGEMENT WITH YOUR MASTER WHICH HE MAY HAVE MENTIONED TO YOU.
AN ARRANGEMENT?
AN ARRANGEMENT, YES.
THEN GO UP, AND BE DAMNED TO YOU. WHEN THE LILIM CLAIM THEIR RIGHT, YOU'LL LAST NO LONGER THAN THE ANGELS. YOU'LL JUST BURN WITH A DIFFERENT COLORED FLAME.
OH, NOTHING WILL BE BURNING BY THEN. EVEN SOLAR FUSION ONLY LASTS SO LONG.
WHO'S THERE, MANU? I HEAR VOICES.
IS IT THE CHALDAEAN BITCH, COME GRUBBING FOR NEWS OF THE DEAD CITIES? OR FALLEN SAMAEL, WITH HIS HURT PRIDE AND HIS SAVAGE TONGUE? WHO'S THERE, I SAY!

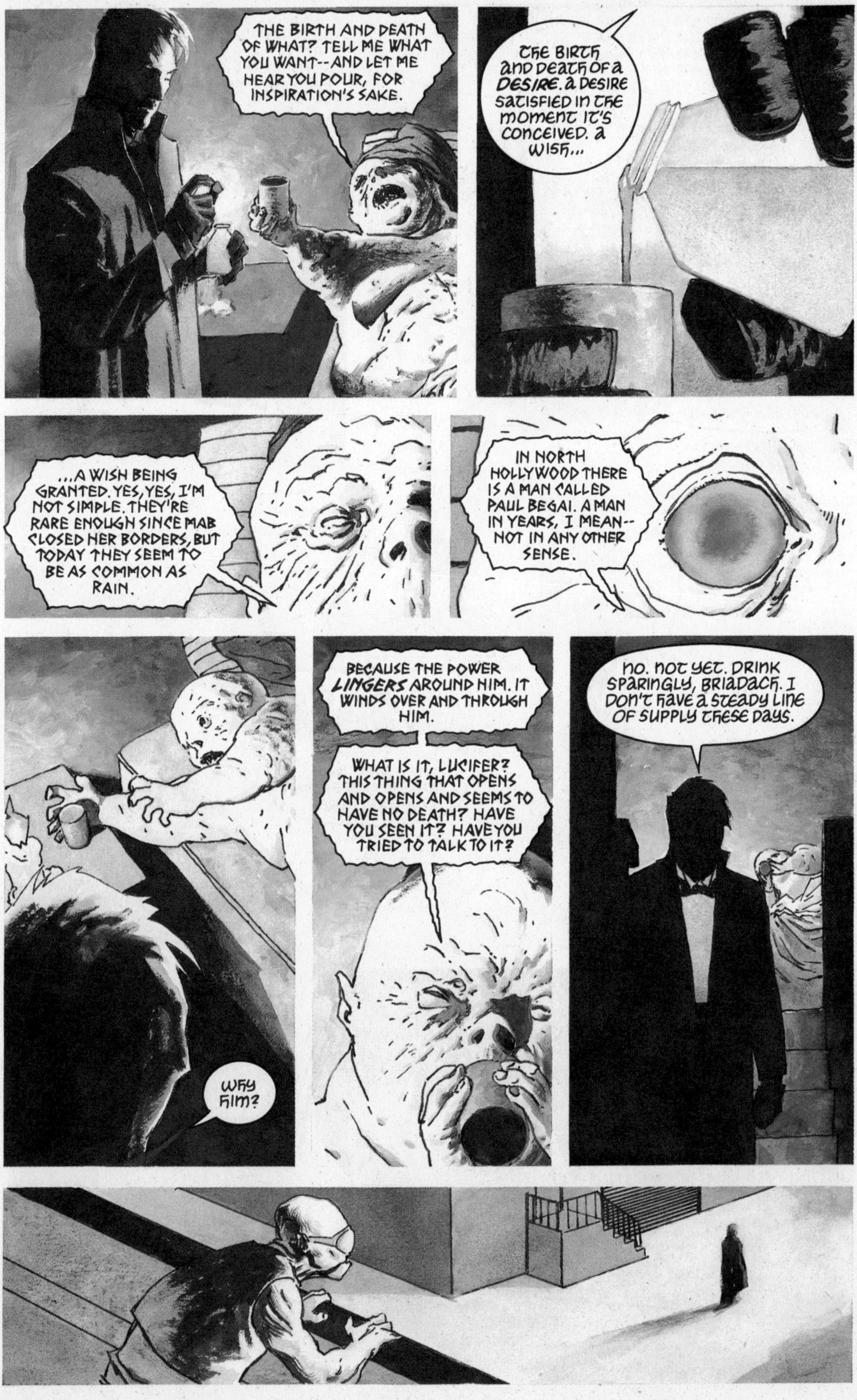
THE BIRTH AND DEATH OF WHAT? TELL ME WHAT YOU WANT--AND LET ME HEAR YOU POUR, FOR INSPIRATION'S SAKE.
THE BIRTH AND DEATH OF A DESIRE. A DESIRE SATISFIED IN THE MOMENT IT'S CONCEIVED. A WISH...
...A WISH BEING GRANTED. YES, YES, I'M NOT SIMPLE. THEY'RE RARE ENOUGH SINCE MAB CLOSED HER BORDERS, BUT TODAY THEY SEEM TO BE AS COMMON AS RAIN.
IN NORTH HOLLYWOOD THERE IS A MAN CALLED PAUL BEGAI. A MAN IN YEARS, I MEAN--NOT IN ANY OTHER SENSE.
WHY HIM?
BECAUSE THE POWER LINGERS AROUND HIM. IT WINDS OVER AND THROUGH HIM.
WHAT IS IT, LUCIFER? THIS THING THAT OPENS AND OPENS AND SEEMS TO HAVE NO DEATH? HAVE YOU SEEN IT? HAVE YOU TRIED TO TALK TO IT?
NO. NOT YET. DRINK SPARINGLY, BRIADACH. I DON'T HAVE A STEADY LINE OF SUPPLY THESE DAYS.

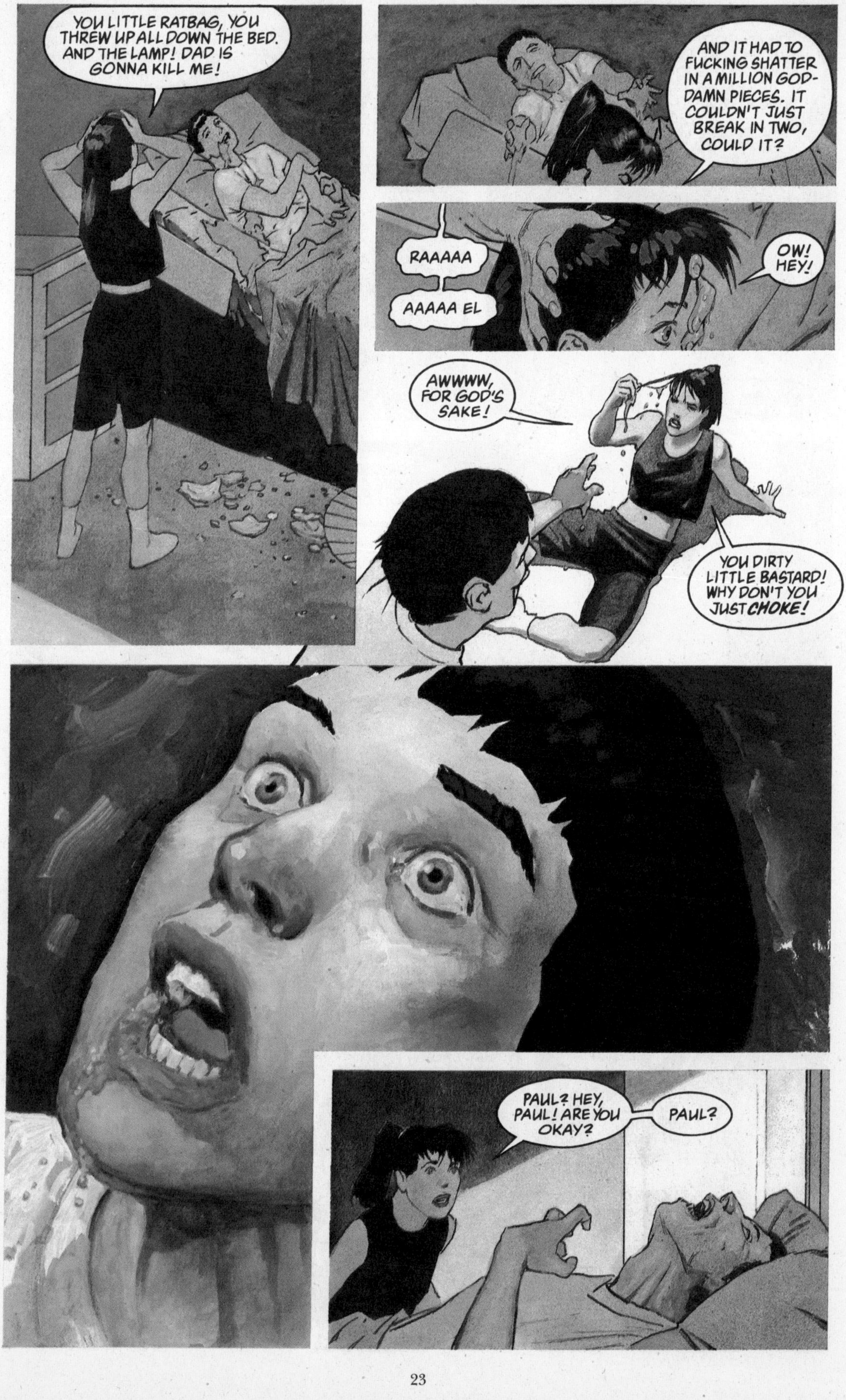
YOU LITTLE RATBAG, YOU THREW UP ALL DOWN THE BED. AND THE LAMP! DAD IS GONNA KILL ME!
AND IT HAD TO FUCKING SHATTER IN A MILLION GOD-DAMN PIECES. IT COULDN'T JUST BREAK IN TWO, COULD IT?
RAAAAA
AAAAA EL
OW! HEY!
AWWWW, FOR GOD'S SAKE!
YOU DIRTY LITTLE BASTARD! WHY DON'T YOU JUST CHOKE!
PAUL? HEY, PAUL! ARE YOU OKAY?
PAUL?

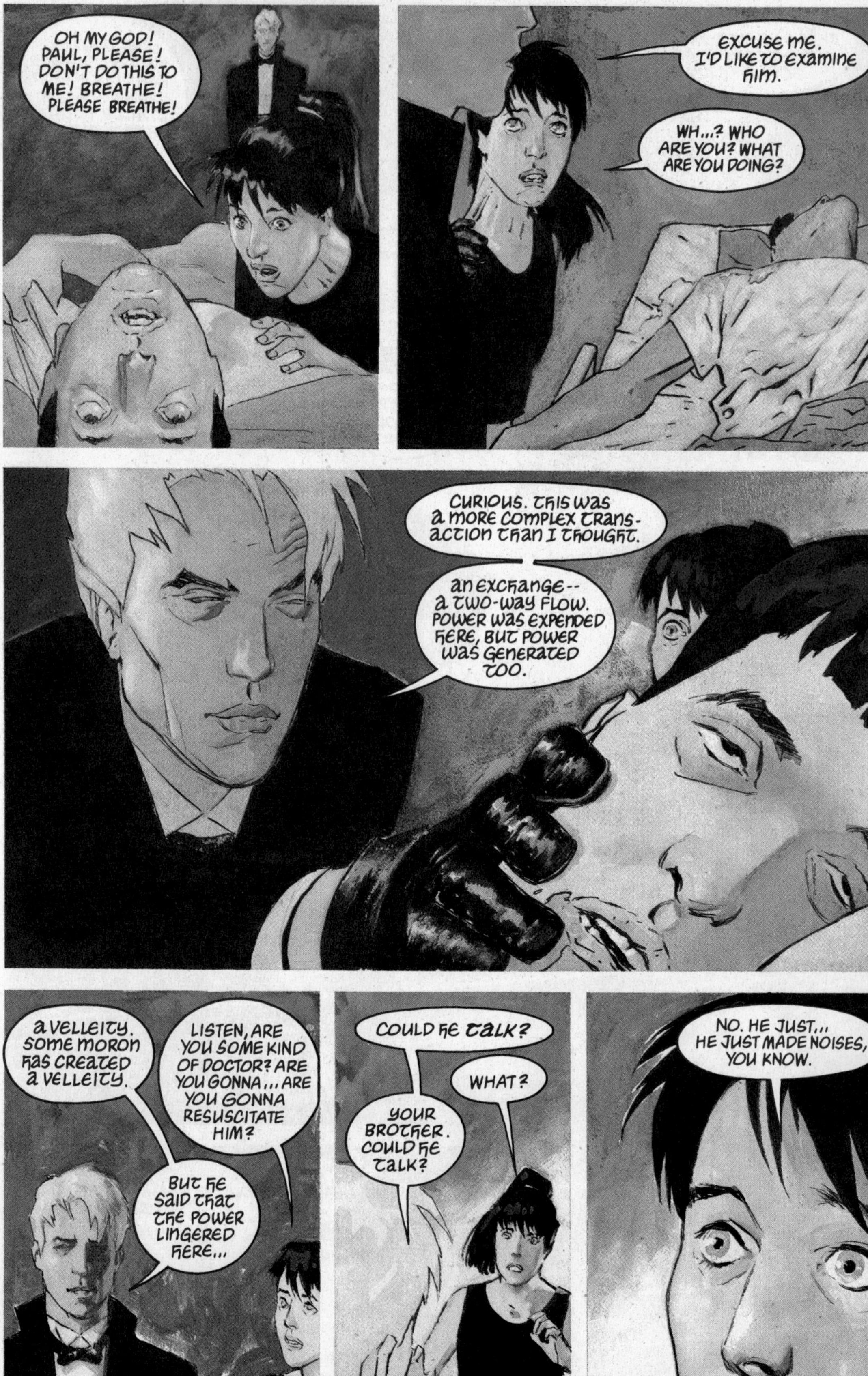
OH MY GOD! PAUL, PLEASE! DON'T DO THIS TO ME! BREATHE! PLEASE BREATHE!
EXCUSE ME. I'D LIKE TO EXAMINE HIM.
WH...? WHO ARE YOU? WHAT ARE YOU DOING?
CURIOUS. THIS WAS A MORE COMPLEX TRANSACTION THAN I THOUGHT.
AN EXCHANGE-- A TWO-WAY FLOW. POWER WAS EXPENDED HERE, BUT POWER WAS GENERATED TOO.
A VELLEITY. SOME MORON HAS CREATED A VELLEITY.
LISTEN, ARE YOU SOME KIND OF DOCTOR? ARE YOU GONNA... ARE YOU GONNA RESUSCITATE HIM?
BUT HE SAID THAT THE POWER LINGERED HERE...
COULD HE TALK?
WHAT?
YOUR BROTHER. COULD HE TALK?
NO. HE JUST... HE JUST MADE NOISES, YOU KNOW.

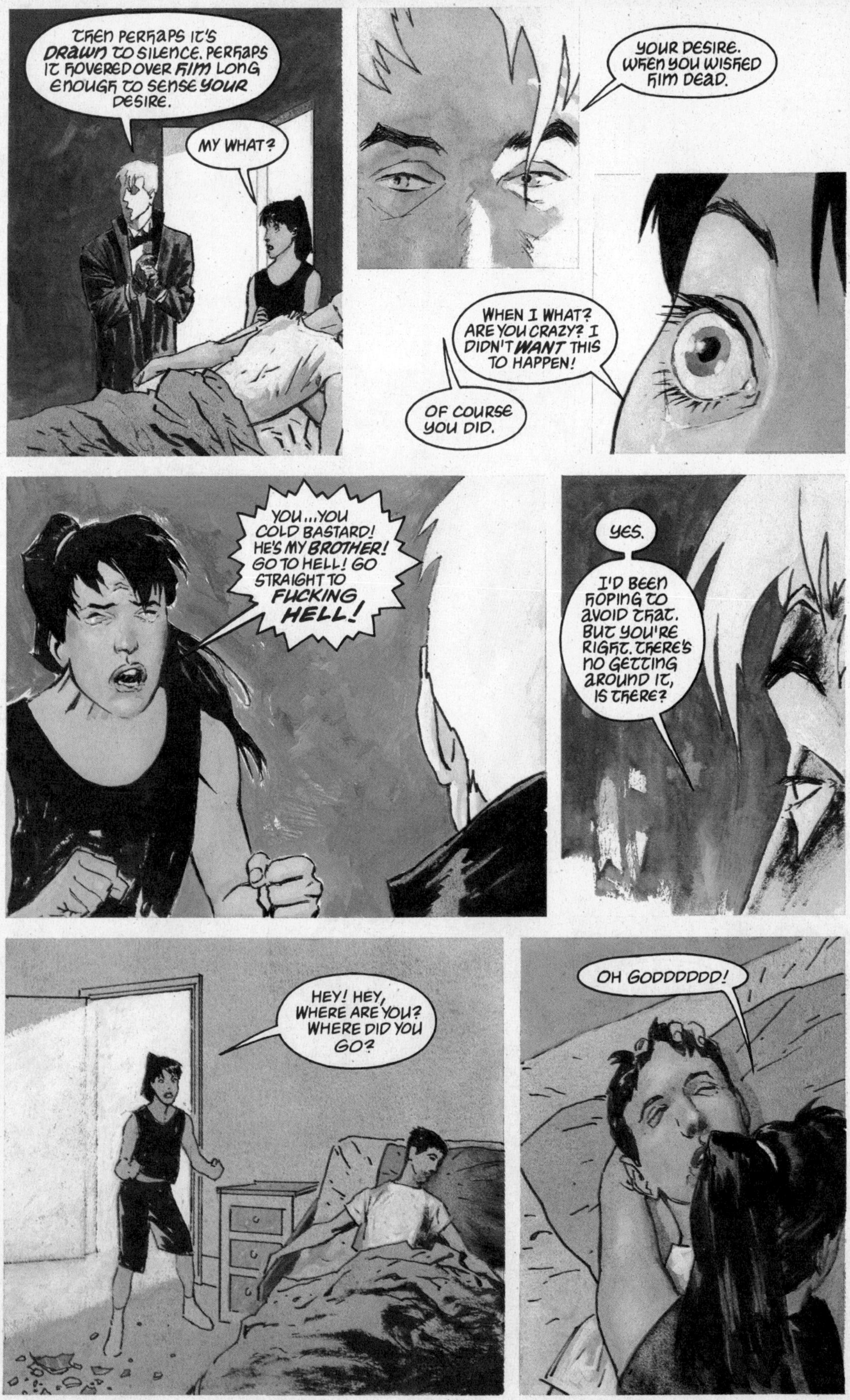
THEN PERHAPS IT'S DRAWN TO SILENCE. PERHAPS IT HOVERED OVER HIM LONG ENOUGH TO SENSE YOUR DESIRE.
MY WHAT?
YOUR DESIRE. WHEN YOU WISHED HIM DEAD.
WHEN I WHAT? ARE YOU CRAZY? I DIDN'T WANT THIS TO HAPPEN!
OF COURSE YOU DID.
YOU...YOU COLD BASTARD! HE'S MY BROTHER! GO TO HELL! GO STRAIGHT TO FUCKING HELL!
YES.
I'D BEEN HOPING TO AVOID THAT. BUT YOU'RE RIGHT. THERE'S NO GETTING AROUND IT, IS THERE?
HEY! HEY, WHERE ARE YOU? WHERE DID YOU GO?
OH GODDDDDD!

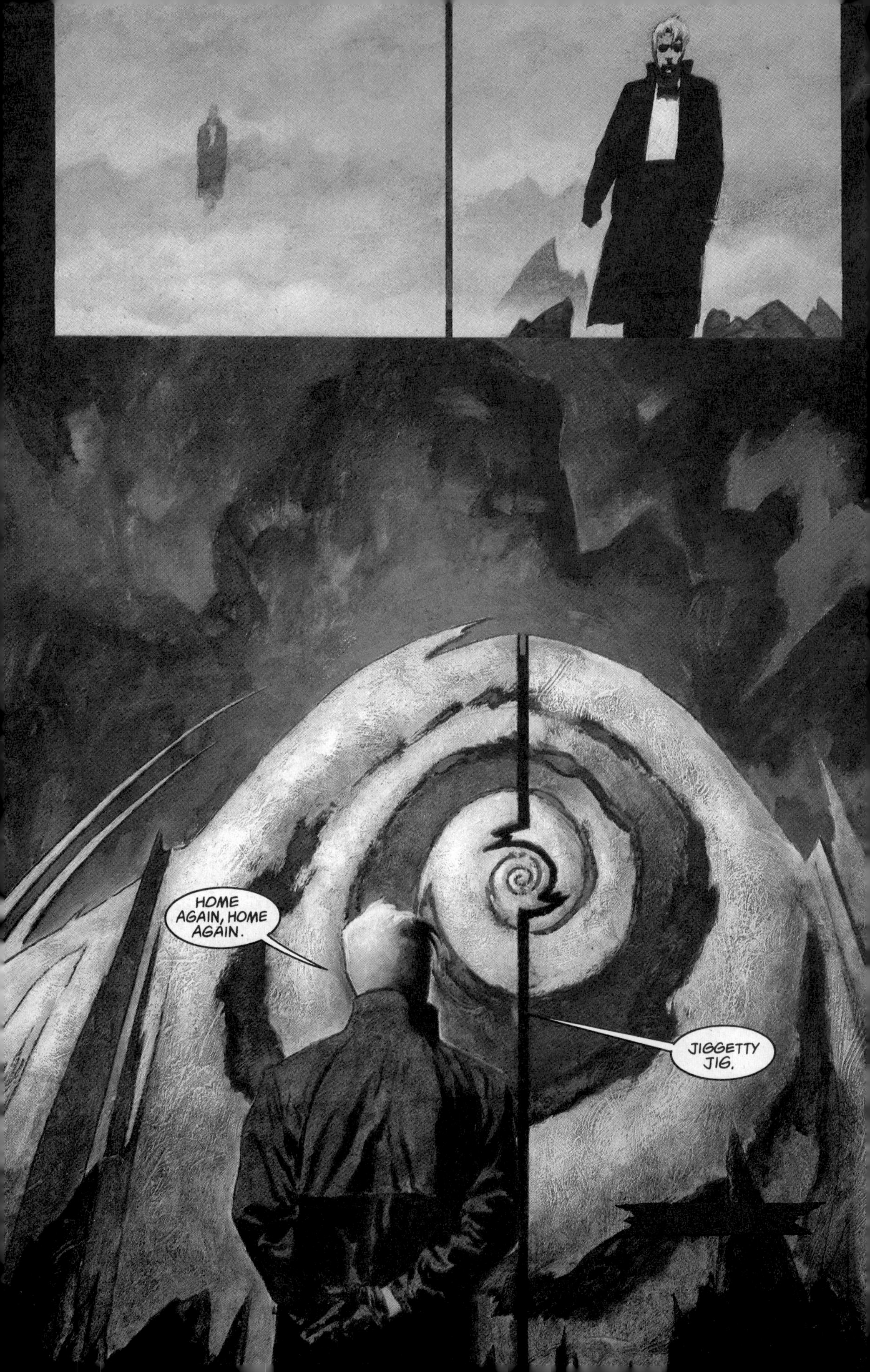
HOME AGAIN, HOME AGAIN.
JIGGETTY JIG.

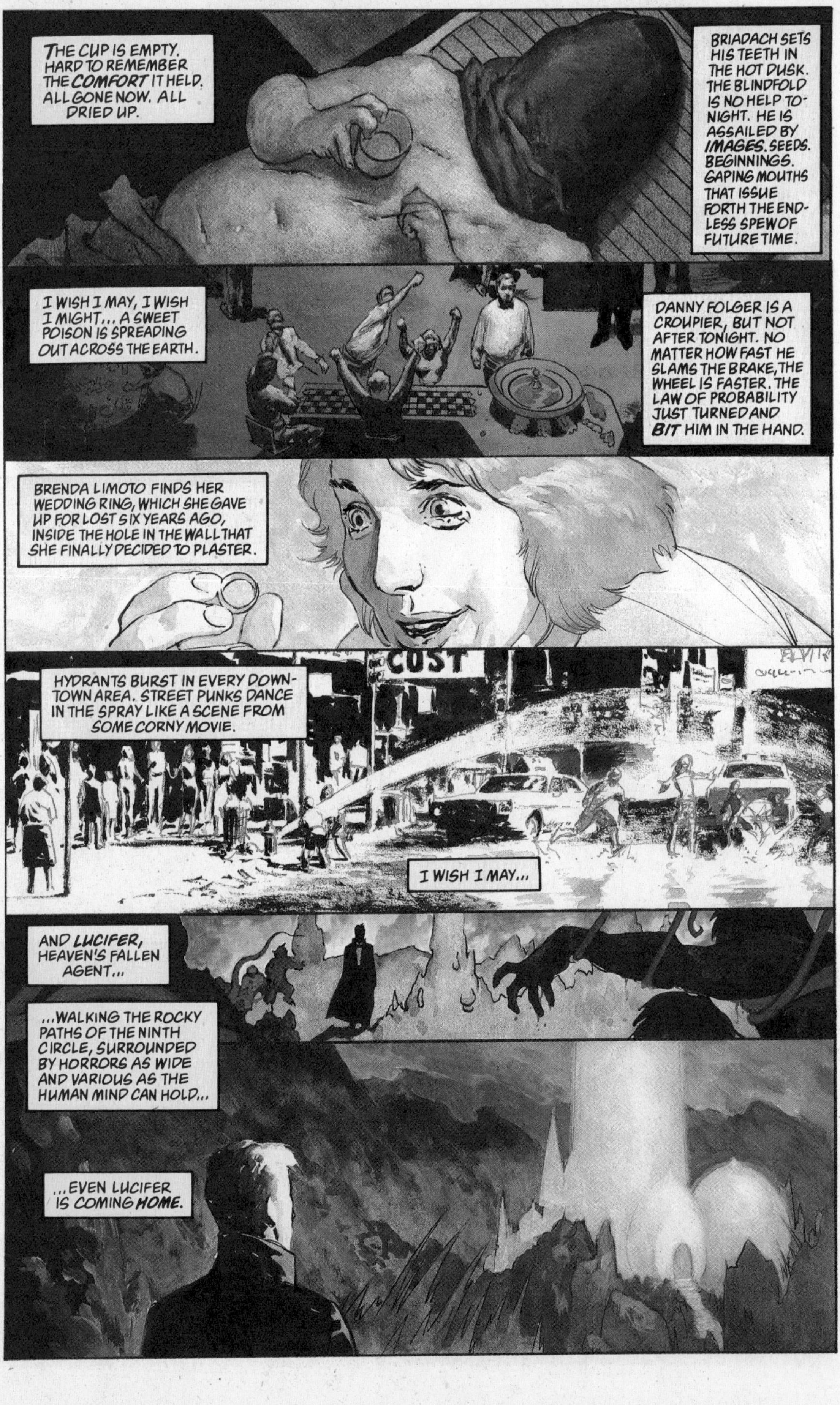
THE CUP IS EMPTY. HARD TO REMEMBER THE COMFORT IT HELD. ALL GONE NOW. ALL DRIED UP.
BRIADACH SETS HIS TEETH IN THE HOT DUSK. THE BLINDFOLD IS NO HELP TO-NIGHT. HE IS ASSAILED BY IMAGES. SEEDS. BEGINNINGS. GAPING MOUTHS THAT ISSUE FORTH THE END-LESS SPEW OF FUTURE TIME.
I WISH I MAY, I WISH I MIGHT... A SWEET POISON IS SPREADING OUT ACROSS THE EARTH.
DANNY FOLGER IS A CROUPIER, BUT NOT AFTER TONIGHT. NO MATTER HOW FAST HE SLAMS THE BRAKE, THE WHEEL IS FASTER. THE LAW OF PROBABILITY JUST TURNED AND BIT HIM IN THE HAND.
BRENDA LIMOTO FINDS HER WEDDING RING, WHICH SHE GAVE UP FOR LOST SIX YEARS AGO, INSIDE THE HOLE IN THE WALL THAT SHE FINALLY DECIDED TO PLASTER.
COST
HYDRANTS BURST IN EVERY DOWN-TOWN AREA. STREET PUNKS DANCE IN THE SPRAY LIKE A SCENE FROM SOME CORNY MOVIE.
I WISH I MAY...
AND LUCIFER, HEAVEN'S FALLEN AGENT...
...WALKING THE ROCKY PATHS OF THE NINTH CIRCLE, SURROUNDED BY HORRORS AS WIDE AND VARIOUS AS THE HUMAN MIND CAN HOLD...
...EVEN LUCIFER IS COMING HOME.

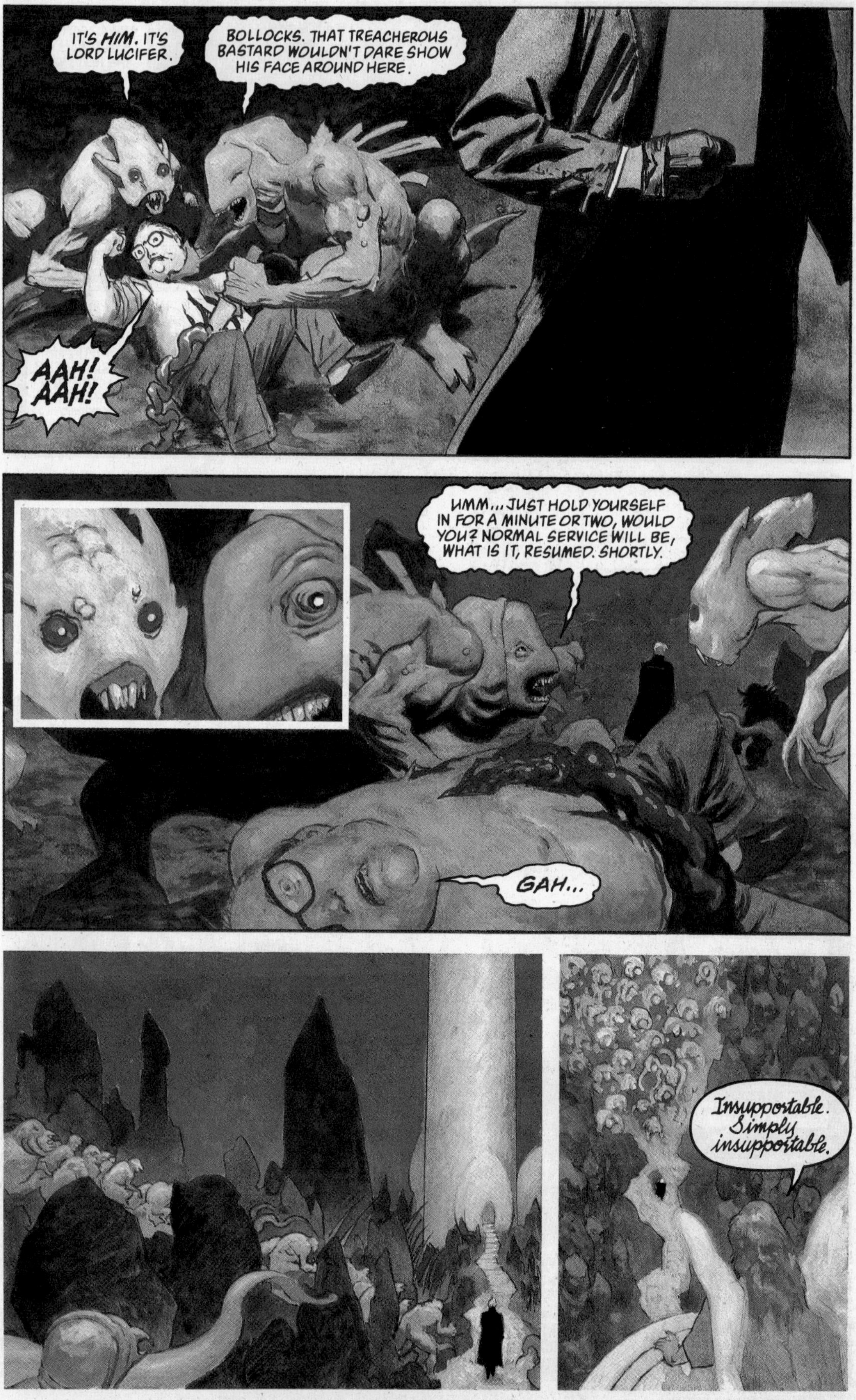
IT'S HIM. IT'S LORD LUCIFER.
BOLLOCKS. THAT TREACHEROUS BASTARD WOULDN'T DARE SHOW HIS FACE AROUND HERE.
AAH! AAH!
UMM... JUST HOLD YOURSELF IN FOR A MINUTE OR TWO, WOULD YOU? NORMAL SERVICE WILL BE, WHAT IS IT, RESUMED. SHORTLY.
GAH...
Insupportable. Simply insupportable.

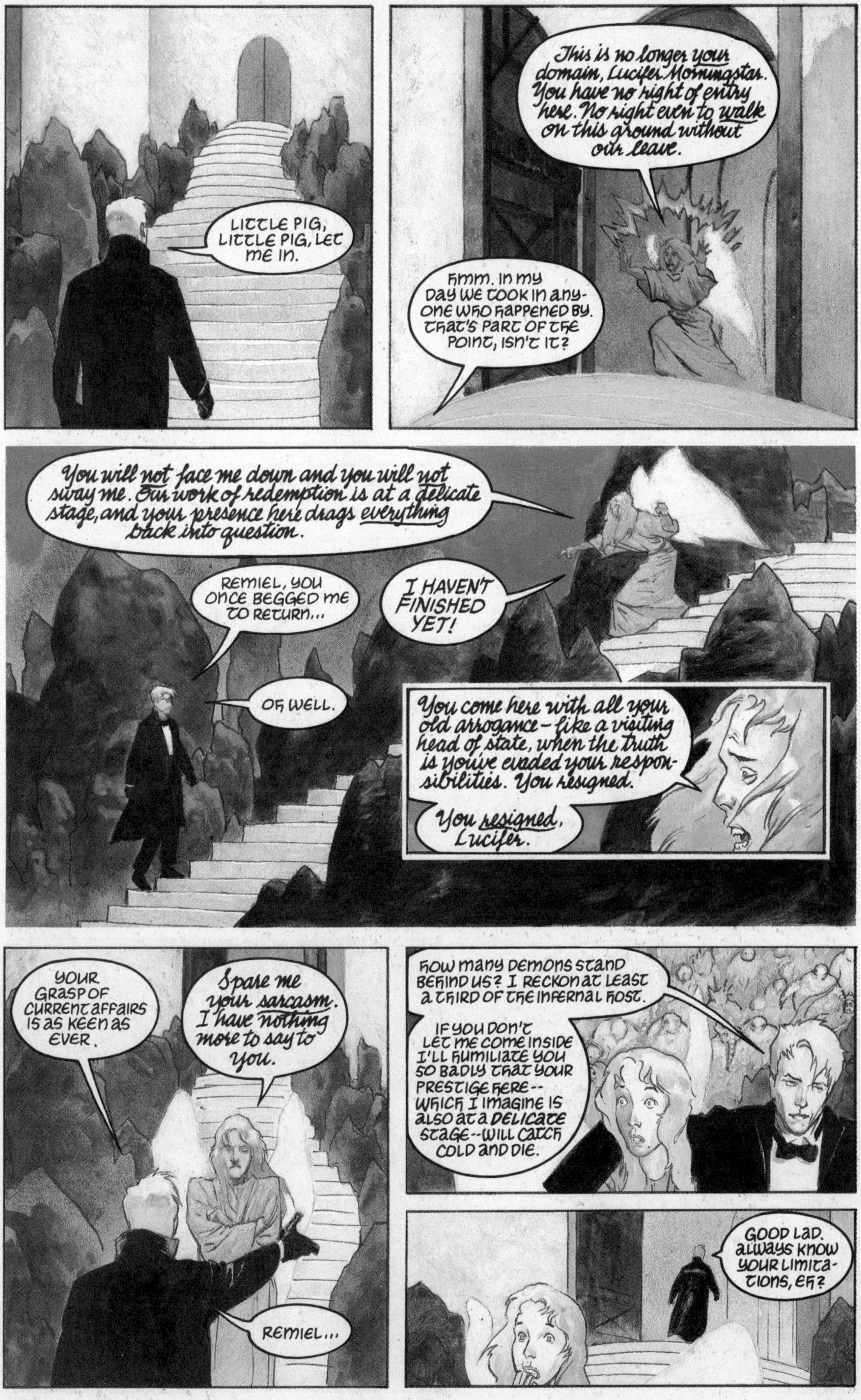
LITTLE PIG, LITTLE PIG, LET ME IN.
This is no longer your domain, Lucifer Morningstar. You have no right of entry here. No right even to walk on this ground without our leave.
HMM. IN MY DAY WE TOOK IN ANYONE WHO HAPPENED BY. THAT'S PART OF THE POINT, ISN'T IT?
You will not face me down and you will not sway me. Our work of redemption is at a delicate stage, and your presence here drags everything back into question.
REMIEL, YOU ONCE BEGGED ME TO RETURN...
I HAVEN'T FINISHED YET!
OH WELL.
You come here with all your old arrogance—like a visiting head of state, when the truth is you've evaded your responsibilities. You resigned.
You resigned, Lucifer.
YOUR GRASP OF CURRENT AFFAIRS IS AS KEEN AS EVER.
Spare me your sarcasm. I have nothing more to say to you.
REMIEL...
HOW MANY DEMONS STAND BEHIND US? I RECKON AT LEAST A THIRD OF THE INFERNAL HOST.
IF YOU DON'T LET ME COME INSIDE I'LL HUMILIATE YOU SO BADLY THAT YOUR PRESTIGE HERE-- WHICH I IMAGINE IS ALSO AT A DELICATE STAGE--WILL CATCH COLD AND DIE.
GOOD LAD. ALWAYS KNOW YOUR LIMITATIONS, EH?

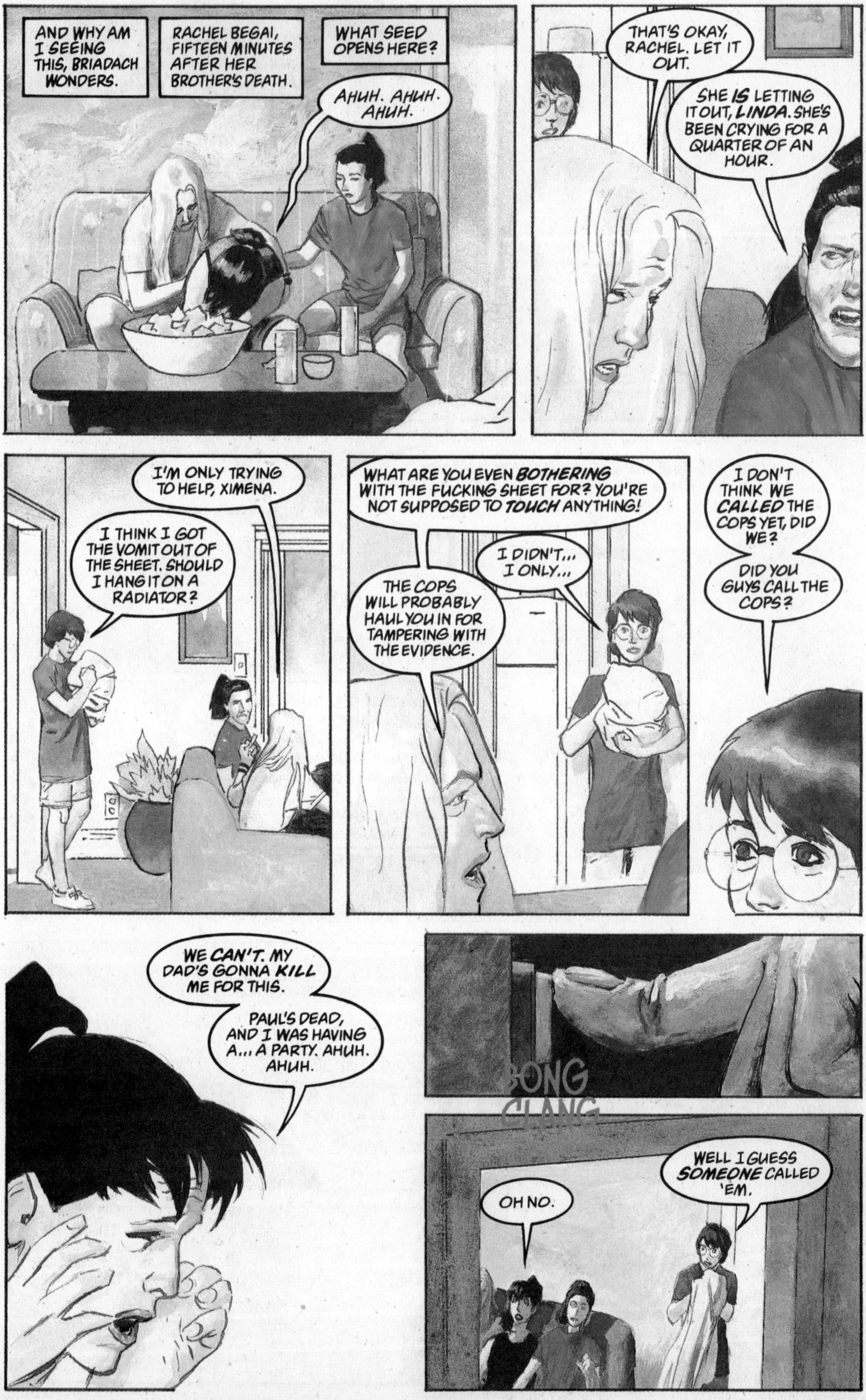
AND WHY AM I SEEING THIS, BRIADACH WONDERS.
RACHEL BEGAI, FIFTEEN MINUTES AFTER HER BROTHER'S DEATH.
WHAT SEED OPENS HERE?
AHUH. AHUH. AHUH.
THAT'S OKAY, RACHEL. LET IT OUT.
SHE IS LETTING IT OUT, LINDA. SHE'S BEEN CRYING FOR A QUARTER OF AN HOUR.
I'M ONLY TRYING TO HELP, XIMENA.
I THINK I GOT THE VOMIT OUT OF THE SHEET. SHOULD I HANG IT ON A RADIATOR?
WHAT ARE YOU EVEN BOTHERING WITH THE FUCKING SHEET FOR? YOU'RE NOT SUPPOSED TO TOUCH ANYTHING!
I DIDN'T... I ONLY...
THE COPS WILL PROBABLY HAUL YOU IN FOR TAMPERING WITH THE EVIDENCE.
I DON'T THINK WE CALLED THE COPS YET, DID WE?
DID YOU GUYS CALL THE COPS?
WE CAN'T. MY DAD'S GONNA KILL ME FOR THIS.
PAUL'S DEAD, AND I WAS HAVING A... A PARTY. AHUH. AHUH.
BONG
CLANG
OH NO.
WELL I GUESS SOMEONE CALLED 'EM.

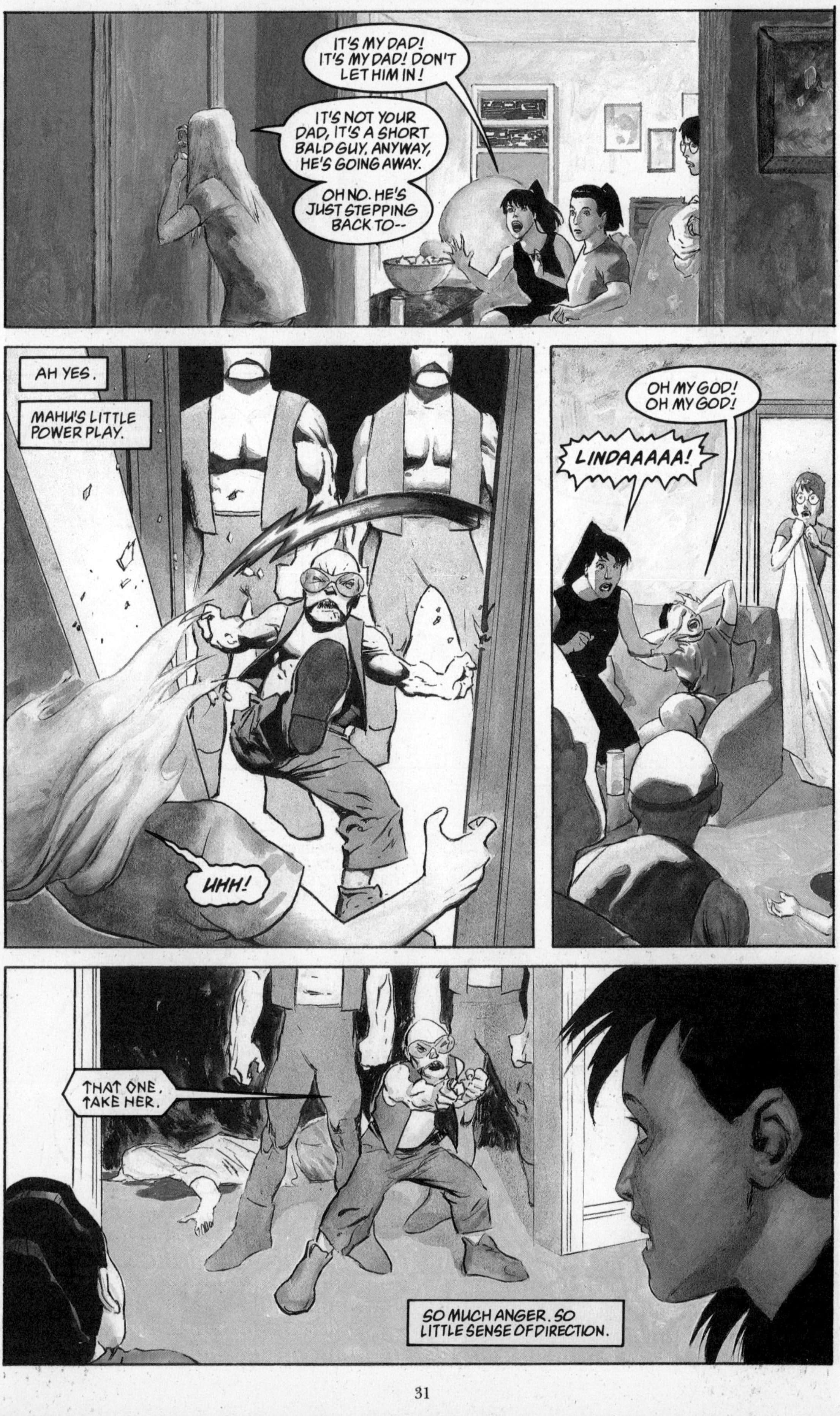
IT'S MY DAD! IT'S MY DAD! DON'T LET HIM IN!
IT'S NOT YOUR DAD, IT'S A SHORT BALD GUY. ANYWAY, HE'S GOING AWAY.
OH NO. HE'S JUST STEPPING BACK TO--
AH YES.
MAHU'S LITTLE POWER PLAY.
UHH!
OH MY GOD! OH MY GOD!
LINDAAAAA!
THAT ONE. TAKE HER.
SO MUCH ANGER. SO LITTLE SENSE OF DIRECTION.

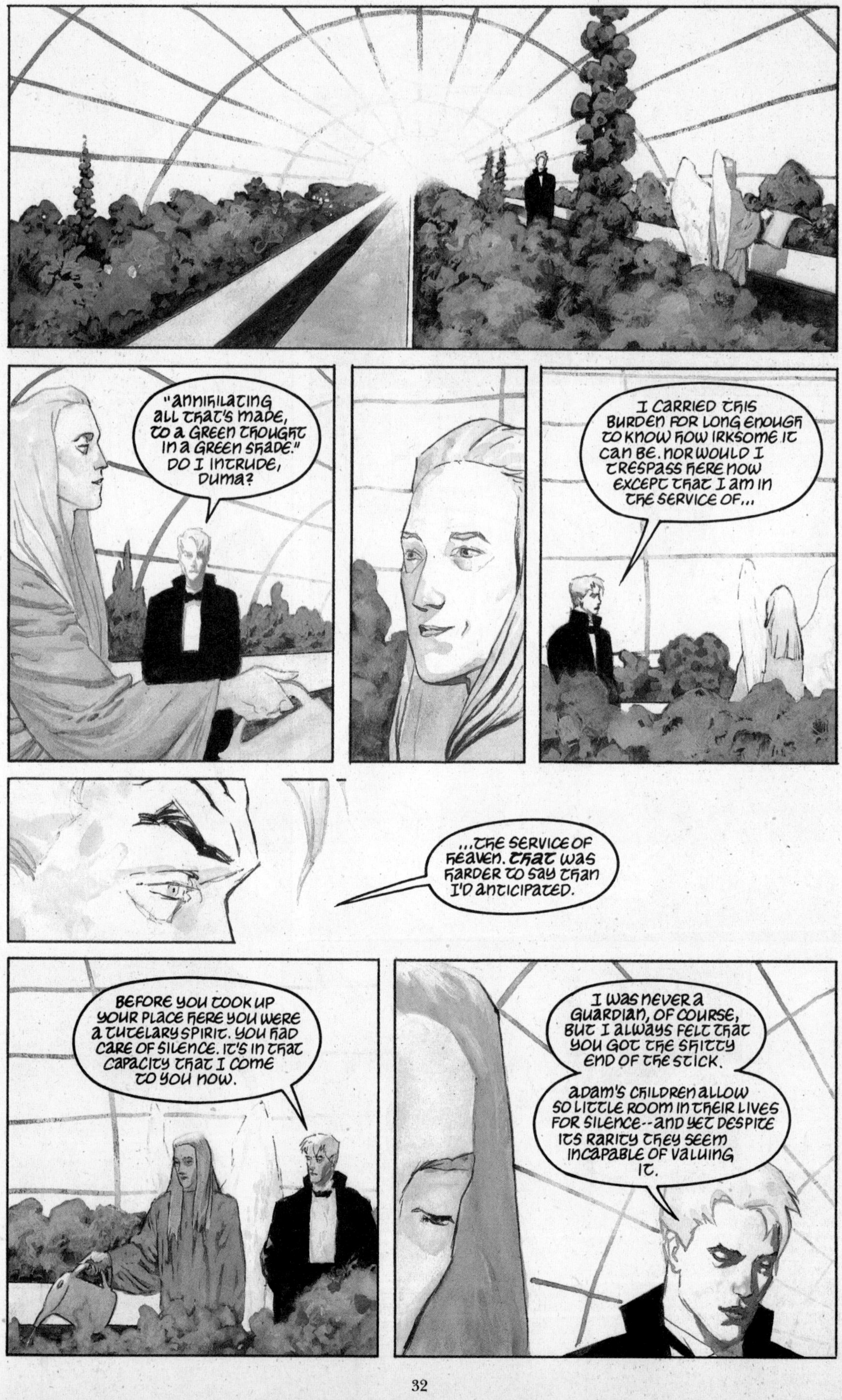
"ANNIHILATING ALL THAT'S MADE, TO A GREEN THOUGHT IN A GREEN SHADE." DO I INTRUDE, DUMA?
I CARRIED THIS BURDEN FOR LONG ENOUGH TO KNOW HOW IRKSOME IT CAN BE. NOR WOULD I TRESPASS HERE NOW EXCEPT THAT I AM IN THE SERVICE OF...
...THE SERVICE OF HEAVEN. THAT WAS HARDER TO SAY THAN I'D ANTICIPATED.
BEFORE YOU TOOK UP YOUR PLACE HERE YOU WERE A TUTELARY SPIRIT. YOU HAD CARE OF SILENCE. IT'S IN THAT CAPACITY THAT I COME TO YOU NOW.
I WAS NEVER A GUARDIAN, OF COURSE, BUT I ALWAYS FELT THAT YOU GOT THE SHITTY END OF THE STICK.
ADAM'S CHILDREN ALLOW SO LITTLE ROOM IN THEIR LIVES FOR SILENCE--AND YET DESPITE ITS RARITY THEY SEEM INCAPABLE OF VALUING IT.

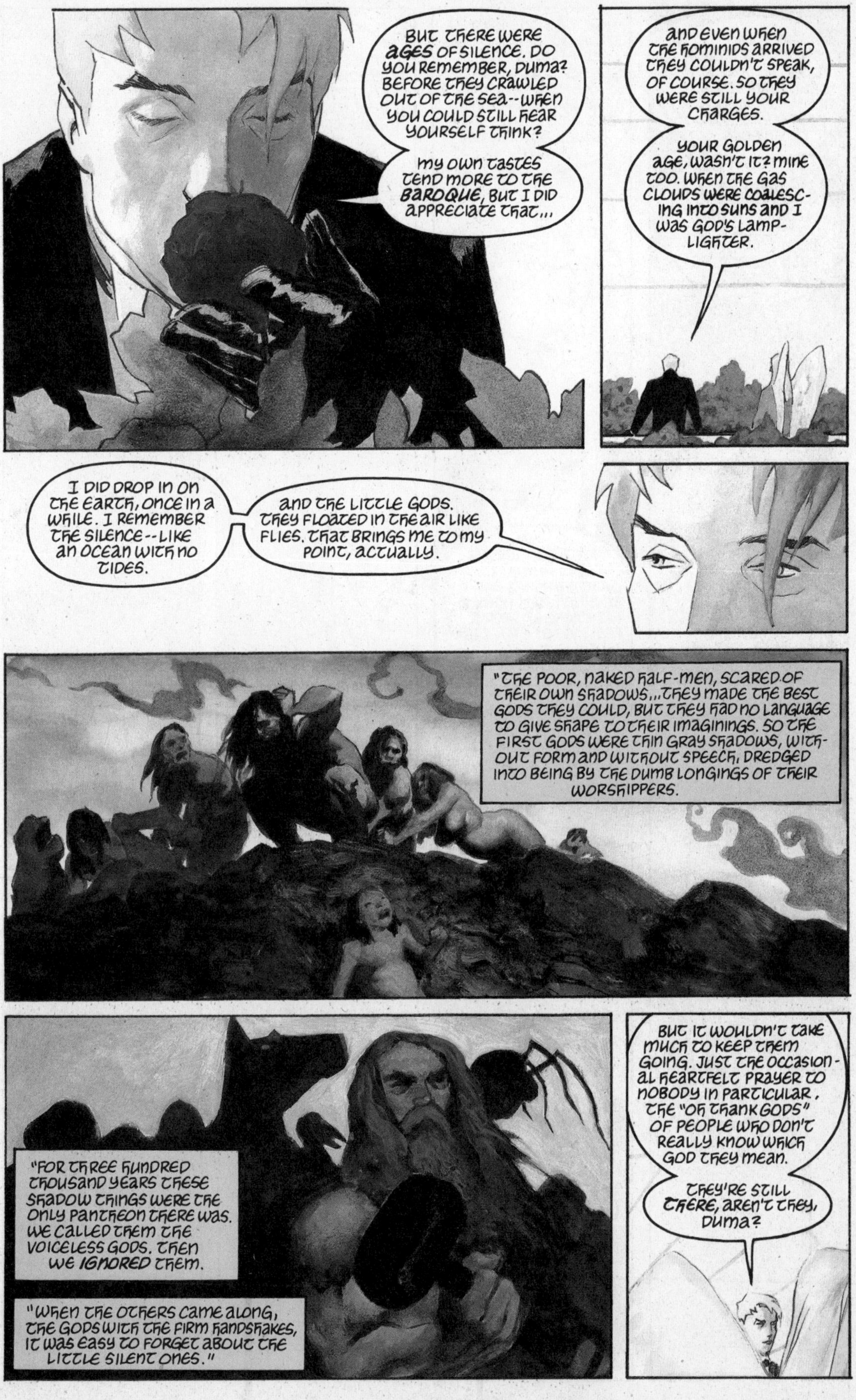
BUT THERE WERE AGES OF SILENCE. DO YOU REMEMBER, DUMA? BEFORE THEY CRAWLED OUT OF THE SEA--WHEN YOU COULD STILL HEAR YOURSELF THINK?
MY OWN TASTES TEND MORE TO THE BAROQUE, BUT I DID APPRECIATE THAT...
AND EVEN WHEN THE HOMINIDS ARRIVED THEY COULDN'T SPEAK, OF COURSE. SO THEY WERE STILL YOUR CHARGES.
YOUR GOLDEN AGE, WASN'T IT? MINE TOO. WHEN THE GAS CLOUDS WERE COALESC-ING INTO SUNS AND I WAS GOD'S LAMP-LIGHTER.
I DID DROP IN ON THE EARTH, ONCE IN A WHILE. I REMEMBER THE SILENCE--LIKE AN OCEAN WITH NO TIDES.
AND THE LITTLE GODS. THEY FLOATED IN THE AIR LIKE FLIES. THAT BRINGS ME TO MY POINT, ACTUALLY.
"THE POOR, NAKED HALF-MEN, SCARED OF THEIR OWN SHADOWS...THEY MADE THE BEST GODS THEY COULD, BUT THEY HAD NO LANGUAGE TO GIVE SHAPE TO THEIR IMAGININGS. SO THE FIRST GODS WERE THIN GRAY SHADOWS, WITH-OUT FORM AND WITHOUT SPEECH, DREDGED INTO BEING BY THE DUMB LONGINGS OF THEIR WORSHIPPERS.
"FOR THREE HUNDRED THOUSAND YEARS THESE SHADOW THINGS WERE THE ONLY PANTHEON THERE WAS. WE CALLED THEM THE VOICELESS GODS. THEN WE IGNORED THEM.
"WHEN THE OTHERS CAME ALONG, THE GODS WITH THE FIRM HANDSHAKES, IT WAS EASY TO FORGET ABOUT THE LITTLE SILENT ONES."
BUT IT WOULDN'T TAKE MUCH TO KEEP THEM GOING. JUST THE OCCASION-AL HEARTFELT PRAYER TO NOBODY IN PARTICULAR. THE "OH THANK GODS" OF PEOPLE WHO DON'T REALLY KNOW WHICH GOD THEY MEAN.
THEY'RE STILL THERE, AREN'T THEY, DUMA?

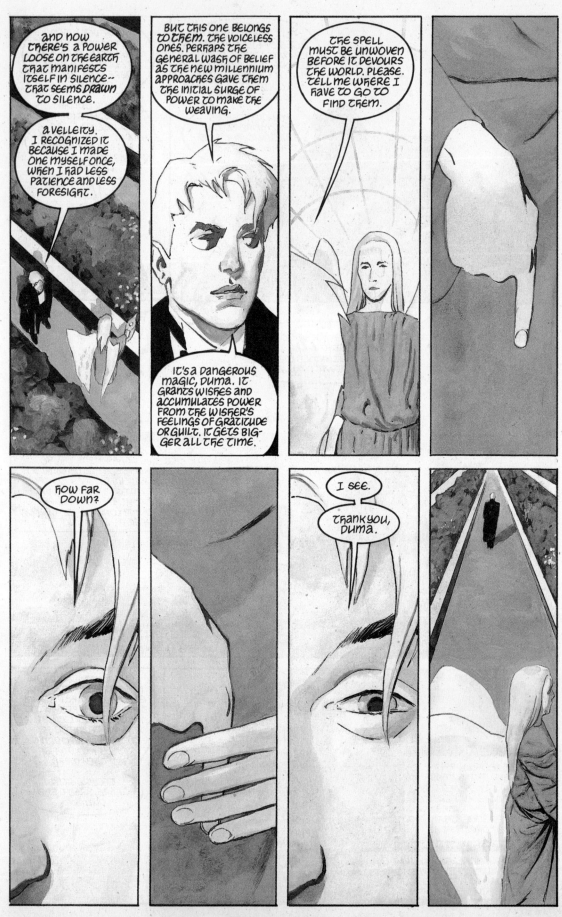

AND NOW THERE'S A POWER LOOSE ON THE EARTH THAT MANIFESTS ITSELF IN SILENCE-- THAT SEEMS DRAWN TO SILENCE.

A VELLEITY. I RECOGNIZED IT BECAUSE I MADE ONE MYSELF ONCE, WHEN I HAD LESS PATIENCE AND LESS FORESIGHT.

BUT THIS ONE BELONGS TO THEM. THE VOICELESS ONES. PERHAPS THE GENERAL WASH OF BELIEF AS THE NEW MILLENNIUM APPROACHES GAVE THEM THE INITIAL SURGE OF POWER TO MAKE THE WEAVING.

IT'S A DANGEROUS MAGIC, DUMA. IT GRANTS WISHES AND ACCUMULATES POWER FROM THE WISHER'S FEELINGS OF GRATITUDE OR GUILT. IT GETS BIG- GER ALL THE TIME.

THE SPELL MUST BE UNWOVEN BEFORE IT DEVOURS THE WORLD. PLEASE. TELL ME WHERE I HAVE TO GO TO FIND THEM.

HOW FAR DOWN?

I SEE.

THANK YOU, DUMA.

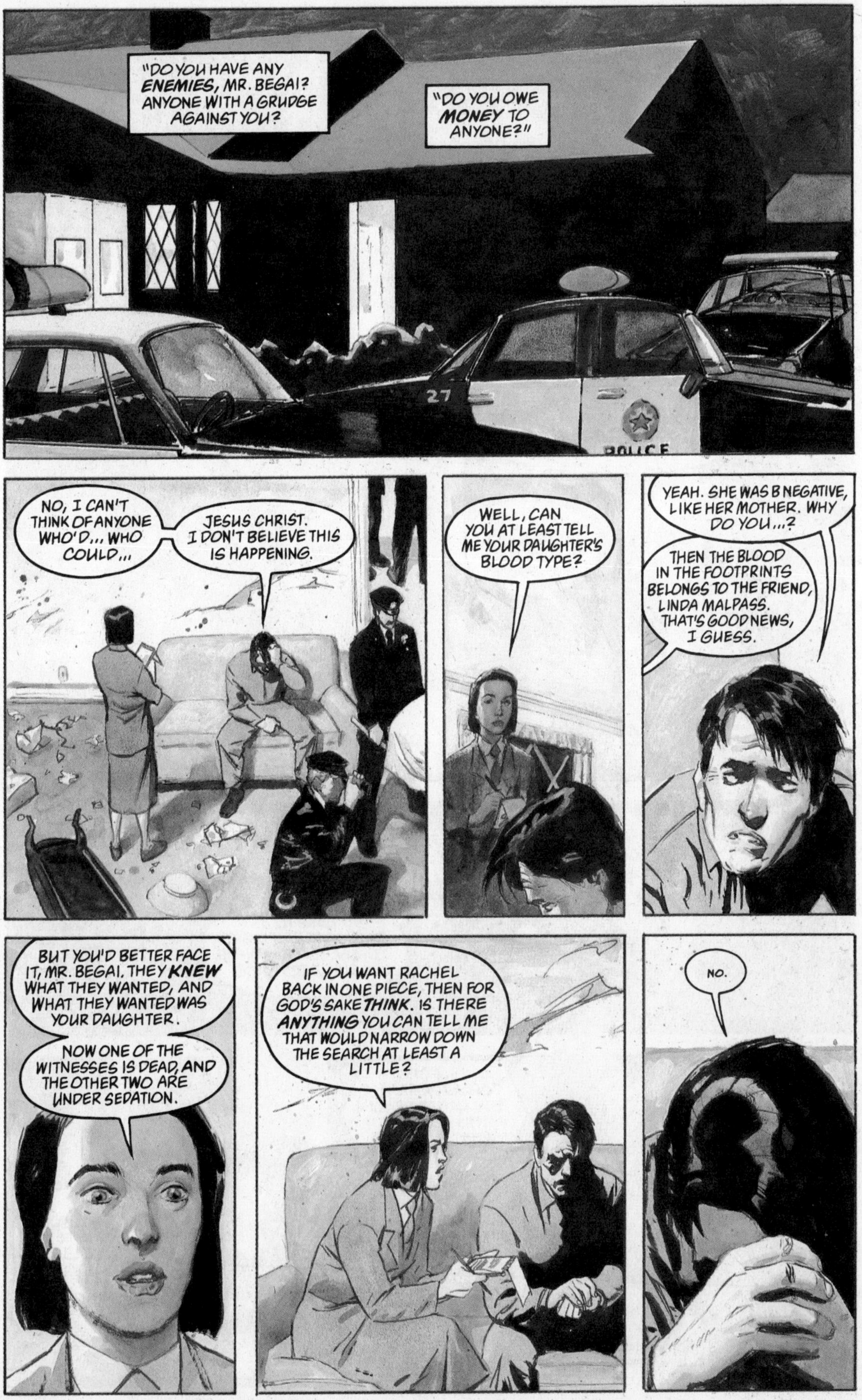
"DO YOU HAVE ANY ENEMIES, MR. BEGAI? ANYONE WITH A GRUDGE AGAINST YOU?
"DO YOU OWE MONEY TO ANYONE?"
POLICE
NO, I CAN'T THINK OF ANYONE WHO'D... WHO COULD...
JESUS CHRIST. I DON'T BELIEVE THIS IS HAPPENING.
WELL, CAN YOU AT LEAST TELL ME YOUR DAUGHTER'S BLOOD TYPE?
YEAH. SHE WAS B NEGATIVE, LIKE HER MOTHER. WHY DO YOU...?
THEN THE BLOOD IN THE FOOTPRINTS BELONGS TO THE FRIEND, LINDA MALPASS. THAT'S GOOD NEWS, I GUESS.
BUT YOU'D BETTER FACE IT, MR. BEGAI. THEY KNEW WHAT THEY WANTED, AND WHAT THEY WANTED WAS YOUR DAUGHTER.
NOW ONE OF THE WITNESSES IS DEAD, AND THE OTHER TWO ARE UNDER SEDATION.
IF YOU WANT RACHEL BACK IN ONE PIECE, THEN FOR GOD'S SAKE THINK. IS THERE ANYTHING YOU CAN TELL ME THAT WOULD NARROW DOWN THE SEARCH AT LEAST A LITTLE?
NO.

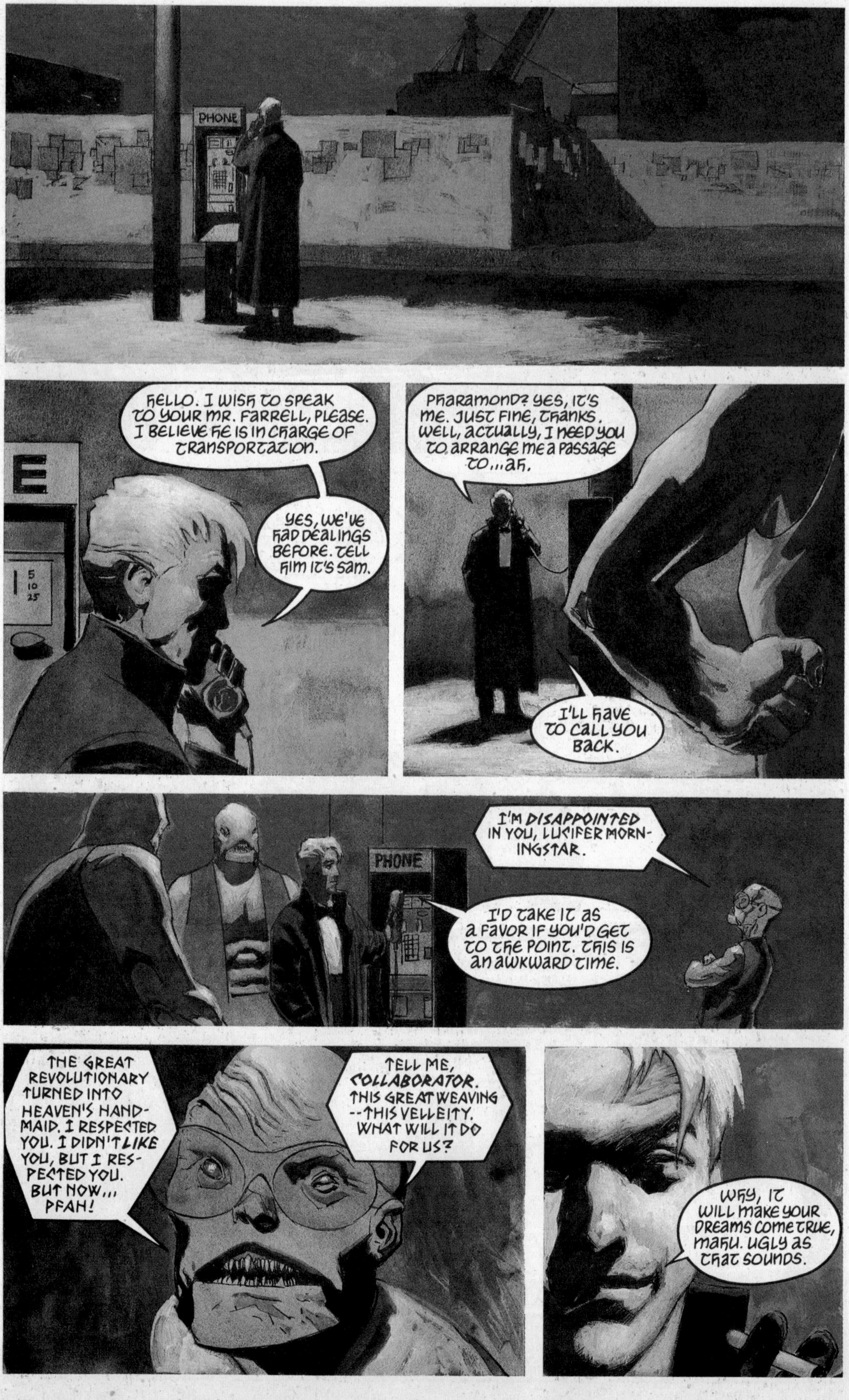
PHONE
HELLO. I WISH TO SPEAK TO YOUR MR. FARRELL, PLEASE. I BELIEVE HE IS IN CHARGE OF TRANSPORTATION.
YES, WE'VE HAD DEALINGS BEFORE. TELL HIM IT'S SAM.
PHARAMOND? YES, IT'S ME. JUST FINE, THANKS. WELL, ACTUALLY, I NEED YOU TO ARRANGE ME A PASSAGE TO...AH.
I'LL HAVE TO CALL YOU BACK.
PHONE
I'M *DISAPPOINTED* IN YOU, LUCIFER MORN-INGSTAR.
I'D TAKE IT AS A FAVOR IF YOU'D GET TO THE POINT. THIS IS AN AWKWARD TIME.
THE GREAT REVOLUTIONARY TURNED INTO HEAVEN'S HAND-MAID. I RESPECTED YOU. I DIDN'T *LIKE* YOU, BUT I RES-PECTED YOU. BUT NOW... PFAH!
TELL ME, *COLLABORATOR*. THIS GREAT WEAVING --THIS VELLEITY. WHAT WILL IT DO FOR US?
WHY, IT WILL MAKE YOUR DREAMS COME TRUE, MAHU. UGLY AS THAT SOUNDS.

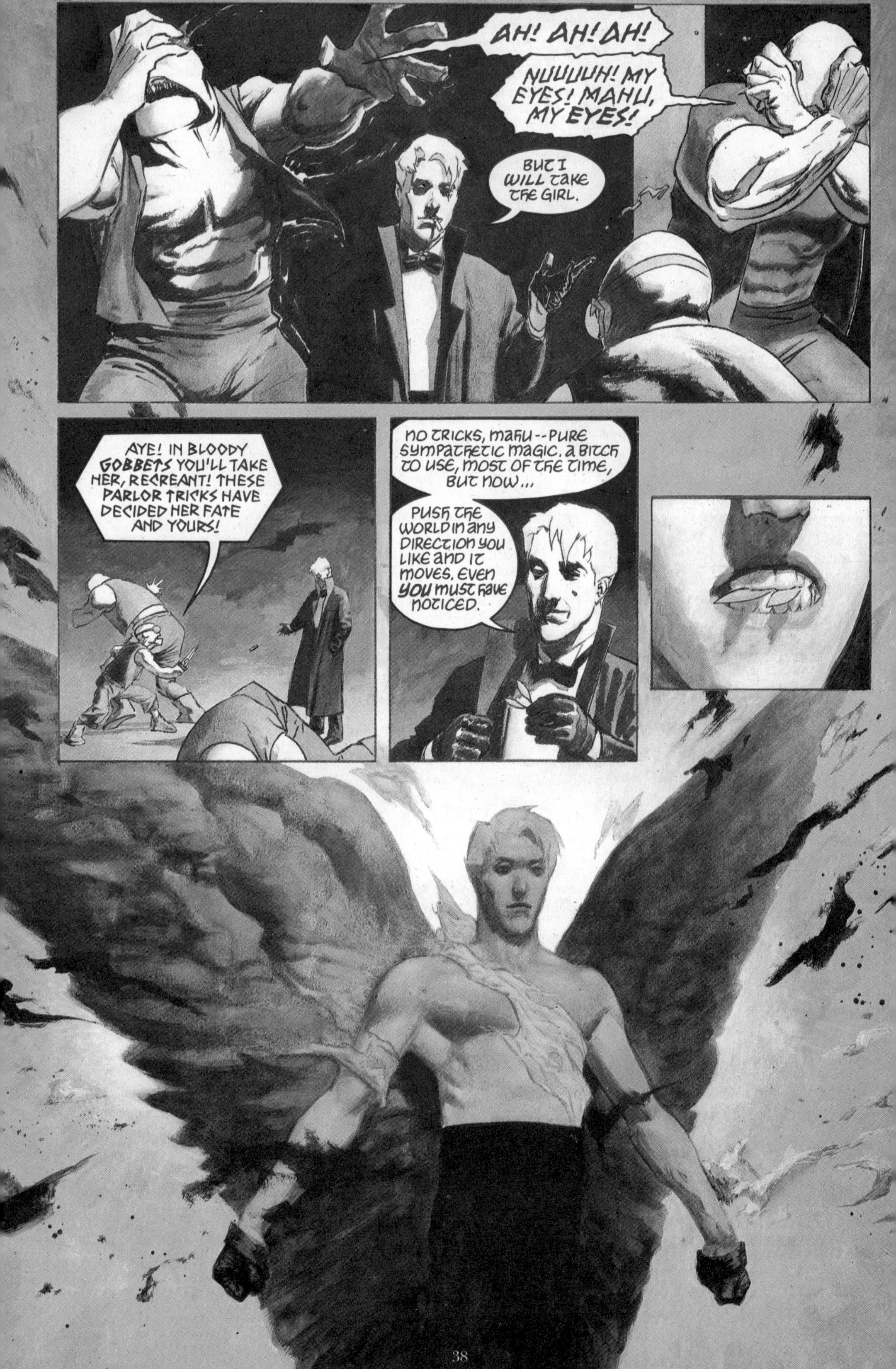
AH! AH! AH!
NUUUUH! MY EYES! MAHU, MY EYES!
BUT I WILL TAKE THE GIRL.
AYE! IN BLOODY GOBBETS YOU'LL TAKE HER, RECREANT! THESE PARLOR TRICKS HAVE DECIDED HER FATE AND YOURS!
NO TRICKS, MAHU--PURE SYMPATHETIC MAGIC. A BITCH TO USE, MOST OF THE TIME, BUT NOW...
PUSH THE WORLD IN ANY DIRECTION YOU LIKE AND IT MOVES. EVEN YOU MUST HAVE NOTICED.

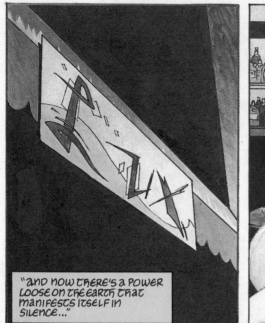

"AND NOW THERE'S A POWER LOOSE ON THE EARTH THAT MANIFESTS ITSELF IN SILENCE..."

"IT'S A DANGEROUS MAGIC..."

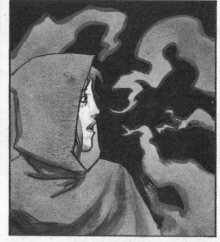

MAZIKEEN, I SHALL REQUIRE YOUR ASSISTANCE.

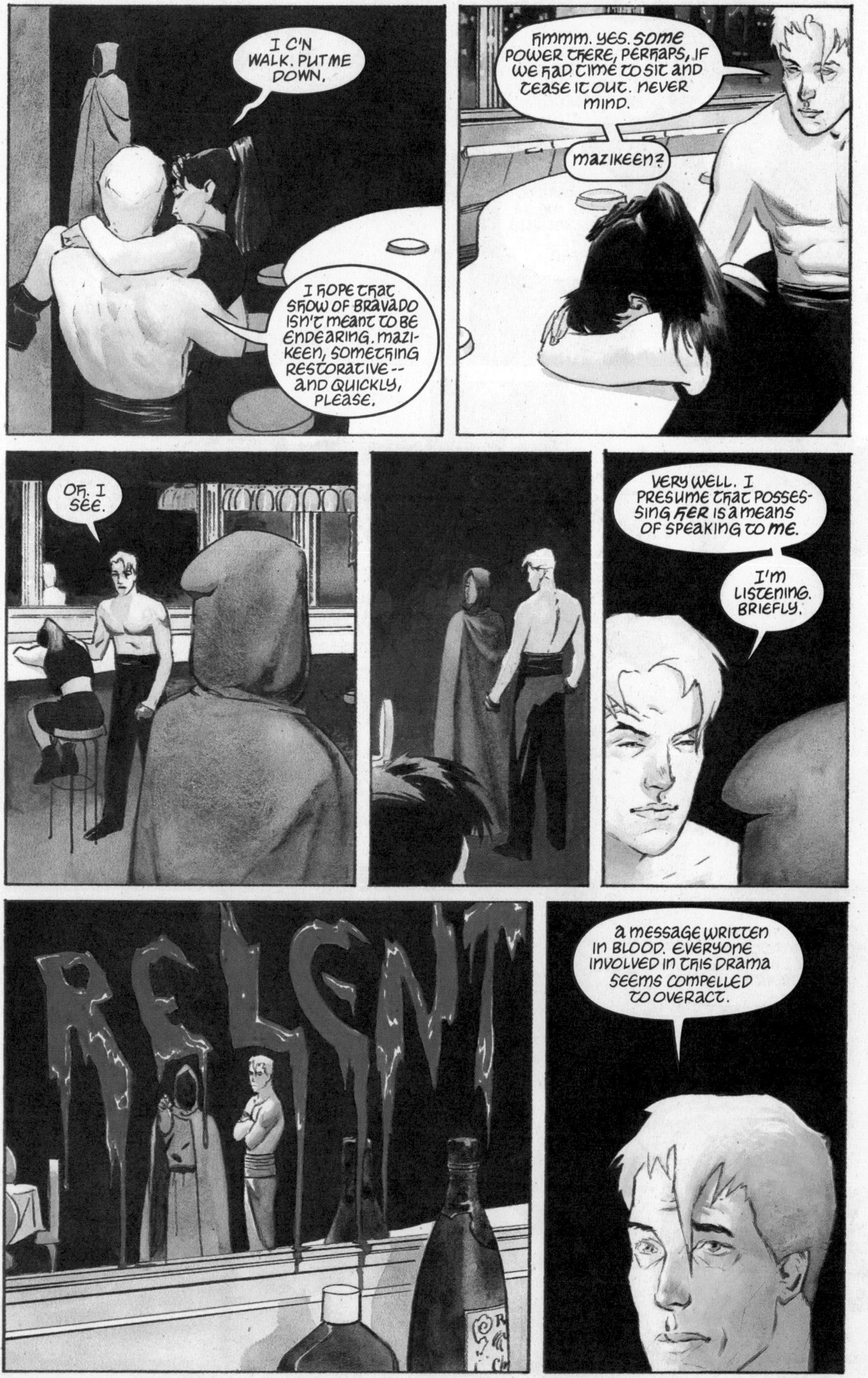
I C'N WALK. PUT ME DOWN.
I HOPE THAT SHOW OF BRAVADO ISN'T MEANT TO BE ENDEARING. MAZIKEEN, SOMETHING RESTORATIVE -- AND QUICKLY, PLEASE.
HMMM. YES. SOME POWER THERE, PERHAPS, IF WE HAD TIME TO SIT AND TEASE IT OUT. NEVER MIND.
MAZIKEEN?
OH. I SEE.
VERY WELL. I PRESUME THAT POSSESSING HER IS A MEANS OF SPEAKING TO ME.
I'M LISTENING. BRIEFLY.
RELENT
A MESSAGE WRITTEN IN BLOOD. EVERYONE INVOLVED IN THIS DRAMA SEEMS COMPELLED TO OVERACT.

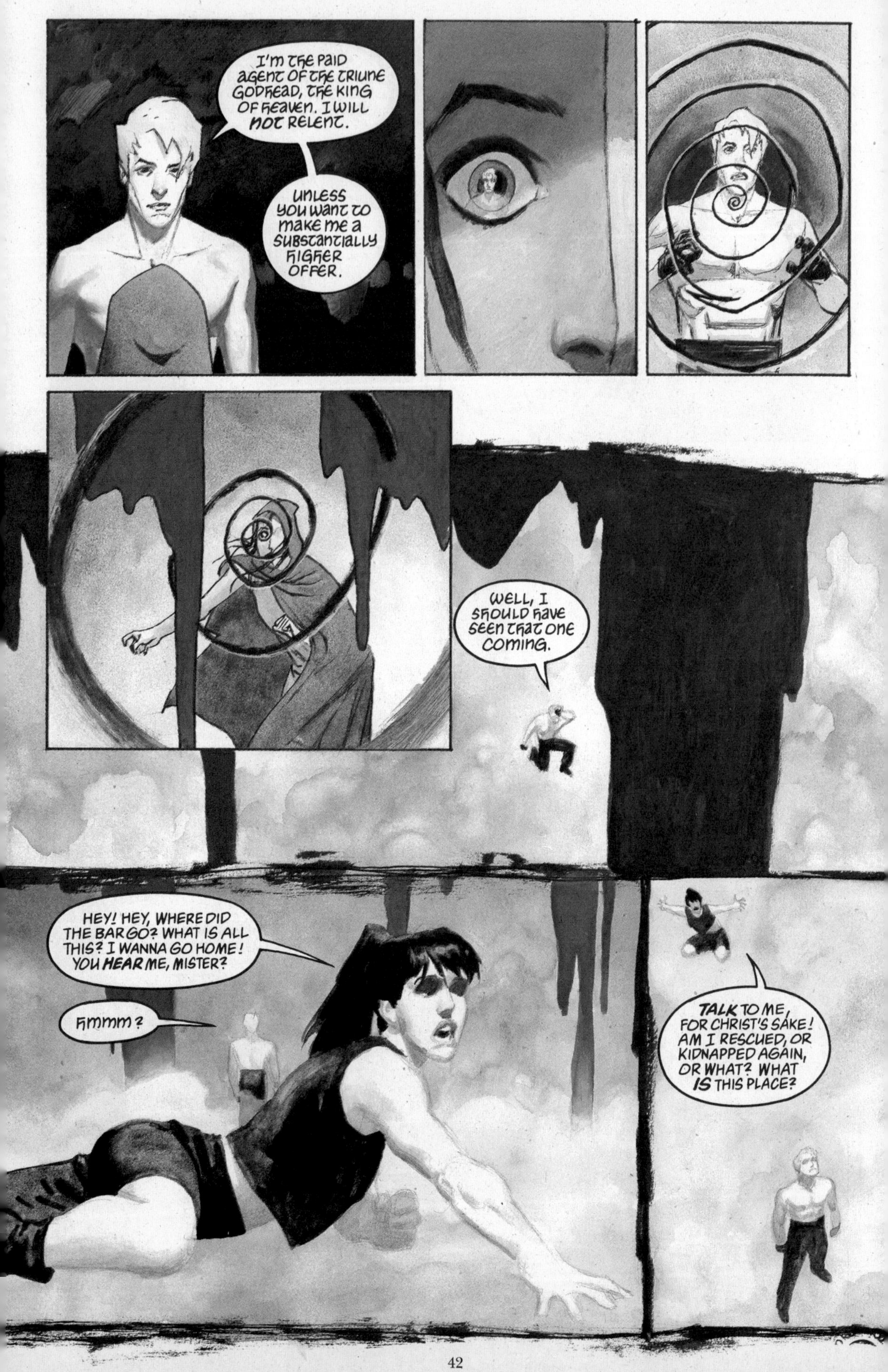
I'M THE PAID AGENT OF THE TRIUNE GODHEAD, THE KING OF HEAVEN. I WILL NOT RELENT.
UNLESS YOU WANT TO MAKE ME A SUBSTANTIALLY HIGHER OFFER.
WELL, I SHOULD HAVE SEEN THAT ONE COMING.
HEY! HEY, WHERE DID THE BAR GO? WHAT IS ALL THIS? I WANNA GO HOME! YOU HEAR ME, MISTER?
HMMM?
TALK TO ME, FOR CHRIST'S SAKE! AM I RESCUED, OR KIDNAPPED AGAIN, OR WHAT? WHAT IS THIS PLACE?

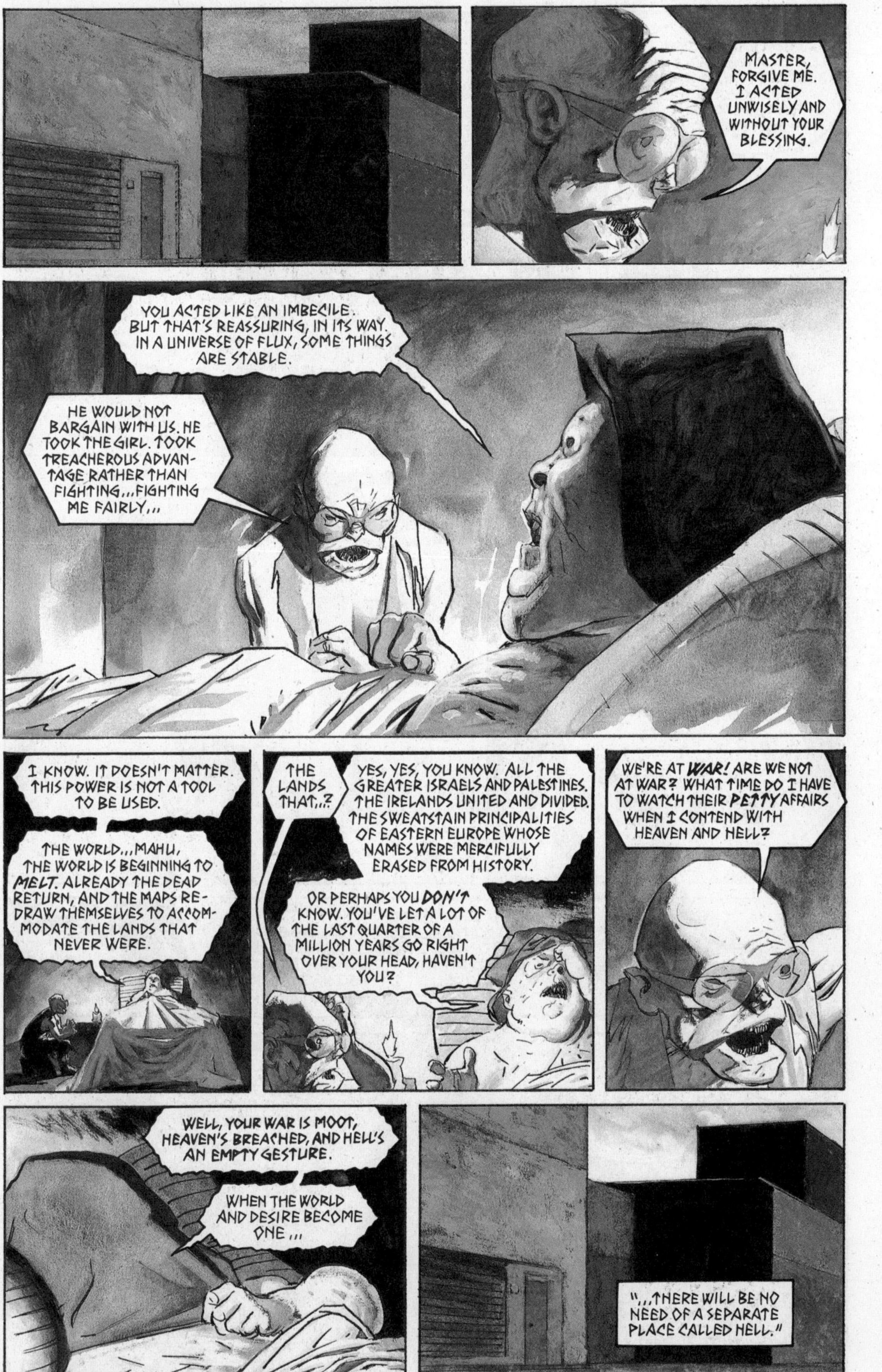

MASTER, FORGIVE ME. I ACTED UNWISELY AND WITHOUT YOUR BLESSING.
YOU ACTED LIKE AN IMBECILE. BUT THAT'S REASSURING, IN ITS WAY. IN A UNIVERSE OF FLUX, SOME THINGS ARE STABLE.
HE WOULD NOT BARGAIN WITH US. HE TOOK THE GIRL. TOOK TREACHEROUS ADVANTAGE RATHER THAN FIGHTING... FIGHTING ME FAIRLY...
I KNOW. IT DOESN'T MATTER. THIS POWER IS NOT A TOOL TO BE USED.
THE WORLD... MAHU, THE WORLD IS BEGINNING TO MELT. ALREADY THE DEAD RETURN, AND THE MAPS REDRAW THEMSELVES TO ACCOMMODATE THE LANDS THAT NEVER WERE.
THE LANDS THAT...?
YES, YES, YOU KNOW. ALL THE GREATER ISRAELS AND PALESTINES. THE IRELANDS UNITED AND DIVIDED. THE SWEATSTAIN PRINCIPALITIES OF EASTERN EUROPE WHOSE NAMES WERE MERCIFULLY ERASED FROM HISTORY.
OR PERHAPS YOU DON'T KNOW. YOU'VE LET A LOT OF THE LAST QUARTER OF A MILLION YEARS GO RIGHT OVER YOUR HEAD, HAVEN'T YOU?
WE'RE AT WAR! ARE WE NOT AT WAR? WHAT TIME DO I HAVE TO WATCH THEIR PETTY AFFAIRS WHEN I CONTEND WITH HEAVEN AND HELL?
WELL, YOUR WAR IS MOOT. HEAVEN'S BREACHED, AND HELL'S AN EMPTY GESTURE.
WHEN THE WORLD AND DESIRE BECOME ONE...
"...THERE WILL BE NO NEED OF A SEPARATE PLACE CALLED HELL."

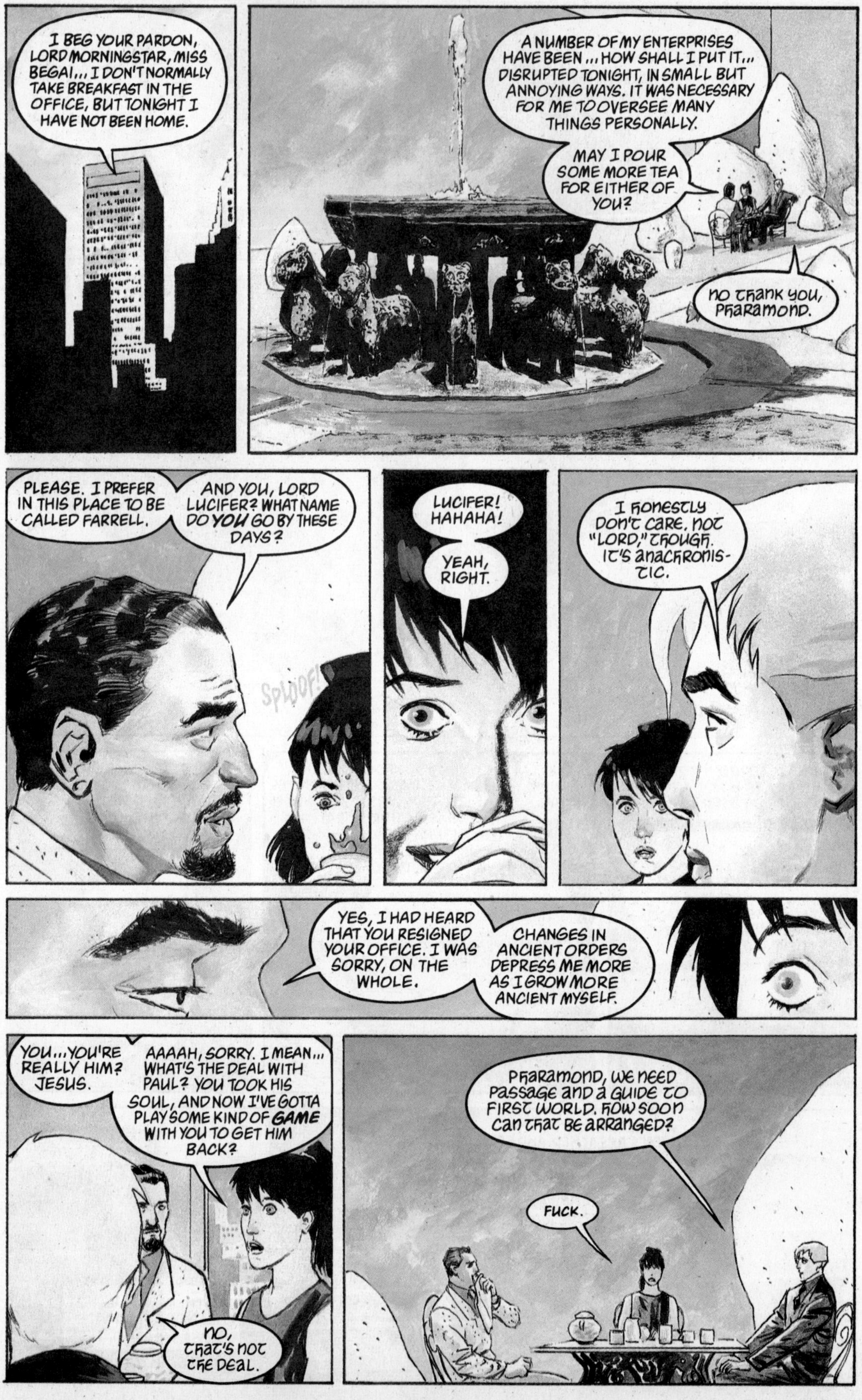
I BEG YOUR PARDON, LORD MORNINGSTAR, MISS BEGAI... I DON'T NORMALLY TAKE BREAKFAST IN THE OFFICE, BUT TONIGHT I HAVE NOT BEEN HOME.
A NUMBER OF MY ENTERPRISES HAVE BEEN... HOW SHALL I PUT IT... DISRUPTED TONIGHT, IN SMALL BUT ANNOYING WAYS. IT WAS NECESSARY FOR ME TO OVERSEE MANY THINGS PERSONALLY.
MAY I POUR SOME MORE TEA FOR EITHER OF YOU?
NO THANK YOU, PHARAMOND.
PLEASE. I PREFER IN THIS PLACE TO BE CALLED FARRELL.
AND YOU, LORD LUCIFER? WHAT NAME DO YOU GO BY THESE DAYS?
SPLOOF!
LUCIFER! HAHAHA!
YEAH, RIGHT.
I HONESTLY DON'T CARE, NOT "LORD," THOUGH. IT'S ANACHRONIS-TIC.
YES, I HAD HEARD THAT YOU RESIGNED YOUR OFFICE. I WAS SORRY, ON THE WHOLE.
CHANGES IN ANCIENT ORDERS DEPRESS ME MORE AS I GROW MORE ANCIENT MYSELF.
YOU... YOU'RE REALLY HIM? JESUS.
AAAAH, SORRY. I MEAN... WHAT'S THE DEAL WITH PAUL? YOU TOOK HIS SOUL, AND NOW I'VE GOTTA PLAY SOME KIND OF GAME WITH YOU TO GET HIM BACK?
NO, THAT'S NOT THE DEAL.
PHARAMOND, WE NEED PASSAGE AND A GUIDE TO FIRST WORLD. HOW SOON CAN THAT BE ARRANGED?
FUCK.

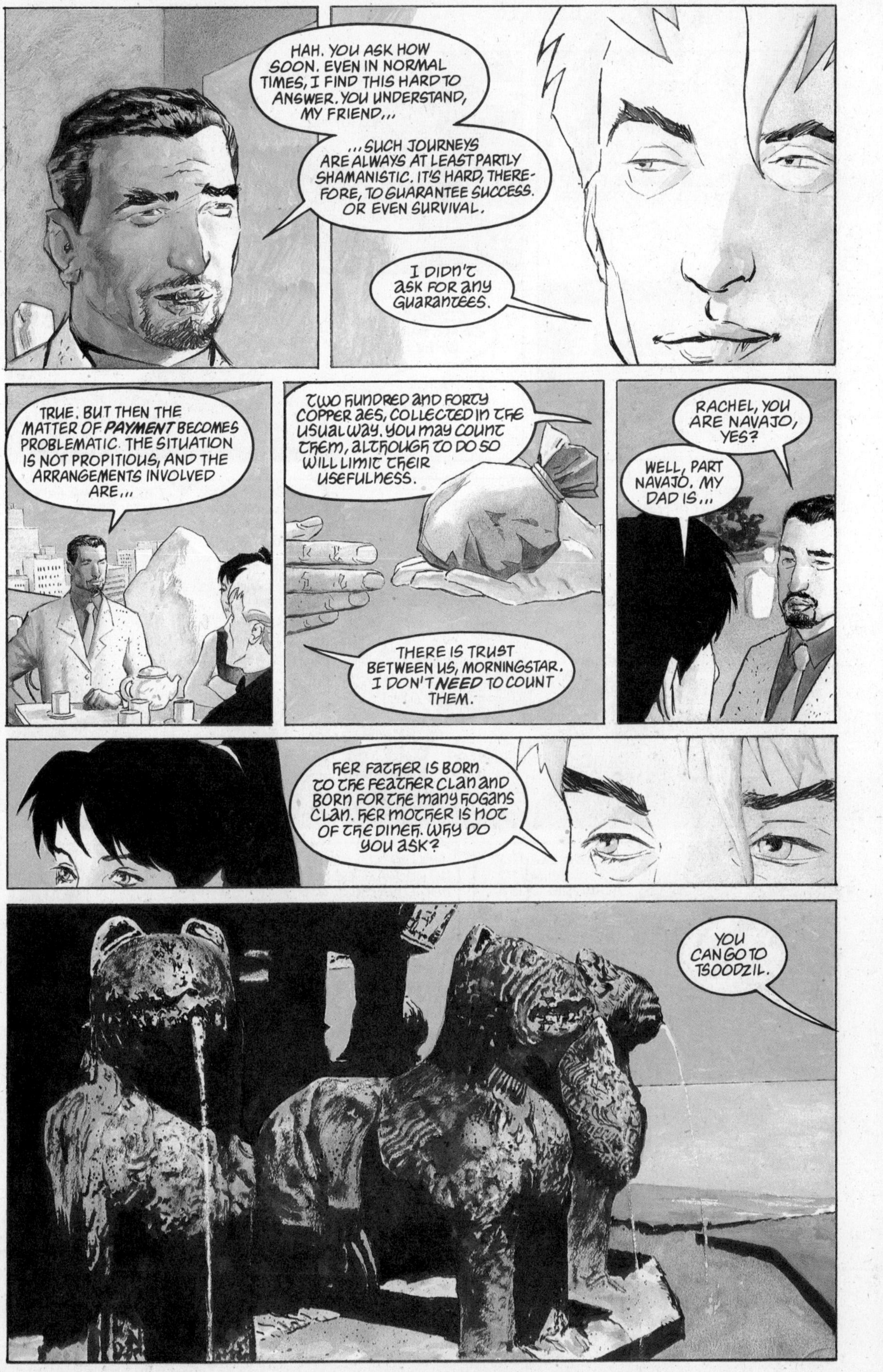
HAH. YOU ASK HOW SOON. EVEN IN NORMAL TIMES, I FIND THIS HARD TO ANSWER. YOU UNDERSTAND, MY FRIEND...
...SUCH JOURNEYS ARE ALWAYS AT LEAST PARTLY SHAMANISTIC. IT'S HARD, THEREFORE, TO GUARANTEE SUCCESS. OR EVEN SURVIVAL.
I DIDN'T ASK FOR ANY GUARANTEES.
TRUE. BUT THEN THE MATTER OF **PAYMENT** BECOMES PROBLEMATIC. THE SITUATION IS NOT PROPITIOUS, AND THE ARRANGEMENTS INVOLVED ARE...
TWO HUNDRED AND FORTY COPPER AES, COLLECTED IN THE USUAL WAY. YOU MAY COUNT THEM, ALTHOUGH TO DO SO WILL LIMIT THEIR USEFULNESS.
THERE IS TRUST BETWEEN US, MORNINGSTAR. I DON'T **NEED** TO COUNT THEM.
RACHEL, YOU ARE NAVAJO, YES?
WELL, PART NAVAJO. MY DAD IS...
HER FATHER IS BORN TO THE FEATHER CLAN AND BORN FOR THE MANY HOGANS CLAN. HER MOTHER IS NOT OF THE DINEH. WHY DO YOU ASK?
YOU CAN GO TO TSOODZIL.

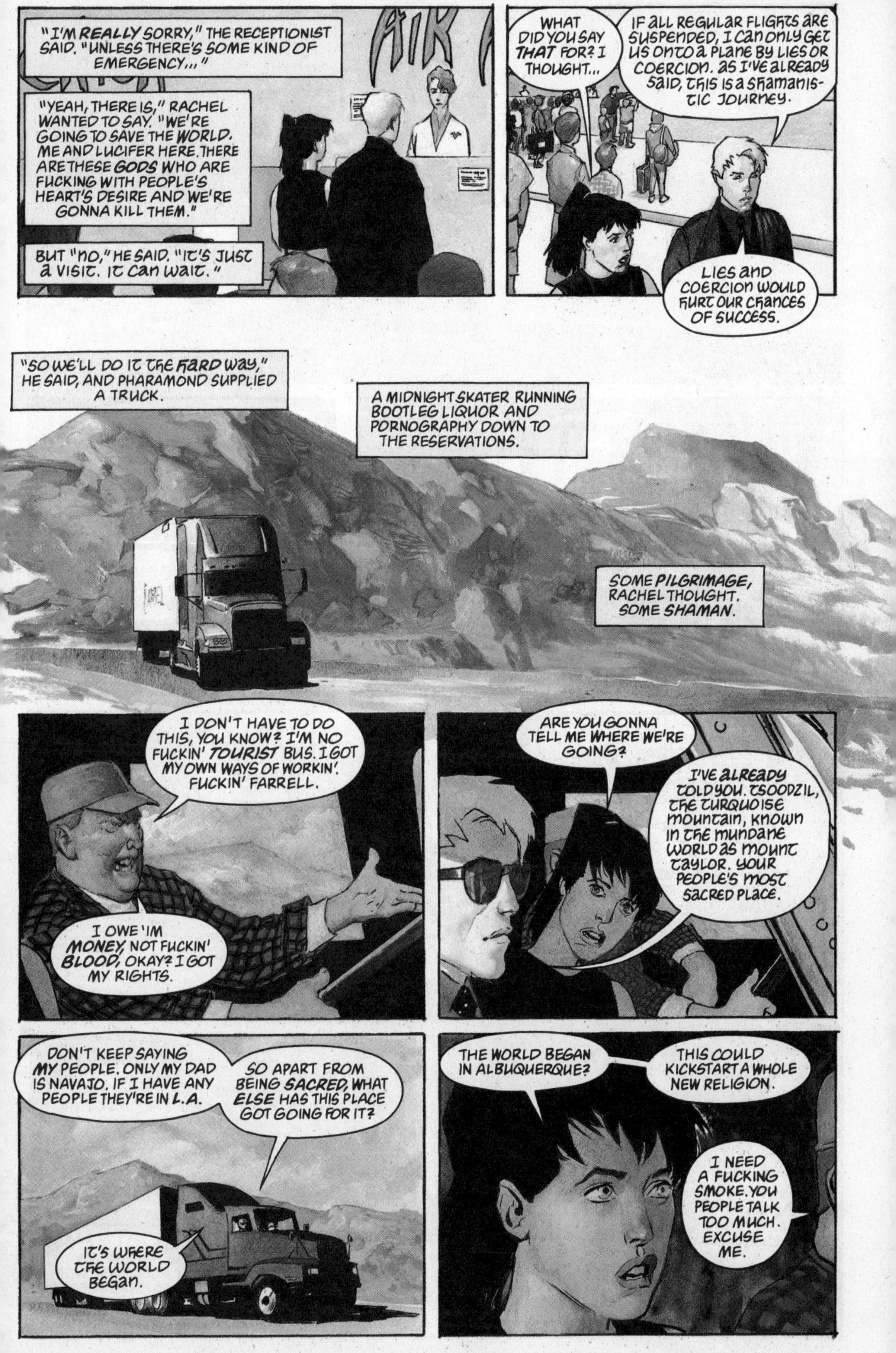
"I'M REALLY SORRY," THE RECEPTIONIST SAID. "UNLESS THERE'S SOME KIND OF EMERGENCY..."
"YEAH, THERE IS," RACHEL WANTED TO SAY. "WE'RE GOING TO SAVE THE WORLD. ME AND LUCIFER HERE. THERE ARE THESE GODS WHO ARE FUCKING WITH PEOPLE'S HEART'S DESIRE AND WE'RE GONNA KILL THEM."
BUT "NO," HE SAID. "IT'S JUST A VISIT. IT CAN WAIT."
WHAT DID YOU SAY THAT FOR? I THOUGHT...
IF ALL REGULAR FLIGHTS ARE SUSPENDED, I CAN ONLY GET US ONTO A PLANE BY LIES OR COERCION. AS I'VE ALREADY SAID, THIS IS A SHAMANISTIC JOURNEY.
LIES AND COERCION WOULD HURT OUR CHANCES OF SUCCESS.
"SO WE'LL DO IT THE HARD WAY," HE SAID, AND PHARAMOND SUPPLIED A TRUCK.
A MIDNIGHT SKATER RUNNING BOOTLEG LIQUOR AND PORNOGRAPHY DOWN TO THE RESERVATIONS.
SOME PILGRIMAGE, RACHEL THOUGHT. SOME SHAMAN.
I DON'T HAVE TO DO THIS, YOU KNOW? I'M NO FUCKIN' TOURIST BUS. I GOT MY OWN WAYS OF WORKIN'. FUCKIN' FARRELL.
I OWE 'IM MONEY, NOT FUCKIN' BLOOD, OKAY? I GOT MY RIGHTS.
ARE YOU GONNA TELL ME WHERE WE'RE GOING?
I'VE ALREADY TOLD YOU. TSOODZIL, THE TURQUOISE MOUNTAIN, KNOWN IN THE MUNDANE WORLD AS MOUNT TAYLOR. YOUR PEOPLE'S MOST SACRED PLACE.
DON'T KEEP SAYING MY PEOPLE. ONLY MY DAD IS NAVAJO. IF I HAVE ANY PEOPLE THEY'RE IN L.A.
SO APART FROM BEING SACRED, WHAT ELSE HAS THIS PLACE GOT GOING FOR IT?
IT'S WHERE THE WORLD BEGAN.
THE WORLD BEGAN IN ALBUQUERQUE?
THIS COULD KICKSTART A WHOLE NEW RELIGION.
I NEED A FUCKING SMOKE. YOU PEOPLE TALK TOO MUCH. EXCUSE ME.

50

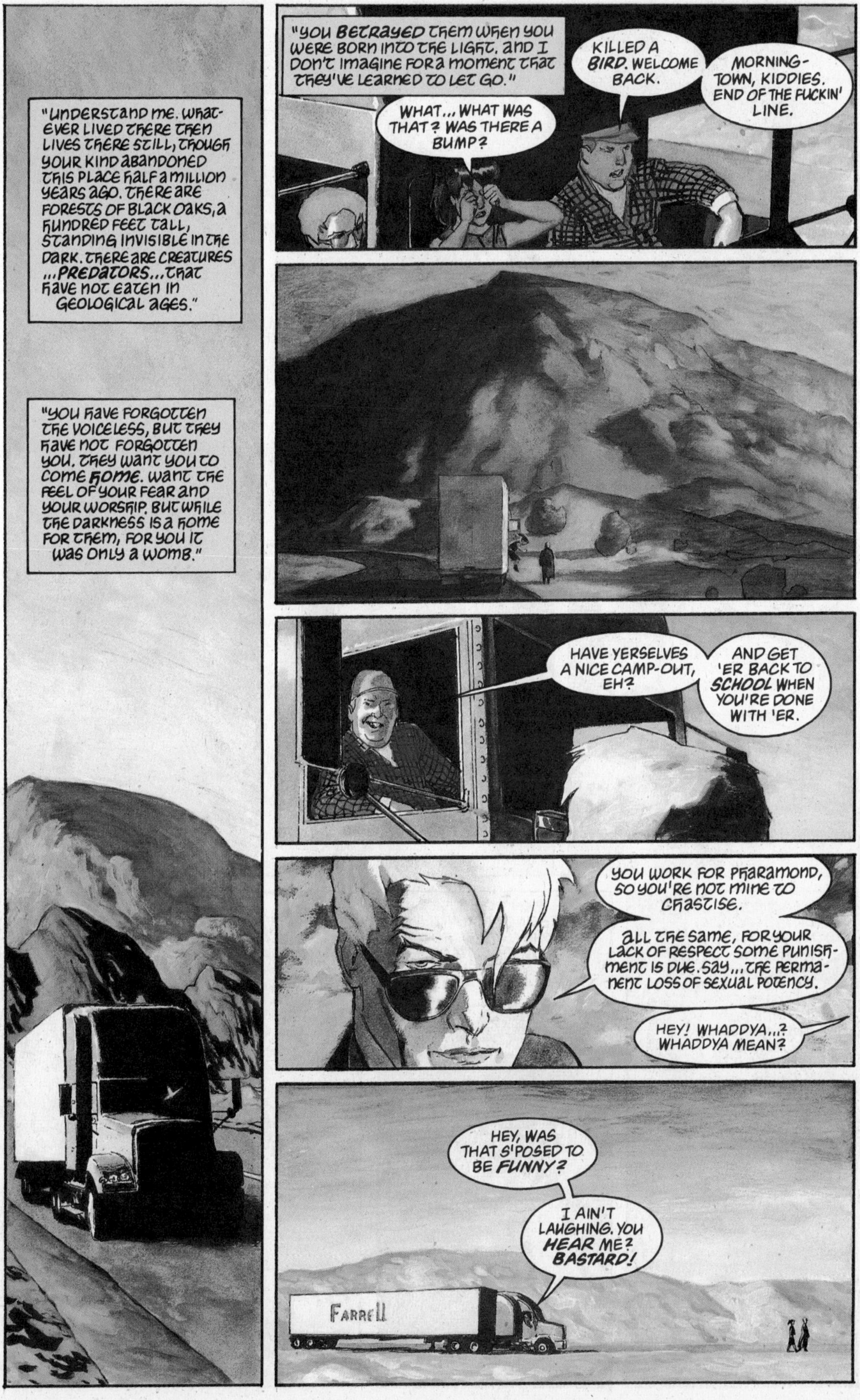
"UNDERSTAND ME. WHATEVER LIVED THERE THEN LIVES THERE STILL, THOUGH YOUR KIND ABANDONED THIS PLACE HALF A MILLION YEARS AGO. THERE ARE FORESTS OF BLACK OAKS, A HUNDRED FEET TALL, STANDING INVISIBLE IN THE DARK. THERE ARE CREATURES ...PREDATORS...THAT HAVE NOT EATEN IN GEOLOGICAL AGES."
"YOU HAVE FORGOTTEN THE VOICELESS, BUT THEY HAVE NOT FORGOTTEN YOU. THEY WANT YOU TO COME HOME. WANT THE FEEL OF YOUR FEAR AND YOUR WORSHIP, BUT WHILE THE DARKNESS IS A HOME FOR THEM, FOR YOU IT WAS ONLY A WOMB."
"YOU BETRAYED THEM WHEN YOU WERE BORN INTO THE LIGHT, AND I DON'T IMAGINE FOR A MOMENT THAT THEY'VE LEARNED TO LET GO."
WHAT... WHAT WAS THAT? WAS THERE A BUMP?
KILLED A BIRD. WELCOME BACK.
MORNING-TOWN, KIDDIES. END OF THE FUCKIN' LINE.
HAVE YERSELVES A NICE CAMP-OUT, EH?
AND GET 'ER BACK TO SCHOOL WHEN YOU'RE DONE WITH 'ER.
YOU WORK FOR PHARAMOND, SO YOU'RE NOT MINE TO CHASTISE.
ALL THE SAME, FOR YOUR LACK OF RESPECT SOME PUNISHMENT IS DUE. SAY... THE PERMANENT LOSS OF SEXUAL POTENCY.
HEY! WHADDYA...? WHADDYA MEAN?
HEY, WAS THAT S'POSED TO BE FUNNY?
I AIN'T LAUGHING. YOU HEAR ME? BASTARD!
FARRELL

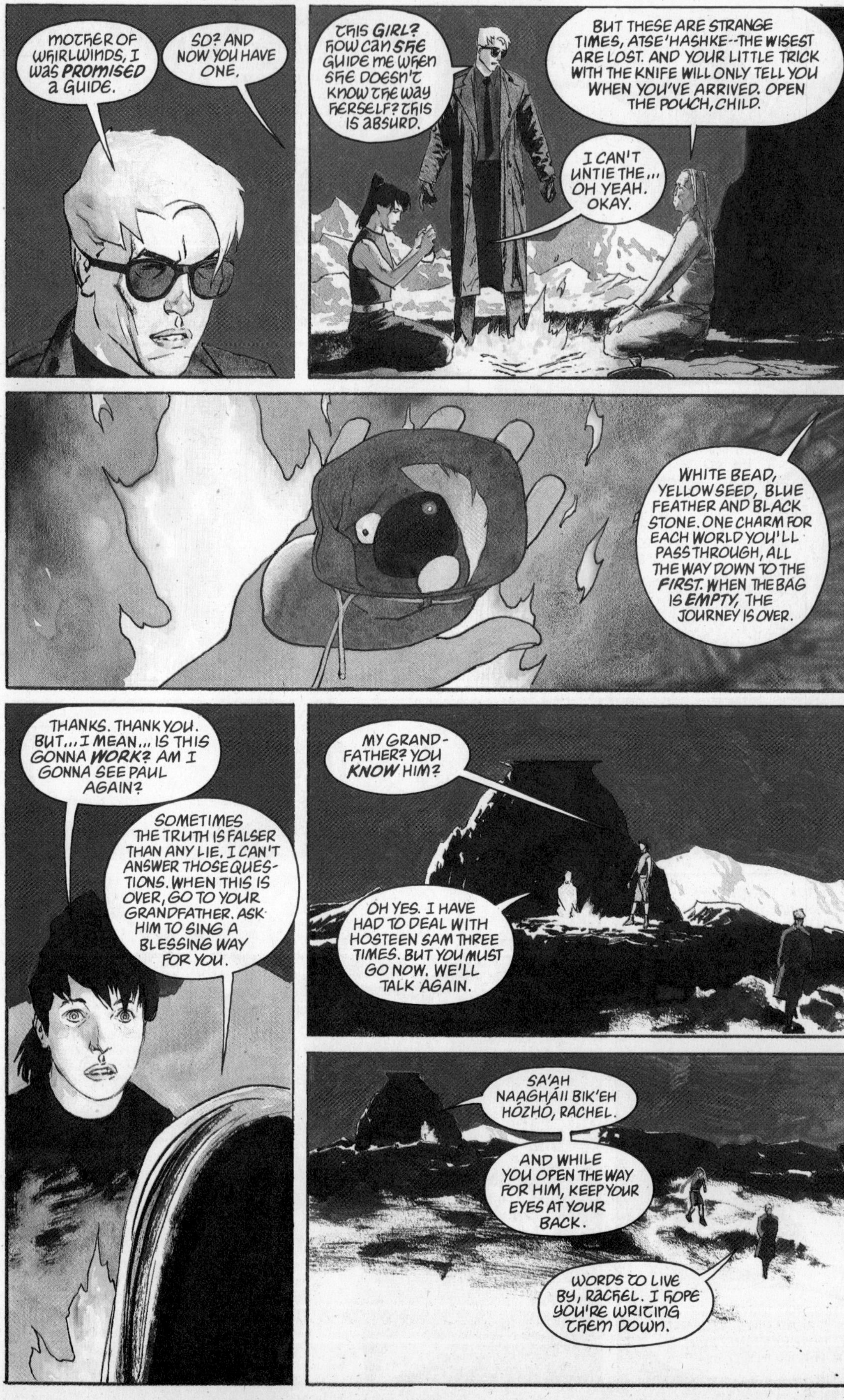
MOTHER OF WHIRLWINDS, I WAS PROMISED A GUIDE.
SO? AND NOW YOU HAVE ONE.
THIS GIRL? HOW CAN SHE GUIDE ME WHEN SHE DOESN'T KNOW THE WAY HERSELF? THIS IS ABSURD.
BUT THESE ARE STRANGE TIMES, ATSE'HASHKE--THE WISEST ARE LOST. AND YOUR LITTLE TRICK WITH THE KNIFE WILL ONLY TELL YOU WHEN YOU'VE ARRIVED. OPEN THE POUCH, CHILD.
I CAN'T UNTIE THE... OH YEAH. OKAY.
WHITE BEAD, YELLOW SEED, BLUE FEATHER AND BLACK STONE. ONE CHARM FOR EACH WORLD YOU'LL PASS THROUGH, ALL THE WAY DOWN TO THE FIRST. WHEN THE BAG IS EMPTY, THE JOURNEY IS OVER.
THANKS. THANK YOU. BUT... I MEAN... IS THIS GONNA WORK? AM I GONNA SEE PAUL AGAIN?
SOMETIMES THE TRUTH IS FALSER THAN ANY LIE. I CAN'T ANSWER THOSE QUESTIONS. WHEN THIS IS OVER, GO TO YOUR GRANDFATHER. ASK HIM TO SING A BLESSING WAY FOR YOU.
MY GRANDFATHER? YOU KNOW HIM?
OH YES. I HAVE HAD TO DEAL WITH HOSTEEN SAM THREE TIMES. BUT YOU MUST GO NOW. WE'LL TALK AGAIN.
SA'AH NAAGHÁII BIK'EH HÓZHÓ, RACHEL.
AND WHILE YOU OPEN THE WAY FOR HIM, KEEP YOUR EYES AT YOUR BACK.
WORDS TO LIVE BY, RACHEL. I HOPE YOU'RE WRITING THEM DOWN.

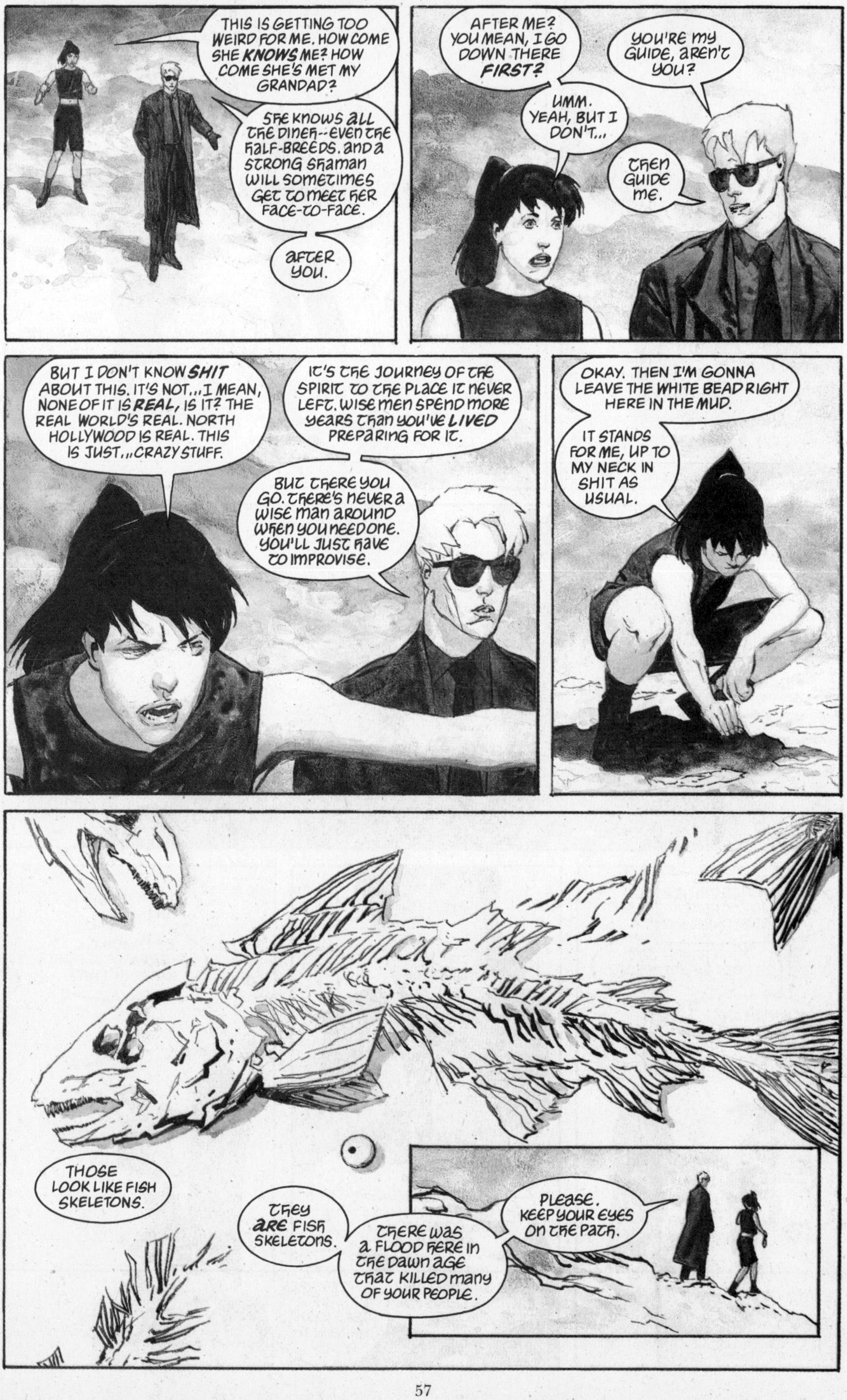
THIS IS GETTING TOO WEIRD FOR ME. HOW COME SHE KNOWS ME? HOW COME SHE'S MET MY GRANDAD?
SHE KNOWS ALL THE DINEH-- EVEN THE HALF-BREEDS. AND A STRONG SHAMAN WILL SOMETIMES GET TO MEET HER FACE-TO-FACE.
AFTER YOU.
AFTER ME? YOU MEAN, I GO DOWN THERE FIRST?
YOU'RE MY GUIDE, AREN'T YOU?
UMM. YEAH, BUT I DON'T...
THEN GUIDE ME.
BUT I DON'T KNOW SHIT ABOUT THIS. IT'S NOT... I MEAN, NONE OF IT IS REAL, IS IT? THE REAL WORLD'S REAL. NORTH HOLLYWOOD IS REAL. THIS IS JUST... CRAZY STUFF.
IT'S THE JOURNEY OF THE SPIRIT TO THE PLACE IT NEVER LEFT. WISE MEN SPEND MORE YEARS THAN YOU'VE LIVED PREPARING FOR IT.
BUT THERE YOU GO. THERE'S NEVER A WISE MAN AROUND WHEN YOU NEED ONE. YOU'LL JUST HAVE TO IMPROVISE.
OKAY. THEN I'M GONNA LEAVE THE WHITE BEAD RIGHT HERE IN THE MUD.
IT STANDS FOR ME, UP TO MY NECK IN SHIT AS USUAL.
THOSE LOOK LIKE FISH SKELETONS.
THEY ARE FISH SKELETONS.
THERE WAS A FLOOD HERE IN THE DAWN AGE THAT KILLED MANY OF YOUR PEOPLE.
PLEASE. KEEP YOUR EYES ON THE PATH.

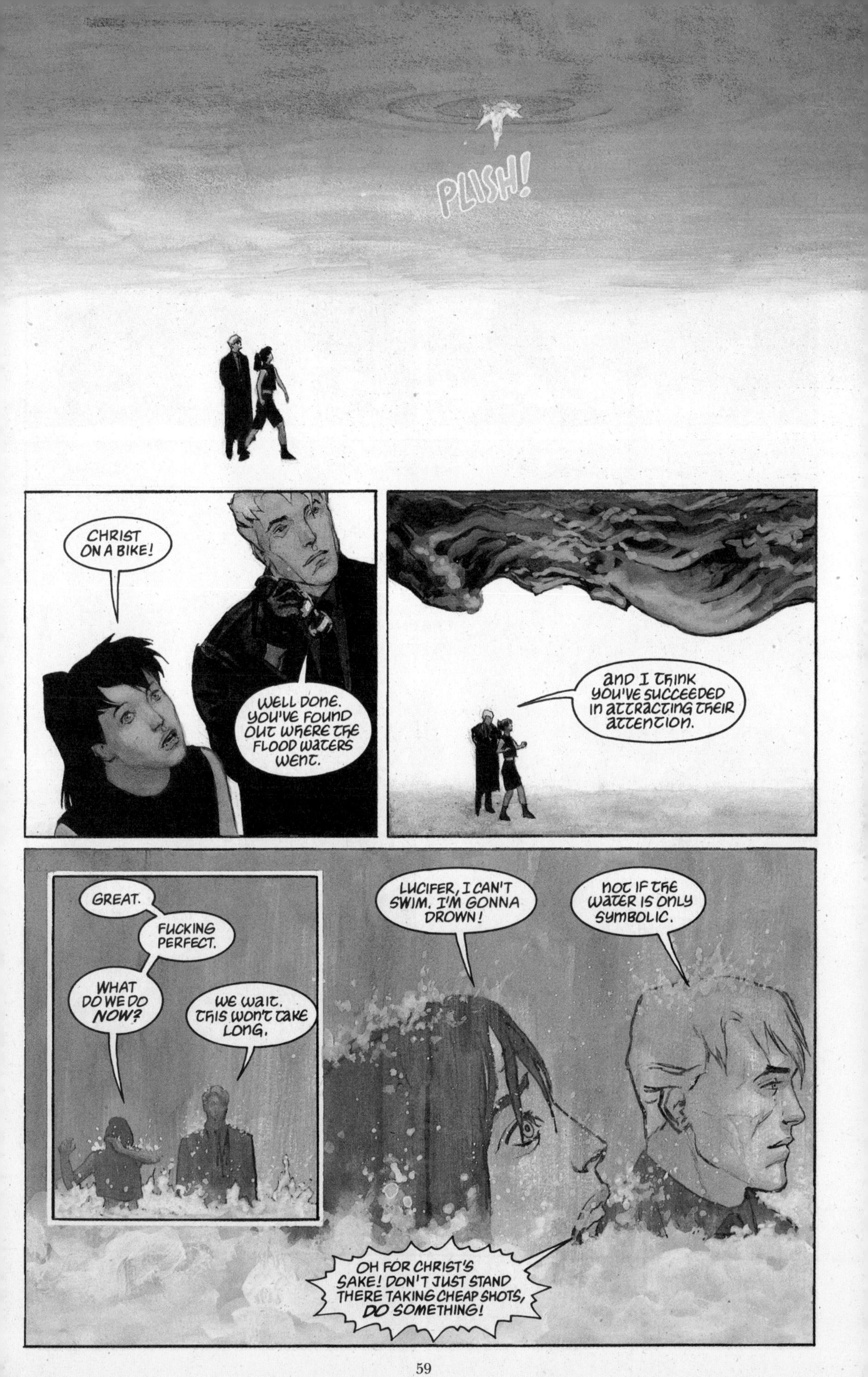
PLISH!
CHRIST ON A BIKE!
WELL DONE. YOU'VE FOUND OUT WHERE THE FLOOD WATERS WENT.
AND I THINK YOU'VE SUCCEEDED IN ATTRACTING THEIR ATTENTION.
GREAT.
FUCKING PERFECT.
WHAT DO WE DO NOW?
WE WAIT. THIS WON'T TAKE LONG.
LUCIFER, I CAN'T SWIM. I'M GONNA DROWN!
NOT IF THE WATER IS ONLY SYMBOLIC.
OH FOR CHRIST'S SAKE! DON'T JUST STAND THERE TAKING CHEAP SHOTS, DO SOMETHING!

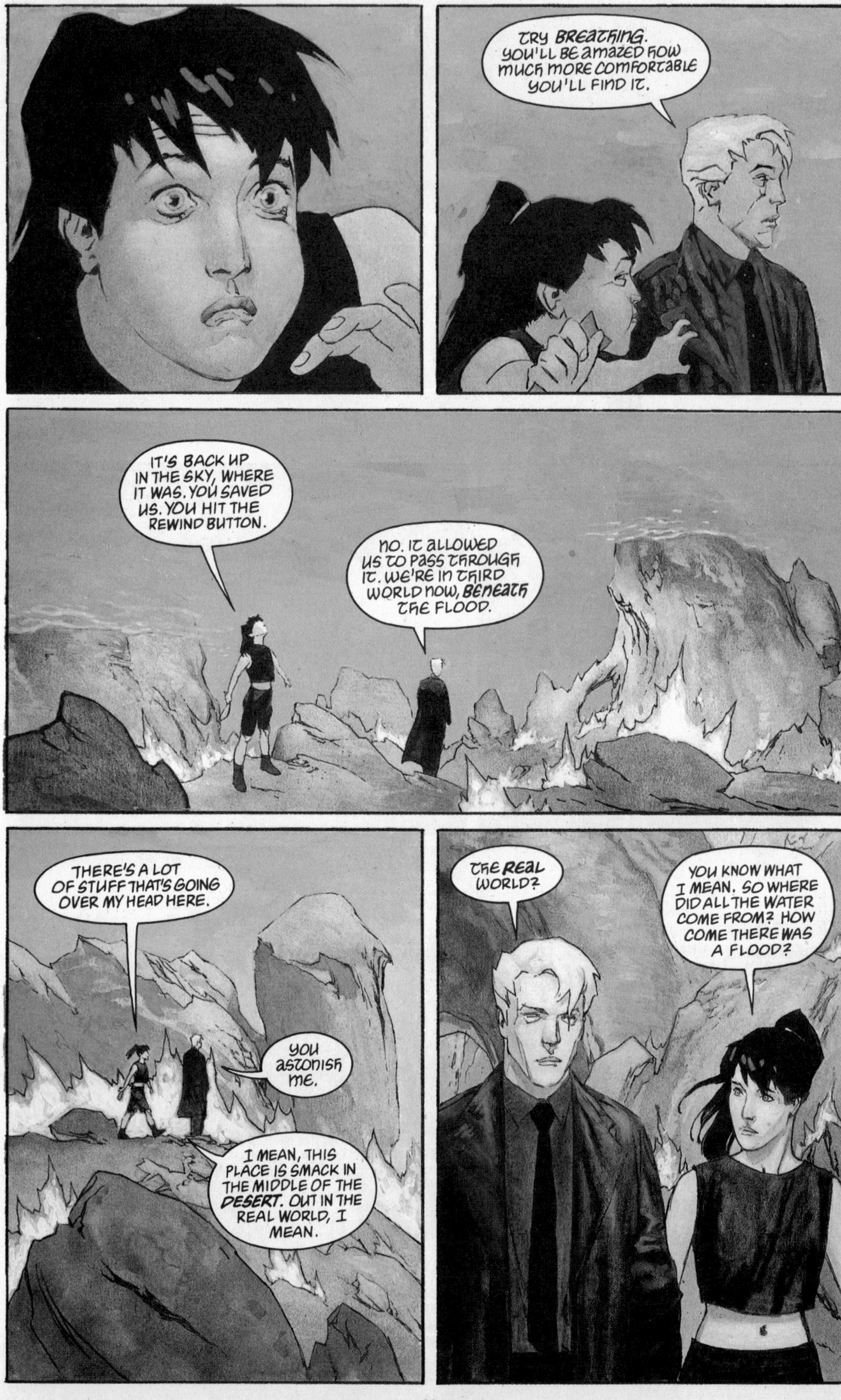

TRY BREATHING. YOU'LL BE AMAZED HOW MUCH MORE COMFORTABLE YOU'LL FIND IT.
IT'S BACK UP IN THE SKY, WHERE IT WAS. YOU SAVED US. YOU HIT THE REWIND BUTTON.
NO. IT ALLOWED US TO PASS THROUGH IT. WE'RE IN THIRD WORLD NOW, BENEATH THE FLOOD.
THERE'S A LOT OF STUFF THAT'S GOING OVER MY HEAD HERE.
YOU ASTONISH ME.
I MEAN, THIS PLACE IS SMACK IN THE MIDDLE OF THE DESERT. OUT IN THE REAL WORLD, I MEAN.
THE REAL WORLD?
YOU KNOW WHAT I MEAN. SO WHERE DID ALL THE WATER COME FROM? HOW COME THERE WAS A FLOOD?

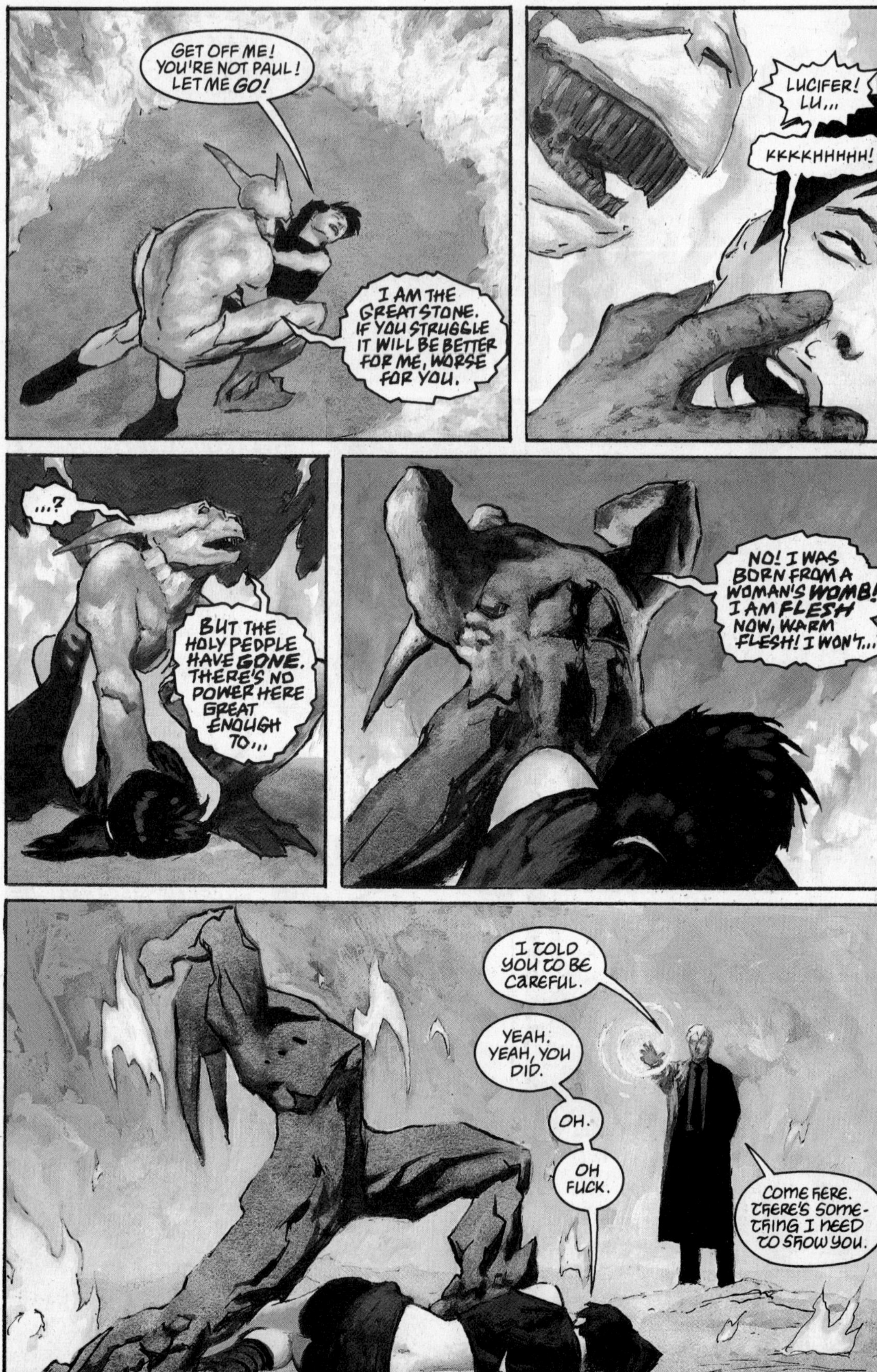
GET OFF ME! YOU'RE NOT PAUL! LET ME GO!
I AM THE GREAT STONE. IF YOU STRUGGLE IT WILL BE BETTER FOR ME, WORSE FOR YOU.
LUCIFER! LU...
KKKKHHHHH!
...?
BUT THE HOLY PEOPLE HAVE GONE. THERE'S NO POWER HERE GREAT ENOUGH TO...
NO! I WAS BORN FROM A WOMAN'S WOMB! I AM FLESH NOW, WARM FLESH! I WON'T...
I TOLD YOU TO BE CAREFUL.
YEAH. YEAH, YOU DID.
OH.
OH FUCK.
COME HERE. THERE'S SOME-THING I NEED TO SHOW YOU.

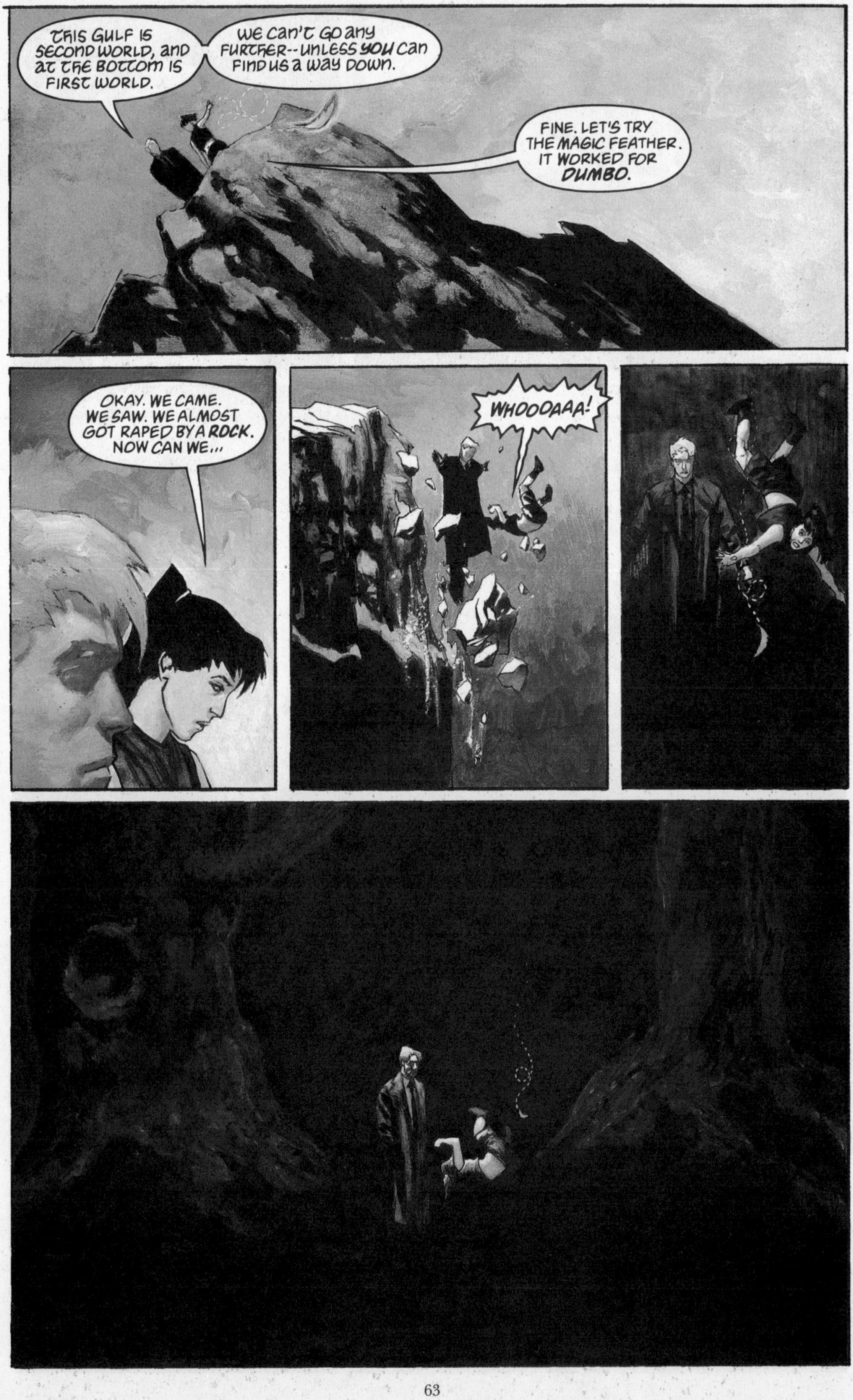

THIS GULF IS SECOND WORLD, AND AT THE BOTTOM IS FIRST WORLD.
WE CAN'T GO ANY FURTHER--UNLESS YOU CAN FIND US A WAY DOWN.
FINE. LET'S TRY THE MAGIC FEATHER. IT WORKED FOR DUMBO.
OKAY. WE CAME. WE SAW. WE ALMOST GOT RAPED BY A ROCK. NOW CAN WE...
WHOOOAAA!

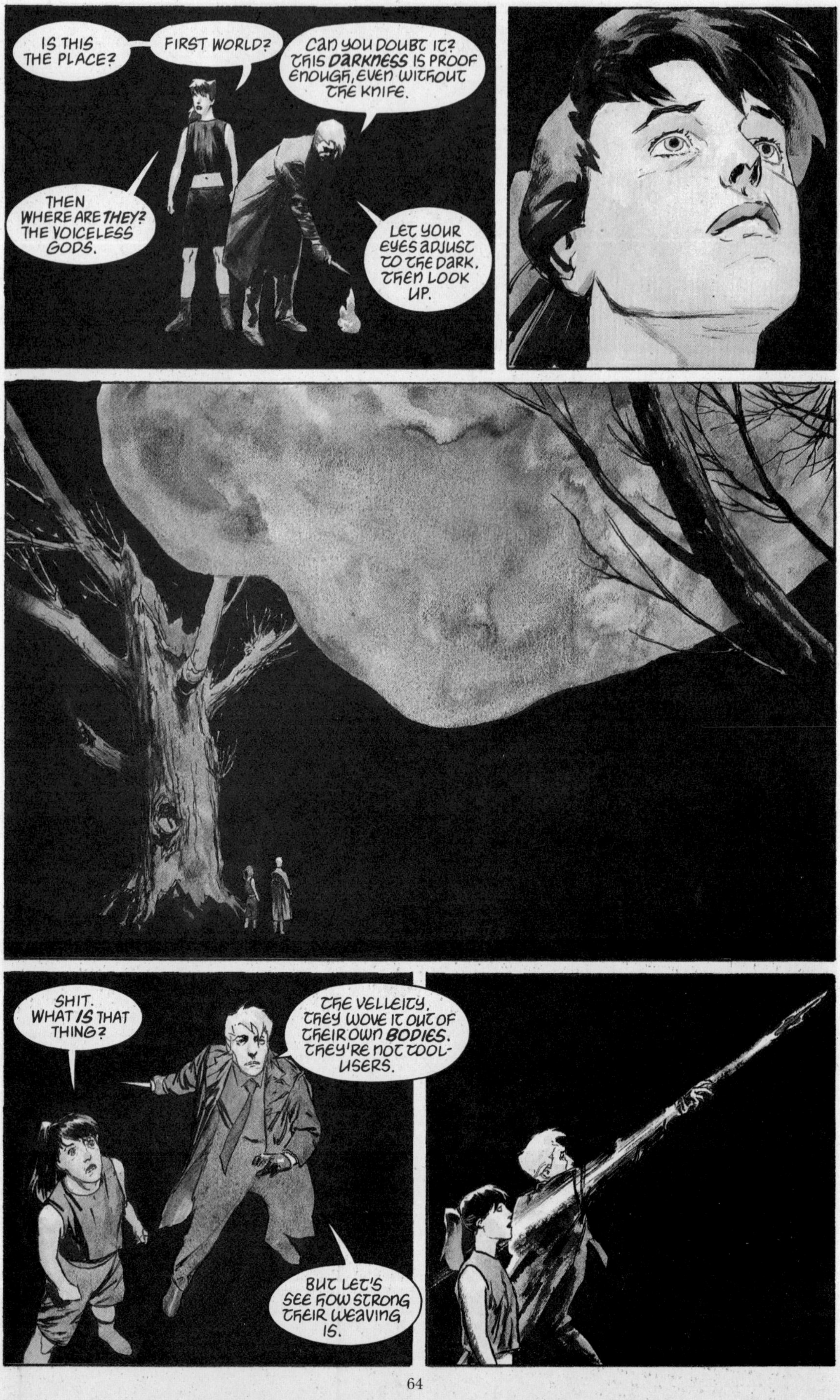
IS THIS THE PLACE?
FIRST WORLD?
CAN YOU DOUBT IT? THIS DARKNESS IS PROOF ENOUGH, EVEN WITHOUT THE KNIFE.
THEN WHERE ARE THEY? THE VOICELESS GODS.
LET YOUR EYES ADJUST TO THE DARK. THEN LOOK UP.
SHIT. WHAT IS THAT THING?
THE VELLEITY. THEY WOVE IT OUT OF THEIR OWN BODIES. THEY'RE NOT TOOL-USERS.
BUT LET'S SEE HOW STRONG THEIR WEAVING IS.

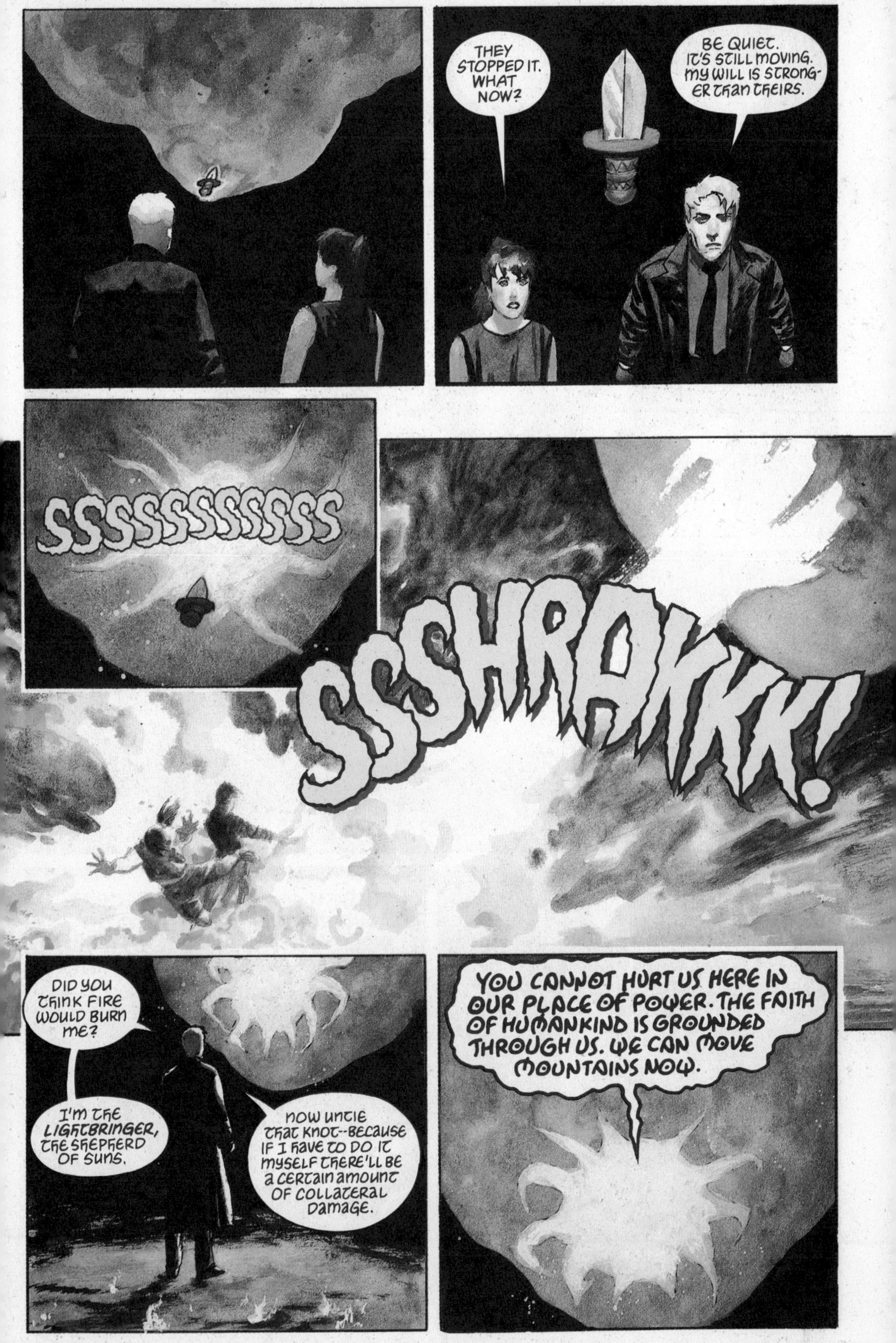
THEY STOPPED IT. WHAT NOW?
BE QUIET. IT'S STILL MOVING. MY WILL IS STRONGER THAN THEIRS.
SSSSSSSSSSS
SSSHRAKKK!
DID YOU THINK FIRE WOULD BURN ME?
I'M THE LIGHTBRINGER, THE SHEPHERD OF SUNS.
NOW UNTIE THAT KNOT--BECAUSE IF I HAVE TO DO IT MYSELF THERE'LL BE A CERTAIN AMOUNT OF COLLATERAL DAMAGE.
YOU CANNOT HURT US HERE IN OUR PLACE OF POWER. THE FAITH OF HUMANKIND IS GROUNDED THROUGH US. WE CAN MOVE MOUNTAINS NOW.

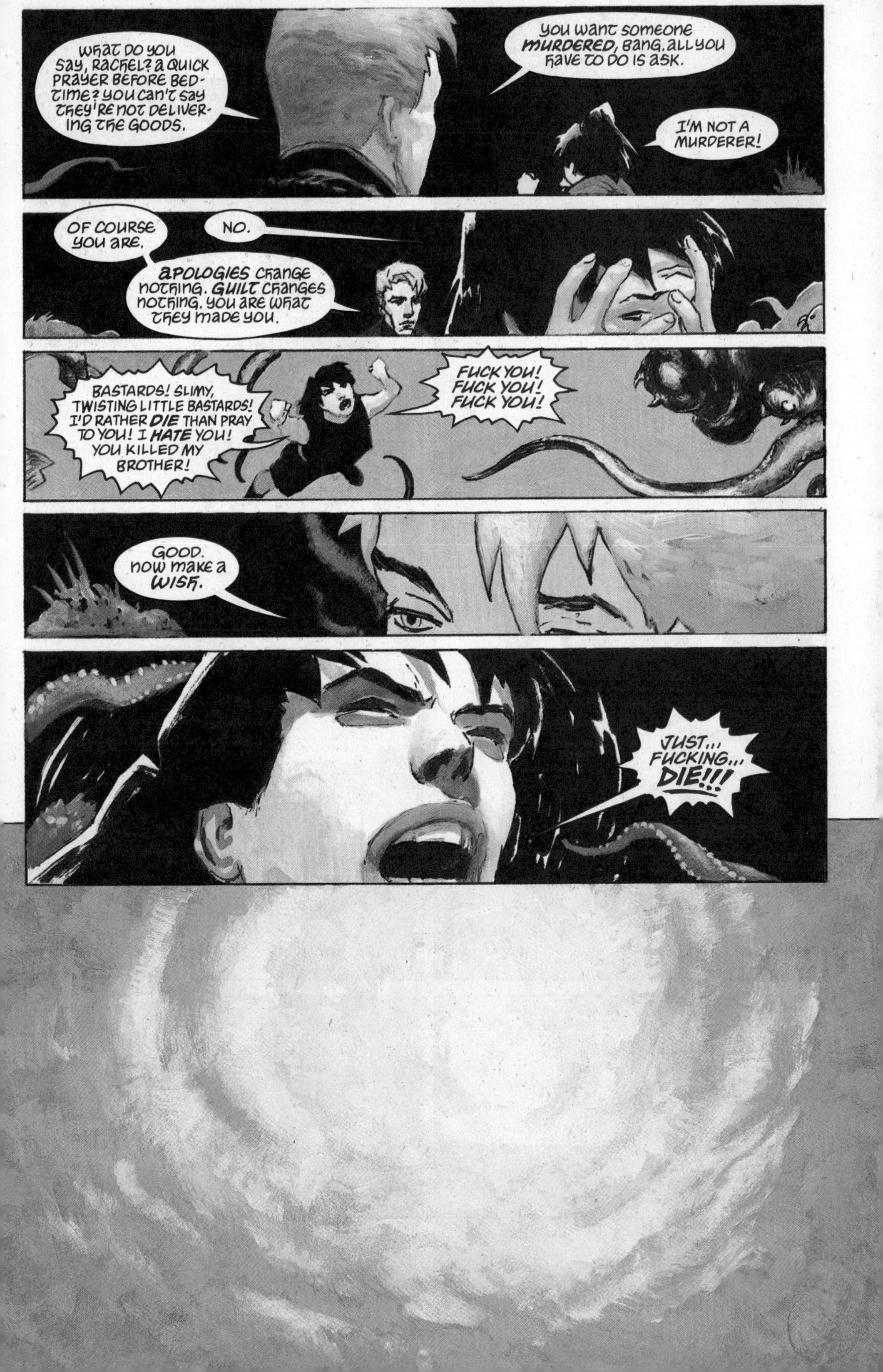
WHAT DO YOU SAY, RACHEL? A QUICK PRAYER BEFORE BED-TIME? YOU CAN'T SAY THEY'RE NOT DELIVER-ING THE GOODS.
YOU WANT SOMEONE MURDERED, BANG. ALL YOU HAVE TO DO IS ASK.
I'M NOT A MURDERER!
OF COURSE YOU ARE.
NO.
APOLOGIES CHANGE NOTHING. GUILT CHANGES NOTHING. YOU ARE WHAT THEY MADE YOU.
BASTARDS! SLIMY, TWISTING LITTLE BASTARDS! I'D RATHER DIE THAN PRAY TO YOU! I HATE YOU! YOU KILLED MY BROTHER!
FUCK YOU! FUCK YOU! FUCK YOU!
GOOD. NOW MAKE A WISH.
JUST... FUCKING... DIE!!!

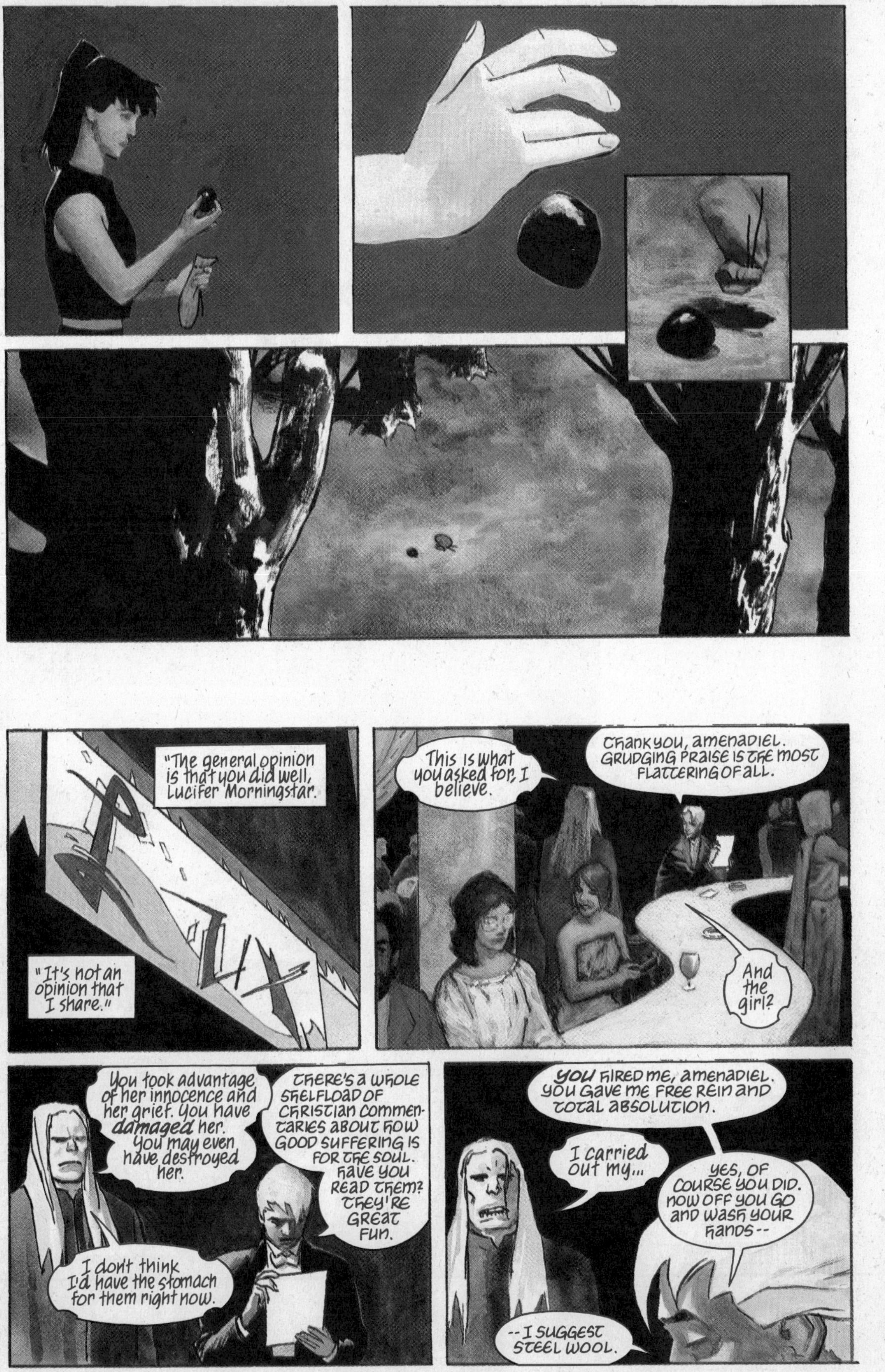
"The general opinion is that you did well, Lucifer Morningstar."
"It's not an opinion that I share."
This is what you asked for, I believe.
THANK YOU, AMENADIEL. GRUDGING PRAISE IS THE MOST FLATTERING OF ALL.
And the girl?
You took advantage of her innocence and her grief. You have damaged her. You may even have destroyed her.
THERE'S A WHOLE SHELFLOAD OF CHRISTIAN COMMENTARIES ABOUT HOW GOOD SUFFERING IS FOR THE SOUL. HAVE YOU READ THEM? THEY'RE GREAT FUN.
I don't think I'd have the stomach for them right now.
YOU HIRED ME, AMENADIEL. YOU GAVE ME FREE REIN AND TOTAL ABSOLUTION.
I carried out my...
YES, OF COURSE YOU DID. NOW OFF YOU GO AND WASH YOUR HANDS--
--I SUGGEST STEEL WOOL.

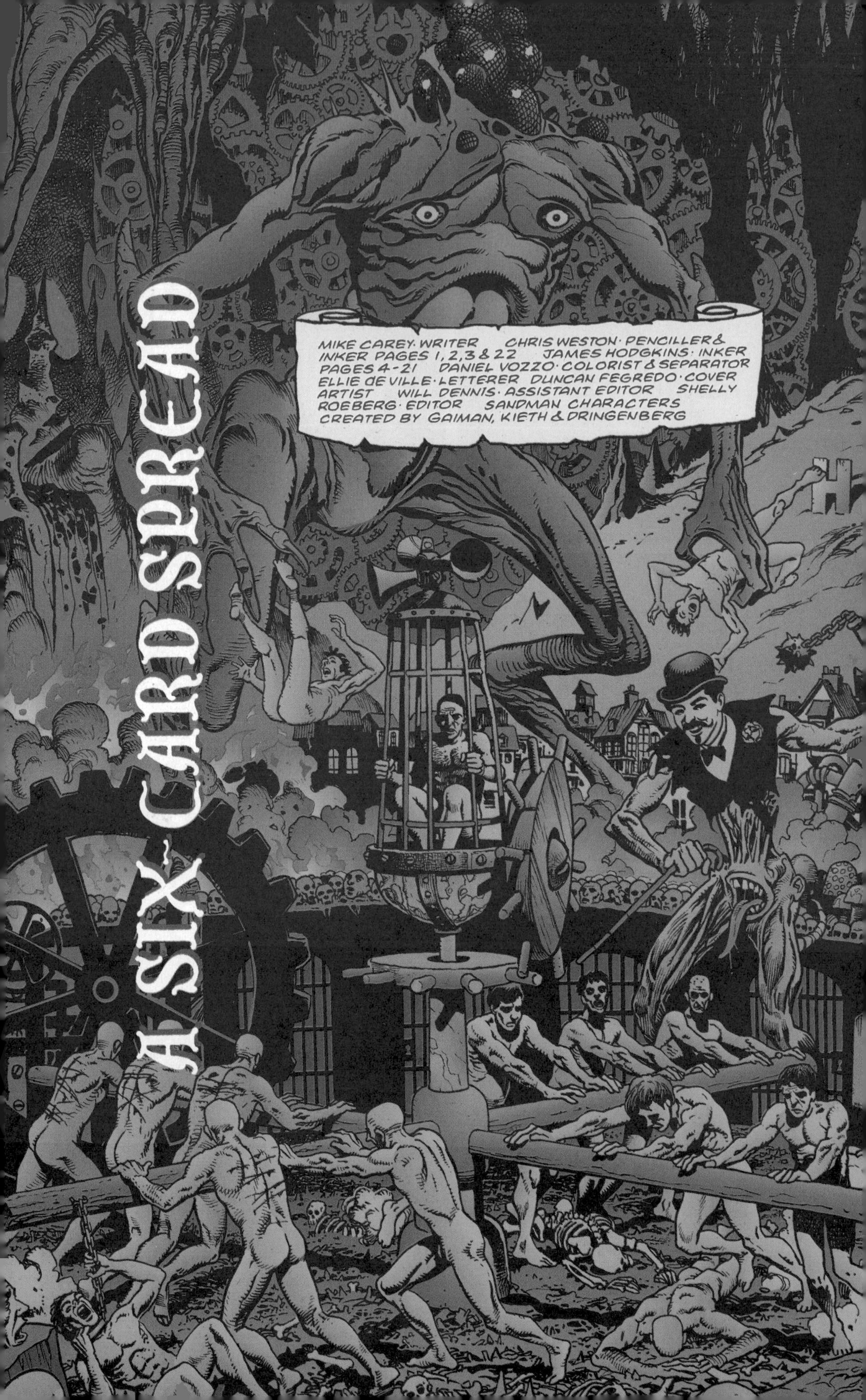
A SIX-CARD SPREAD
MIKE CAREY· WRITER CHRIS WESTON· PENCILLER & INKER PAGES 1, 2, 3 & 22 JAMES HODGKINS· INKER PAGES 4-21 DANIEL VOZZO· COLORIST & SEPARATOR ELLIE DE VILLE· LETTERER DUNCAN FEGREDO· COVER ARTIST WILL DENNIS· ASSISTANT EDITOR SHELLY ROEBERG· EDITOR SANDMAN CHARACTERS CREATED BY GAIMAN, KIETH & DRINGENBERG

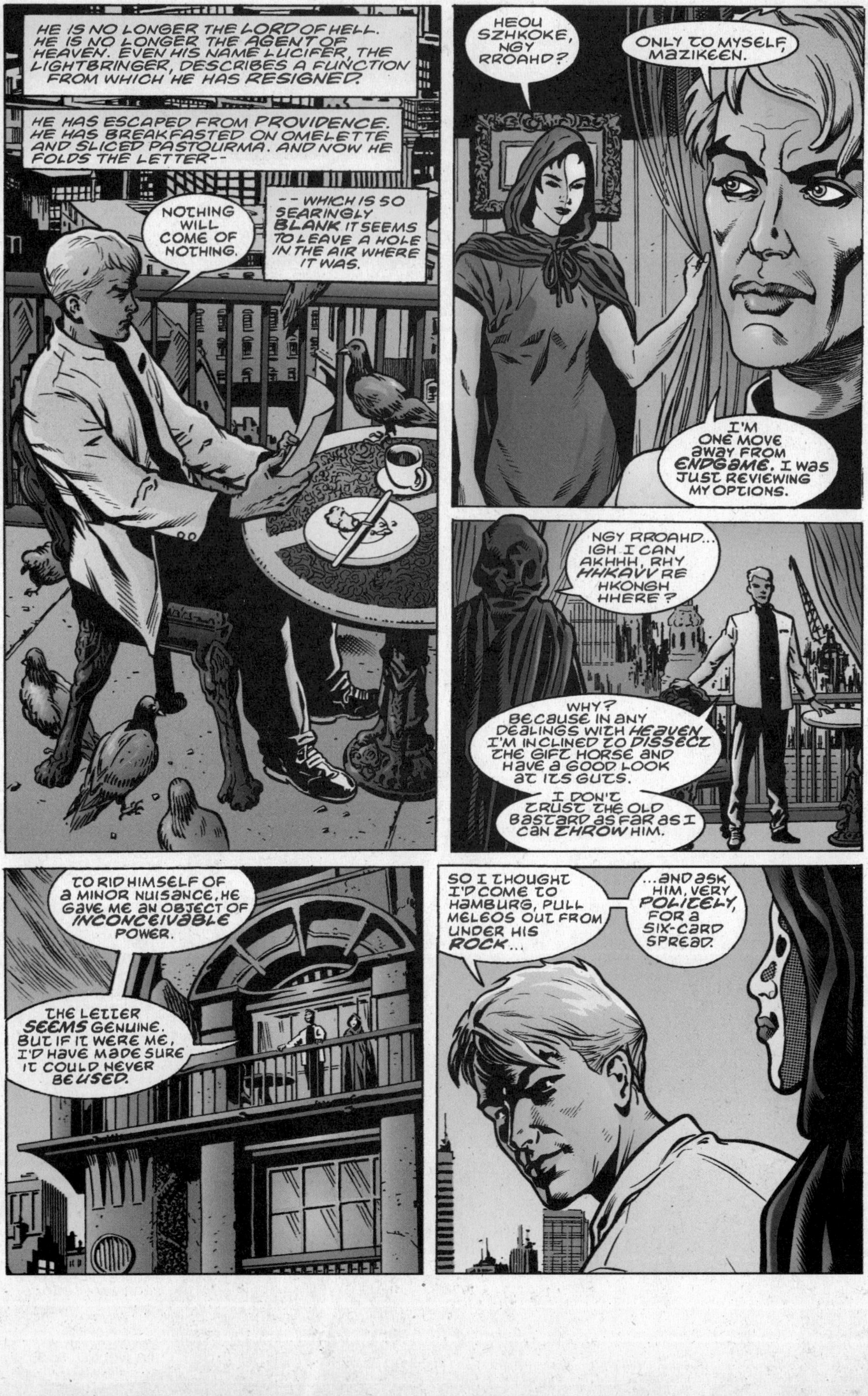
HE IS NO LONGER THE LORD OF HELL. HE IS NO LONGER THE AGENT OF HEAVEN. EVEN HIS NAME LUCIFER, THE LIGHTBRINGER, DESCRIBES A FUNCTION FROM WHICH HE HAS RESIGNED.
HE HAS ESCAPED FROM PROVIDENCE. HE HAS BREAKFASTED ON OMELETTE AND SLICED PASTOURMA. AND NOW HE FOLDS THE LETTER--
NOTHING WILL COME OF NOTHING.
--WHICH IS SO SEARINGLY BLANK IT SEEMS TO LEAVE A HOLE IN THE AIR WHERE IT WAS.
HEOU SZHKOKE, NGY RROAHD?
ONLY TO MYSELF, MAZIKEEN.
I'M ONE MOVE AWAY FROM ENDGAME. I WAS JUST REVIEWING MY OPTIONS.
NGY RROAHD... IGH I CAN AKHHH, RHY HHKAVV RE HKONGH HHERE?
WHY? BECAUSE IN ANY DEALINGS WITH HEAVEN I'M INCLINED TO DISSECT THE GIFT HORSE AND HAVE A GOOD LOOK AT ITS GUTS.
I DON'T TRUST THE OLD BASTARD AS FAR AS I CAN THROW HIM.
TO RID HIMSELF OF A MINOR NUISANCE, HE GAVE ME AN OBJECT OF INCONCEIVABLE POWER.
THE LETTER SEEMS GENUINE. BUT IF IT WERE ME, I'D HAVE MADE SURE IT COULD NEVER BE USED.
SO I THOUGHT I'D COME TO HAMBURG, PULL MELEOS OUT FROM UNDER HIS ROCK...
...AND ASK HIM, VERY POLITELY, FOR A SIX-CARD SPREAD.

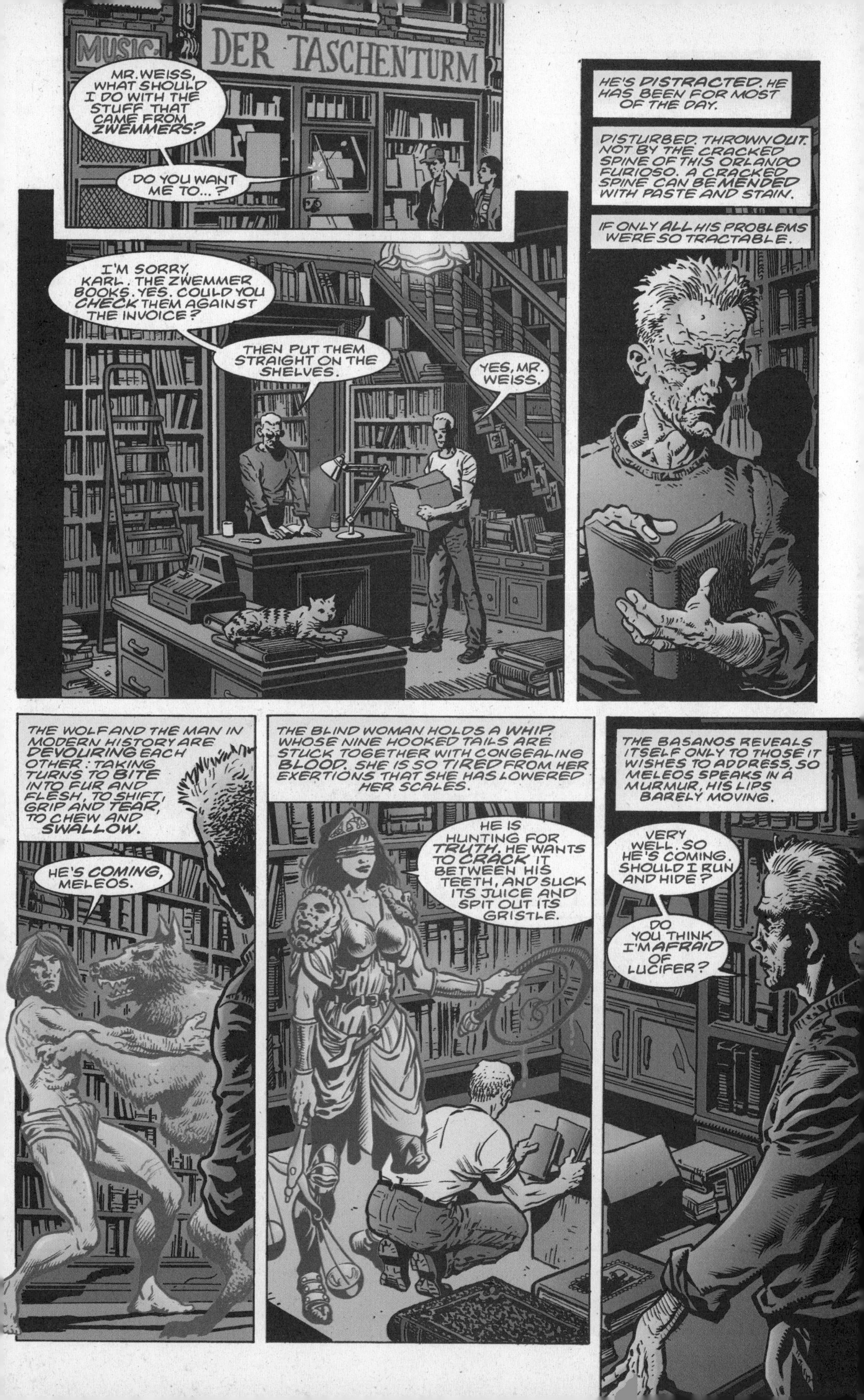
MUSIC
DER TASCHENTURM
MR. WEISS, WHAT SHOULD I DO WITH THE STUFF THAT CAME FROM ZWEMMERS?
DO YOU WANT ME TO...?
HE'S DISTRACTED. HE HAS BEEN FOR MOST OF THE DAY.
DISTURBED. THROWN OUT. NOT BY THE CRACKED SPINE OF THIS ORLANDO FURIOSO. A CRACKED SPINE CAN BE MENDED WITH PASTE AND STAIN.
IF ONLY ALL HIS PROBLEMS WERE SO TRACTABLE.
I'M SORRY, KARL. THE ZWEMMER BOOKS. YES. COULD YOU CHECK THEM AGAINST THE INVOICE?
THEN PUT THEM STRAIGHT ON THE SHELVES.
YES, MR. WEISS.
THE WOLF AND THE MAN IN MODERN HISTORY ARE DEVOURING EACH OTHER: TAKING TURNS TO BITE INTO FUR AND FLESH, TO SHIFT, GRIP AND TEAR, TO CHEW AND SWALLOW.
HE'S COMING, MELEOS.
THE BLIND WOMAN HOLDS A WHIP, WHOSE NINE HOOKED TAILS ARE STUCK TOGETHER WITH CONGEALING BLOOD. SHE IS SO TIRED FROM HER EXERTIONS THAT SHE HAS LOWERED HER SCALES.
HE IS HUNTING FOR TRUTH. HE WANTS TO CRACK IT BETWEEN HIS TEETH, AND SUCK ITS JUICE AND SPIT OUT ITS GRISTLE.
THE BASANOS REVEALS ITSELF ONLY TO THOSE IT WISHES TO ADDRESS, SO MELEOS SPEAKS IN A MURMUR, HIS LIPS BARELY MOVING.
VERY WELL. SO HE'S COMING. SHOULD I RUN AND HIDE?
DO YOU THINK I'M AFRAID OF LUCIFER?

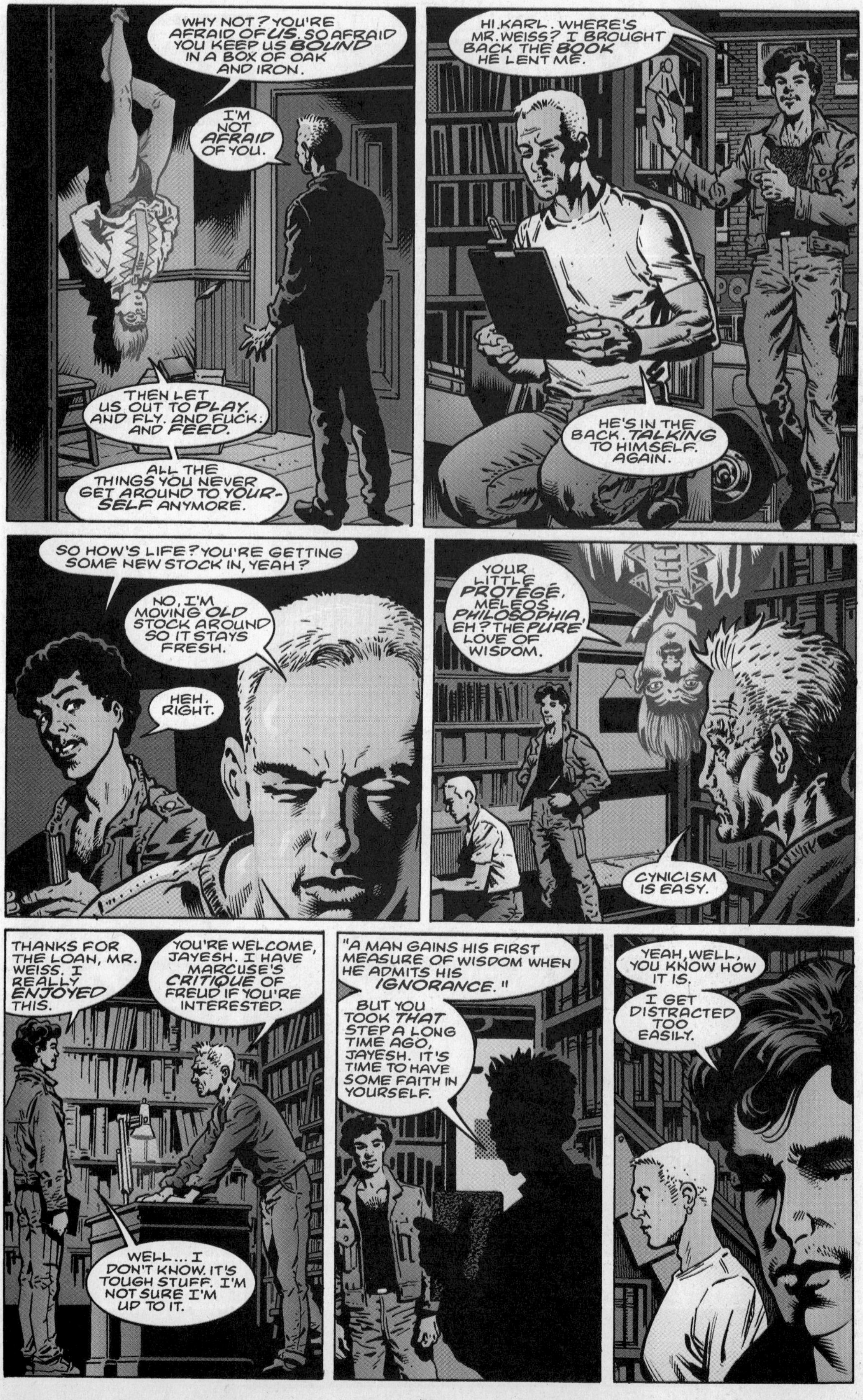
WHY NOT? YOU'RE AFRAID OF US. SO AFRAID YOU KEEP US BOUND IN A BOX OF OAK AND IRON.
I'M NOT AFRAID OF YOU.
THEN LET US OUT TO PLAY. AND FLY. AND FUCK. AND FEED.
ALL THE THINGS YOU NEVER GET AROUND TO YOURSELF ANYMORE.
HI KARL. WHERE'S MR. WEISS? I BROUGHT BACK THE BOOK HE LENT ME.
HE'S IN THE BACK. TALKING TO HIMSELF. AGAIN.
SO HOW'S LIFE? YOU'RE GETTING SOME NEW STOCK IN, YEAH?
NO, I'M MOVING OLD STOCK AROUND SO IT STAYS FRESH.
HEH. RIGHT.
YOUR LITTLE PROTEGÉ, MELEOS. PHILOSOPHIA, EH? THE PURE LOVE OF WISDOM.
CYNICISM IS EASY.
THANKS FOR THE LOAN, MR. WEISS. I REALLY ENJOYED THIS.
YOU'RE WELCOME, JAYESH. I HAVE MARCUSE'S CRITIQUE OF FREUD IF YOU'RE INTERESTED.
WELL... I DON'T KNOW. IT'S TOUGH STUFF. I'M NOT SURE I'M UP TO IT.
"A MAN GAINS HIS FIRST MEASURE OF WISDOM WHEN HE ADMITS HIS IGNORANCE."
BUT YOU TOOK THAT STEP A LONG TIME AGO, JAYESH. IT'S TIME TO HAVE SOME FAITH IN YOURSELF.
YEAH, WELL, YOU KNOW HOW IT IS.
I GET DISTRACTED TOO EASILY.

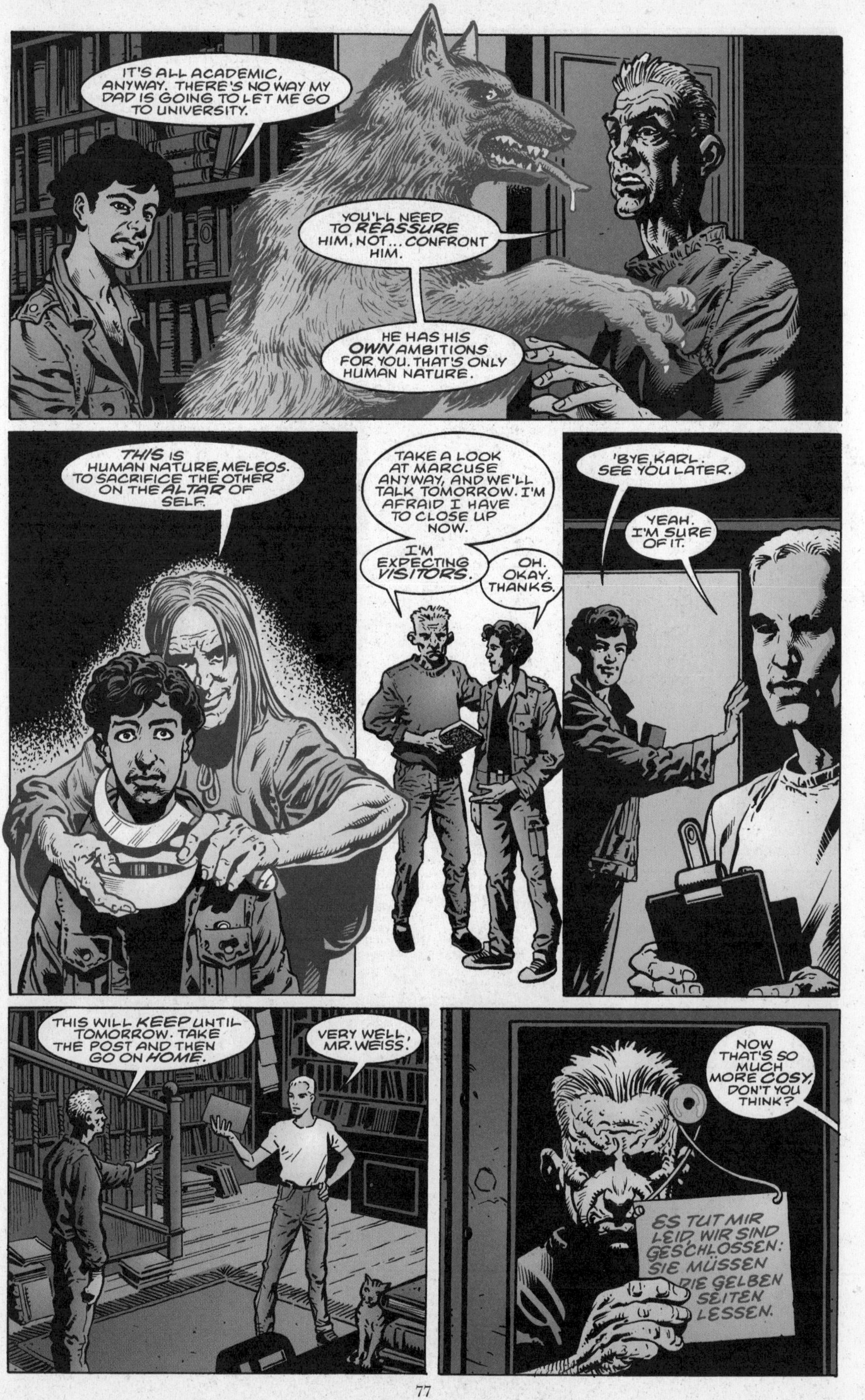

IT'S ALL ACADEMIC, ANYWAY. THERE'S NO WAY MY DAD IS GOING TO LET ME GO TO UNIVERSITY.
YOU'LL NEED TO REASSURE HIM, NOT... CONFRONT HIM.
HE HAS HIS OWN AMBITIONS FOR YOU. THAT'S ONLY HUMAN NATURE.
THIS IS HUMAN NATURE, MELEOS. TO SACRIFICE THE OTHER ON THE ALTAR OF SELF.
TAKE A LOOK AT MARCUSE ANYWAY, AND WE'LL TALK TOMORROW. I'M AFRAID I HAVE TO CLOSE UP NOW.
I'M EXPECTING VISITORS.
OH. OKAY. THANKS.
'BYE, KARL. SEE YOU LATER.
YEAH. I'M SURE OF IT.
THIS WILL KEEP UNTIL TOMORROW. TAKE THE POST AND THEN GO ON HOME.
VERY WELL, MR. WEISS.
NOW THAT'S SO MUCH MORE COSY, DON'T YOU THINK?
ES TUT MIR LEID WIR SIND GESCHLOSSEN: SIE MÜSSEN DIE GELBEN SEITEN LESSEN.

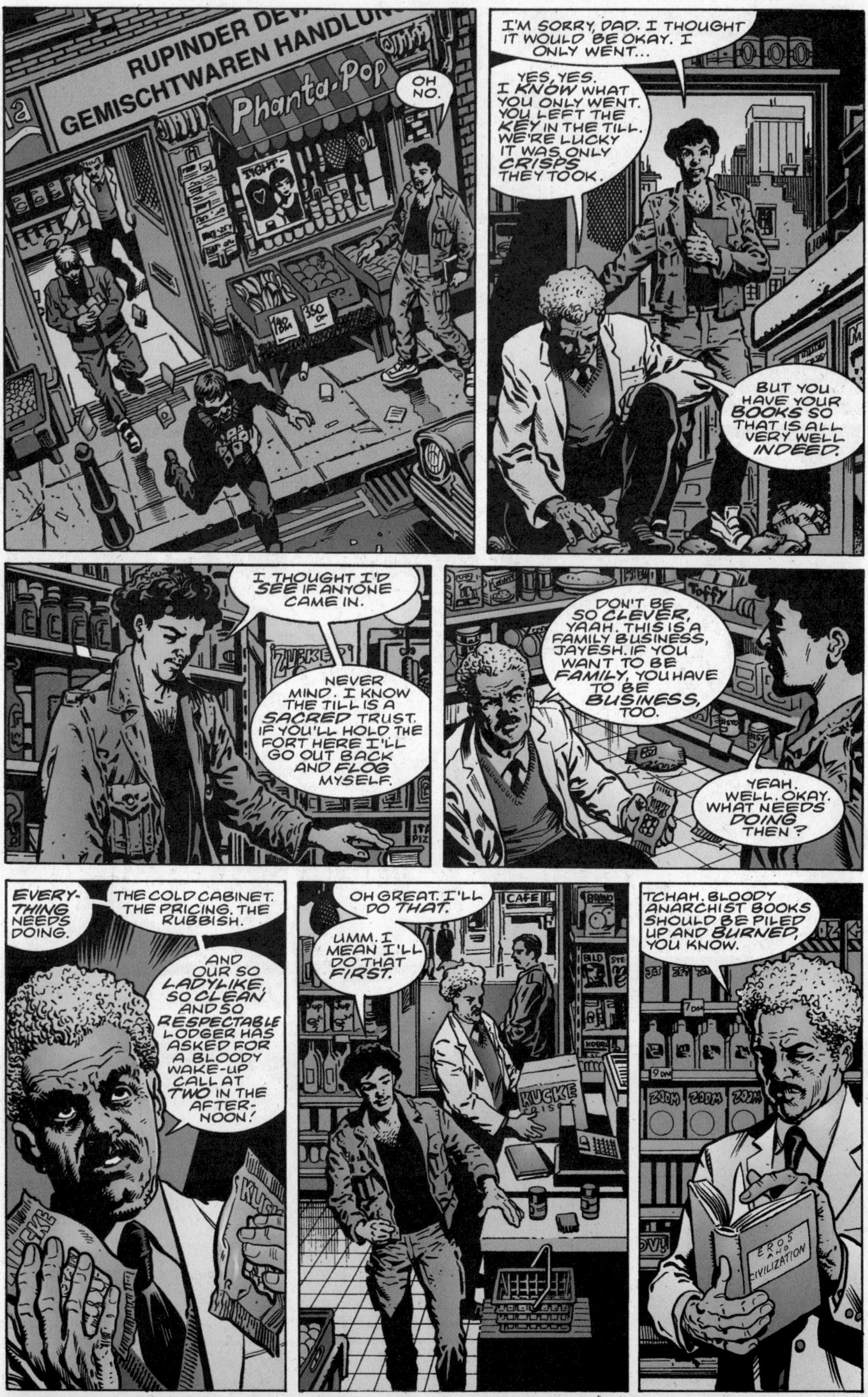
RUPINDER DEV
GEMISCHTWAREN HANDLUN
Phanta-Pop
OH NO.
I'M SORRY, DAD. I THOUGHT IT WOULD BE OKAY. I ONLY WENT...
YES, YES. I KNOW WHAT YOU ONLY WENT. YOU LEFT THE KEY IN THE TILL. WE'RE LUCKY IT WAS ONLY CRISPS THEY TOOK.
BUT YOU HAVE YOUR BOOKS SO THAT IS ALL VERY WELL INDEED.
I THOUGHT I'D SEE IF ANYONE CAME IN.
NEVER MIND. I KNOW THE TILL IS A SACRED TRUST. IF YOU'LL HOLD THE FORT HERE I'LL GO OUT BACK AND FLOG MYSELF.
DON'T BE SO CLEVER, YAAH. THIS IS A FAMILY BUSINESS, JAYESH. IF YOU WANT TO BE FAMILY, YOU HAVE TO BE BUSINESS, TOO.
YEAH. WELL. OKAY. WHAT NEEDS DOING THEN?
EVERY-THING NEEDS DOING.
THE COLD CABINET. THE PRICING. THE RUBBISH.
AND OUR SO LADYLIKE, SO CLEAN AND SO RESPECTABLE LODGER HAS ASKED FOR A BLOODY WAKE-UP CALL AT TWO IN THE AFTER-NOON!
OH GREAT. I'LL DO THAT.
UMM. I MEAN I'LL DO THAT FIRST.
KUCKE
TCHAH. BLOODY ANARCHIST BOOKS SHOULD BE PILED UP AND BURNED, YOU KNOW.
EROS AND CIVILIZATION

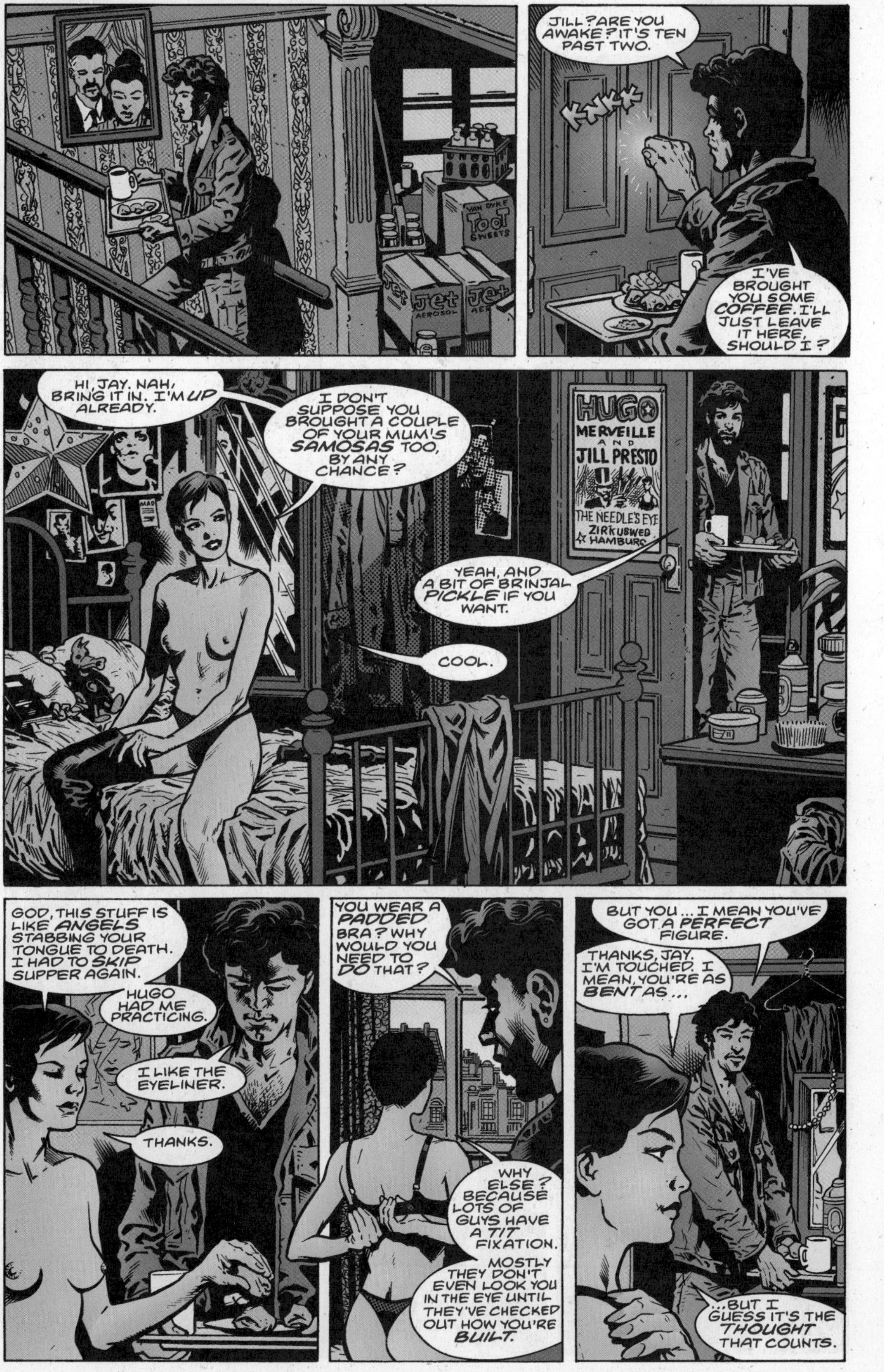
VAN DYKE
TOOT
SWEETS
JET
AEROSOL
JILL? ARE YOU AWAKE? IT'S TEN PAST TWO.
KNK K
I'VE BROUGHT YOU SOME COFFEE. I'LL JUST LEAVE IT HERE, SHOULD I?
HI, JAY. NAH, BRING IT IN. I'M UP ALREADY.
I DON'T SUPPOSE YOU BROUGHT A COUPLE OF YOUR MUM'S SAMOSAS TOO, BY ANY CHANCE?
HUGO
MERVEILLE
AND
JILL PRESTO
THE NEEDLE'S EYE
ZIRKUSWED
HAMBURG
YEAH, AND A BIT OF BRINJAL PICKLE IF YOU WANT.
COOL.
GOD, THIS STUFF IS LIKE ANGELS STABBING YOUR TONGUE TO DEATH. I HAD TO SKIP SUPPER AGAIN.
HUGO HAD ME PRACTICING.
I LIKE THE EYELINER.
THANKS.
YOU WEAR A PADDED BRA? WHY WOULD YOU NEED TO DO THAT?
WHY ELSE? BECAUSE LOTS OF GUYS HAVE A TIT FIXATION.
MOSTLY THEY DON'T EVEN LOOK YOU IN THE EYE UNTIL THEY'VE CHECKED OUT HOW YOU'RE BUILT.
BUT YOU ... I MEAN YOU'VE GOT A PERFECT FIGURE.
THANKS, JAY. I'M TOUCHED. I MEAN, YOU'RE AS BENT AS ...
... BUT I GUESS IT'S THE THOUGHT THAT COUNTS.

80

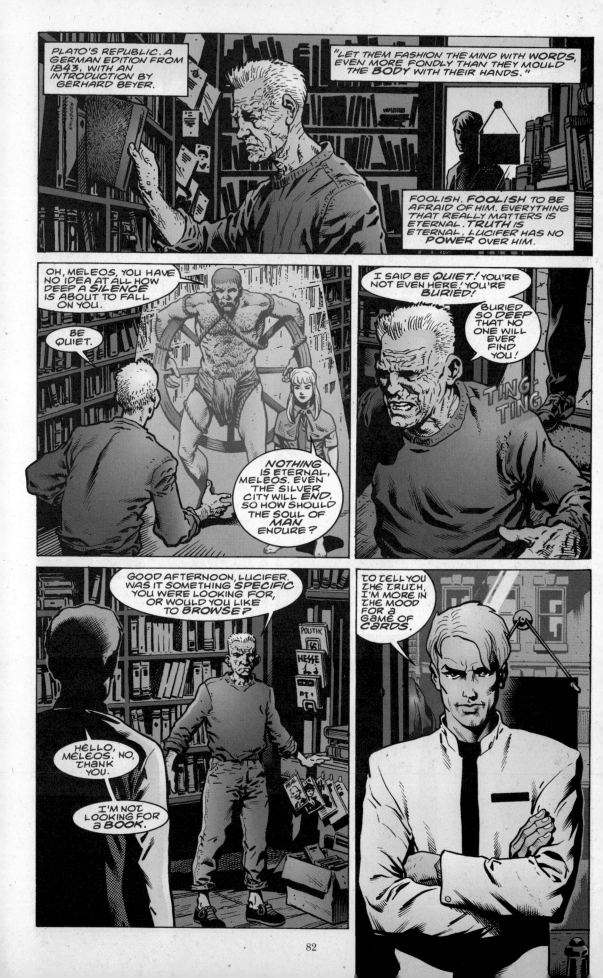

PLATO'S REPUBLIC. A GERMAN EDITION FROM 1843, WITH AN INTRODUCTION BY GERHARD BEYER.

"LET THEM FASHION THE MIND WITH WORDS, EVEN MORE FONDLY THAN THEY MOULD THE BODY WITH THEIR HANDS."

FOOLISH. FOOLISH TO BE AFRAID OF HIM. EVERYTHING THAT REALLY MATTERS IS ETERNAL. TRUTH IS ETERNAL. LUCIFER HAS NO POWER OVER HIM.

OH, MELEOS, YOU HAVE NO IDEA AT ALL HOW DEEP A SILENCE IS ABOUT TO FALL ON YOU.

BE QUIET.

NOTHING IS ETERNAL, MELEOS. EVEN THE SILVER CITY WILL END, SO HOW SHOULD THE SOUL OF MAN ENDURE?

I SAID BE QUIET! YOU'RE NOT EVEN HERE! YOU'RE BURIED!

BURIED SO DEEP THAT NO ONE WILL EVER FIND YOU!

TING-TING

GOOD AFTERNOON, LUCIFER. WAS IT SOMETHING SPECIFIC YOU WERE LOOKING FOR, OR WOULD YOU LIKE TO BROWSE?

HELLO, MELEOS. NO, THANK YOU.

I'M NOT LOOKING FOR A BOOK.

TO TELL YOU THE TRUTH, I'M MORE IN THE MOOD FOR A GAME OF CARDS.

POLITIK

HESSE

82

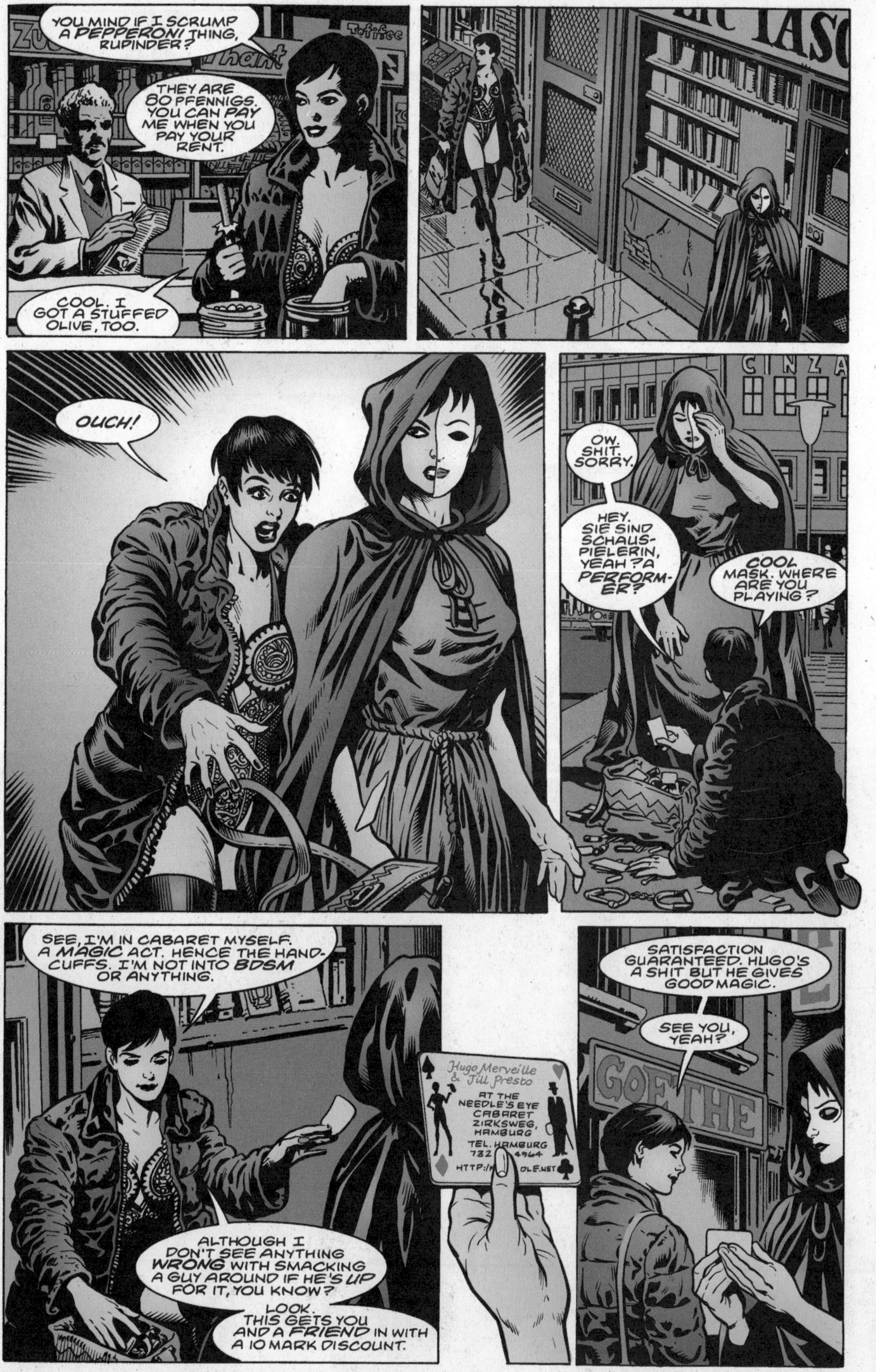
YOU MIND IF I SCRUMP A PEPPERONI THING, RUPINDER?
THEY ARE 80 PFENNIGS. YOU CAN PAY ME WHEN YOU PAY YOUR RENT.
COOL. I GOT A STUFFED OLIVE, TOO.
OUCH!
CINZA
OW. SHIT. SORRY.
HEY. SIE SIND SCHAUS-PIELERIN, YEAH? A PERFORM-ER?
COOL MASK. WHERE ARE YOU PLAYING?
SEE, I'M IN CABARET MYSELF. A MAGIC ACT. HENCE THE HAND-CUFFS. I'M NOT INTO BDSM OR ANYTHING.
ALTHOUGH I DON'T SEE ANYTHING WRONG WITH SMACKING A GUY AROUND IF HE'S UP FOR IT, YOU KNOW?
LOOK. THIS GETS YOU AND A FRIEND IN WITH A 10 MARK DISCOUNT.
Hugo Merveille & Jill Presto
AT THE NEEDLE'S EYE CABARET ZIRKSWEG, HAMBURG
TEL. HAMBURG 732 4964
SATISFACTION GUARANTEED. HUGO'S A SHIT BUT HE GIVES GOOD MAGIC.
SEE YOU, YEAH?
GOETHE

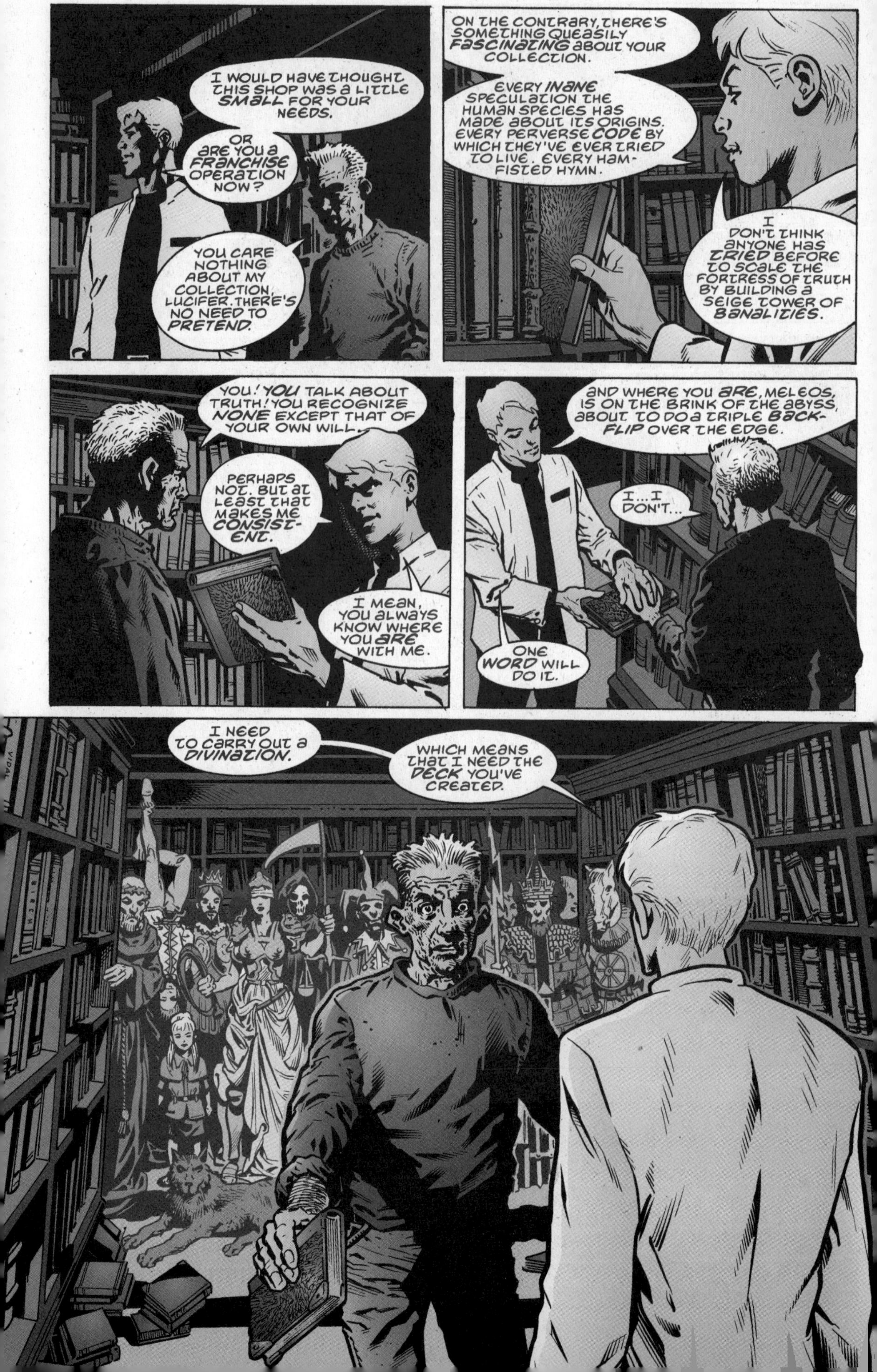
I WOULD HAVE THOUGHT THIS SHOP WAS A LITTLE SMALL FOR YOUR NEEDS.
OR ARE YOU A FRANCHISE OPERATION NOW?
YOU CARE NOTHING ABOUT MY COLLECTION, LUCIFER. THERE'S NO NEED TO PRETEND.
ON THE CONTRARY, THERE'S SOMETHING QUEASILY FASCINATING ABOUT YOUR COLLECTION.
EVERY INANE SPECULATION THE HUMAN SPECIES HAS MADE ABOUT ITS ORIGINS. EVERY PERVERSE CODE BY WHICH THEY'VE EVER TRIED TO LIVE. EVERY HAM-FISTED HYMN.
I DON'T THINK ANYONE HAS TRIED BEFORE TO SCALE THE FORTRESS OF TRUTH BY BUILDING A SEIGE TOWER OF BANALITIES.
YOU! YOU TALK ABOUT TRUTH! YOU RECOGNIZE NONE EXCEPT THAT OF YOUR OWN WILL.
PERHAPS NOT. BUT AT LEAST THAT MAKES ME CONSISTENT.
I MEAN, YOU ALWAYS KNOW WHERE YOU ARE WITH ME.
AND WHERE YOU ARE, MELEOS, IS ON THE BRINK OF THE ABYSS, ABOUT TO DO A TRIPLE BACK-FLIP OVER THE EDGE.
I... I DON'T...
ONE WORD WILL DO IT.
I NEED TO CARRY OUT A DIVINATION.
WHICH MEANS THAT I NEED THE DECK YOU'VE CREATED.

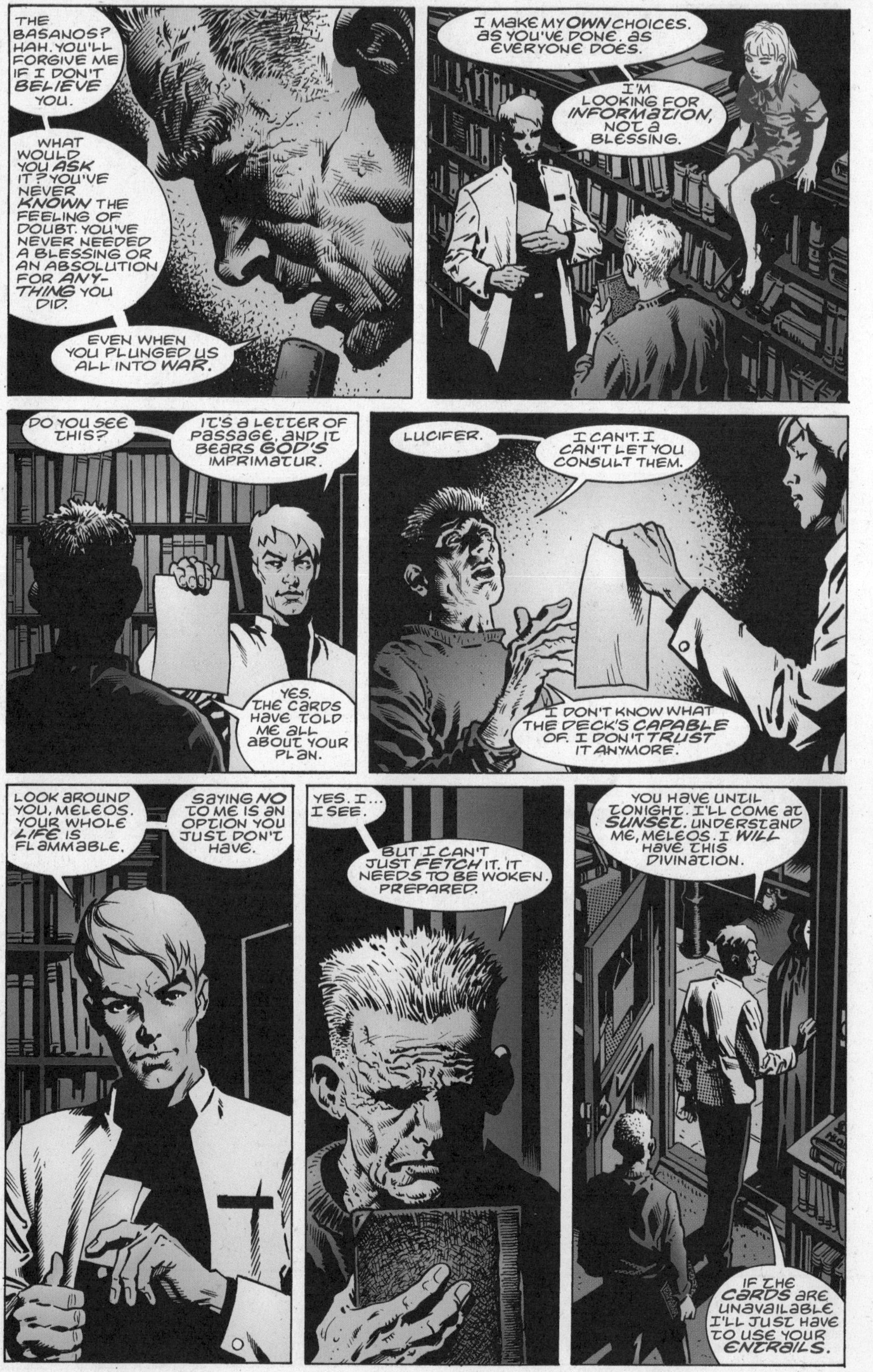
THE BASANOS? HAH. YOU'LL FORGIVE ME IF I DON'T BELIEVE YOU.
WHAT WOULD YOU ASK IT? YOU'VE NEVER KNOWN THE FEELING OF DOUBT. YOU'VE NEVER NEEDED A BLESSING OR AN ABSOLUTION FOR ANY-THING YOU DID.
EVEN WHEN YOU PLUNGED US ALL INTO WAR.
I MAKE MY OWN CHOICES. AS YOU'VE DONE. AS EVERYONE DOES.
I'M LOOKING FOR INFORMATION, NOT A BLESSING.
DO YOU SEE THIS?
IT'S A LETTER OF PASSAGE, AND IT BEARS GOD'S IMPRIMATUR.
YES. THE CARDS HAVE TOLD ME ALL ABOUT YOUR PLAN.
LUCIFER.
I CAN'T. I CAN'T LET YOU CONSULT THEM.
I DON'T KNOW WHAT THE DECK'S CAPABLE OF. I DON'T TRUST IT ANYMORE.
LOOK AROUND YOU, MELEOS. YOUR WHOLE LIFE IS FLAMMABLE.
SAYING NO TO ME IS AN OPTION YOU JUST DON'T HAVE.
YES. I... I SEE.
BUT I CAN'T JUST FETCH IT. IT NEEDS TO BE WOKEN. PREPARED.
YOU HAVE UNTIL TONIGHT. I'LL COME AT SUNSET. UNDERSTAND ME, MELEOS. I WILL HAVE THIS DIVINATION.
IF THE CARDS ARE UNAVAILABLE I'LL JUST HAVE TO USE YOUR ENTRAILS.

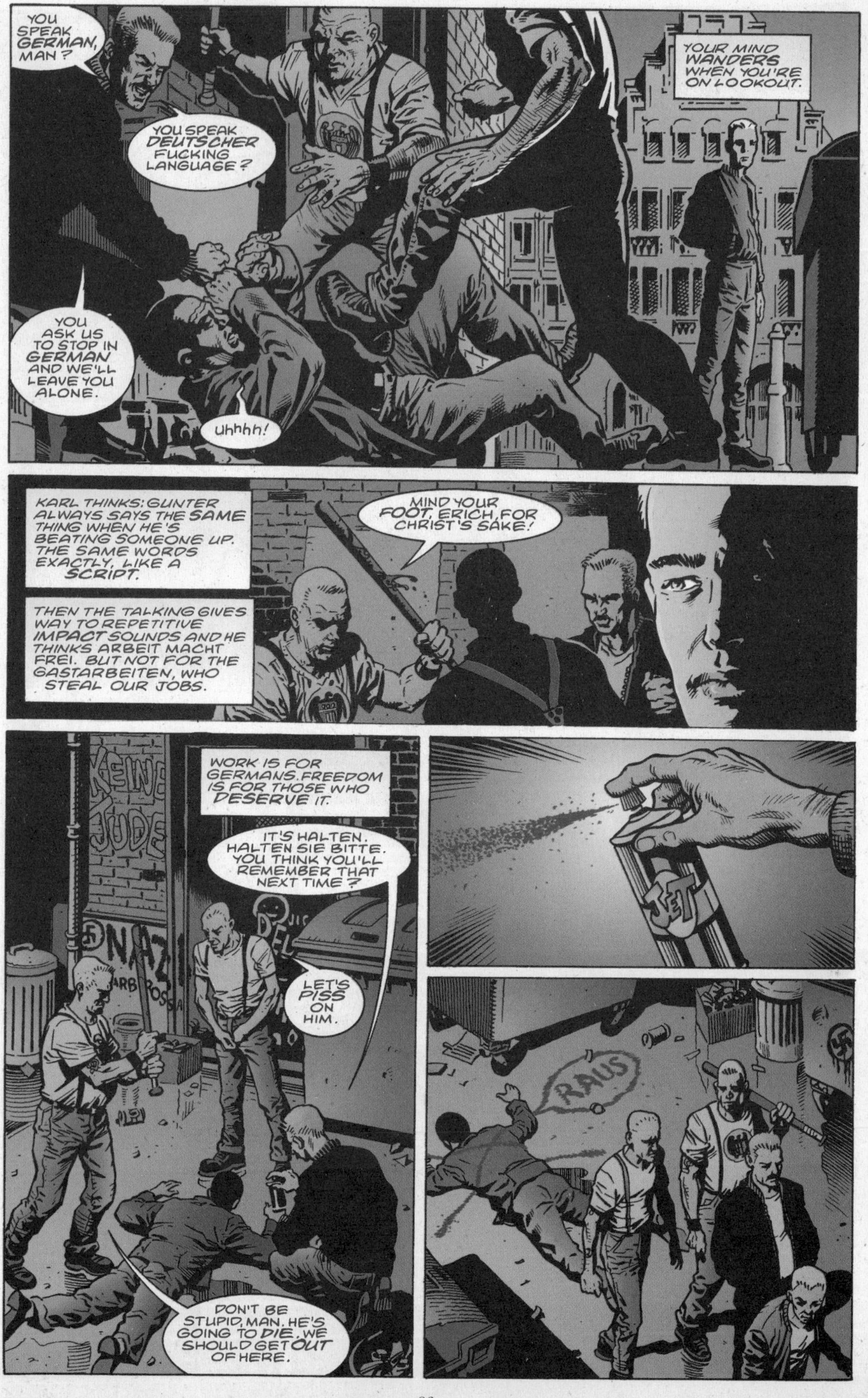
YOU SPEAK GERMAN, MAN?
YOU SPEAK DEUTSCHER FUCKING LANGUAGE?
YOUR MIND WANDERS WHEN YOU'RE ON LOOKOUT.
YOU ASK US TO STOP IN GERMAN AND WE'LL LEAVE YOU ALONE.
uhhhh!
KARL THINKS: GUNTER ALWAYS SAYS THE SAME THING WHEN HE'S BEATING SOMEONE UP. THE SAME WORDS EXACTLY, LIKE A SCRIPT.
THEN THE TALKING GIVES WAY TO REPETITIVE IMPACT SOUNDS AND HE THINKS ARBEIT MACHT FREI. BUT NOT FOR THE GASTARBEITEN, WHO STEAL OUR JOBS.
MIND YOUR FOOT, ERICH, FOR CHRIST'S SAKE!
WORK IS FOR GERMANS. FREEDOM IS FOR THOSE WHO DESERVE IT.
IT'S HALTEN. HALTEN SIE BITTE. YOU THINK YOU'LL REMEMBER THAT NEXT TIME?
LET'S PISS ON HIM.
DON'T BE STUPID, MAN. HE'S GOING TO DIE, WE SHOULD GET OUT OF HERE.
JET
RAUS

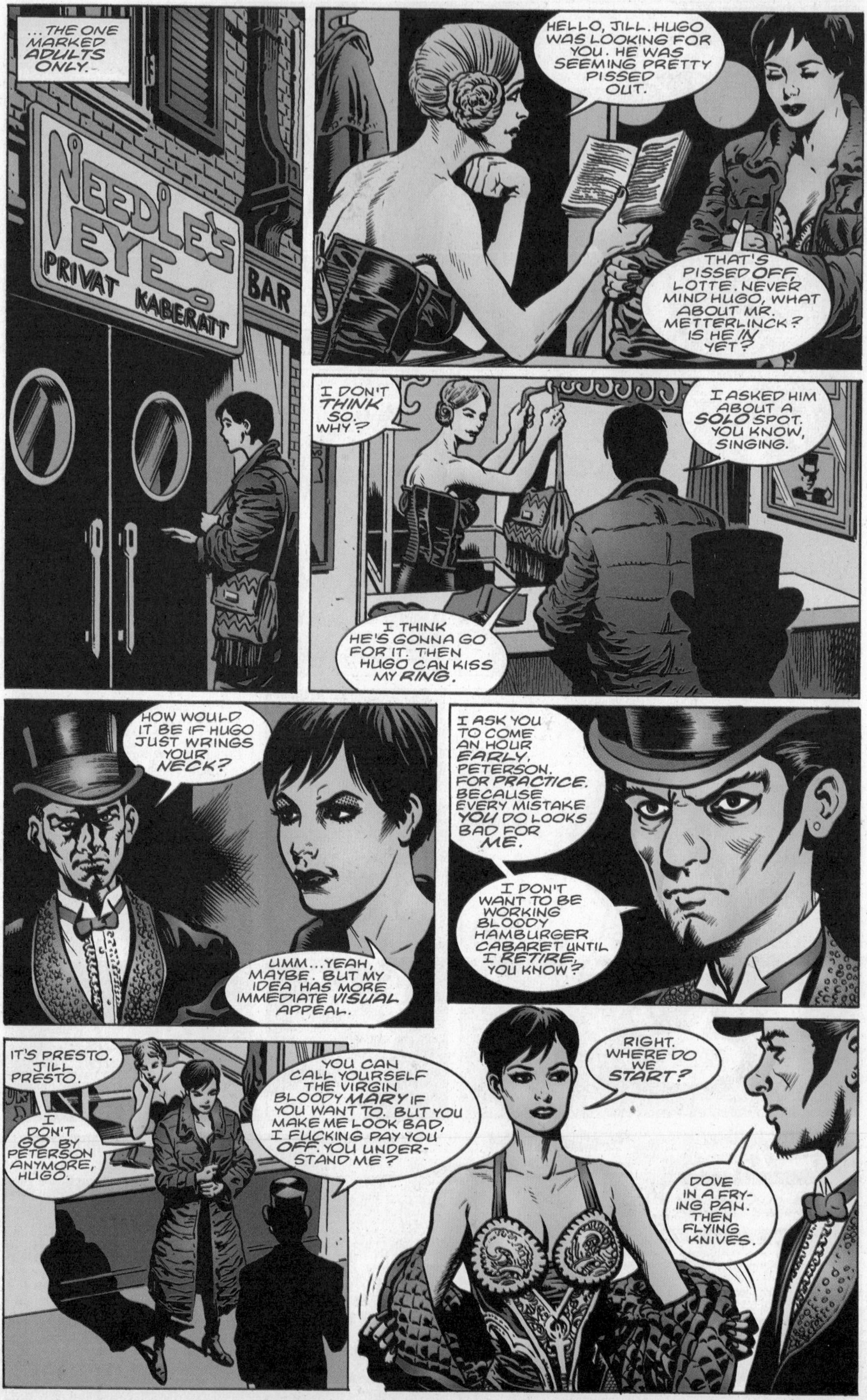

...THE ONE MARKED ADULTS ONLY.
NEEDLE'S EYE PRIVAT KABERATT
BAR
HELLO, JILL. HUGO WAS LOOKING FOR YOU. HE WAS SEEMING PRETTY PISSED OUT.
THAT'S PISSED OFF, LOTTE. NEVER MIND HUGO, WHAT ABOUT MR. METTERLINCK? IS HE IN YET?
I DON'T THINK SO. WHY?
I ASKED HIM ABOUT A SOLO SPOT. YOU KNOW, SINGING.
I THINK HE'S GONNA GO FOR IT. THEN HUGO CAN KISS MY RING.
HOW WOULD IT BE IF HUGO JUST WRINGS YOUR NECK?
UMM...YEAH, MAYBE. BUT MY IDEA HAS MORE IMMEDIATE VISUAL APPEAL.
I ASK YOU TO COME AN HOUR EARLY, PETERSON. FOR PRACTICE. BECAUSE EVERY MISTAKE YOU DO LOOKS BAD FOR ME.
I DON'T WANT TO BE WORKING BLOODY HAMBURGER CABARET UNTIL I RETIRE, YOU KNOW?
IT'S PRESTO. JILL PRESTO.
I DON'T GO BY PETERSON ANYMORE, HUGO.
YOU CAN CALL YOURSELF THE VIRGIN BLOODY MARY IF YOU WANT TO. BUT YOU MAKE ME LOOK BAD, I FUCKING PAY YOU OFF. YOU UNDERSTAND ME?
RIGHT. WHERE DO WE START?
DOVE IN A FRYING PAN. THEN FLYING KNIVES.

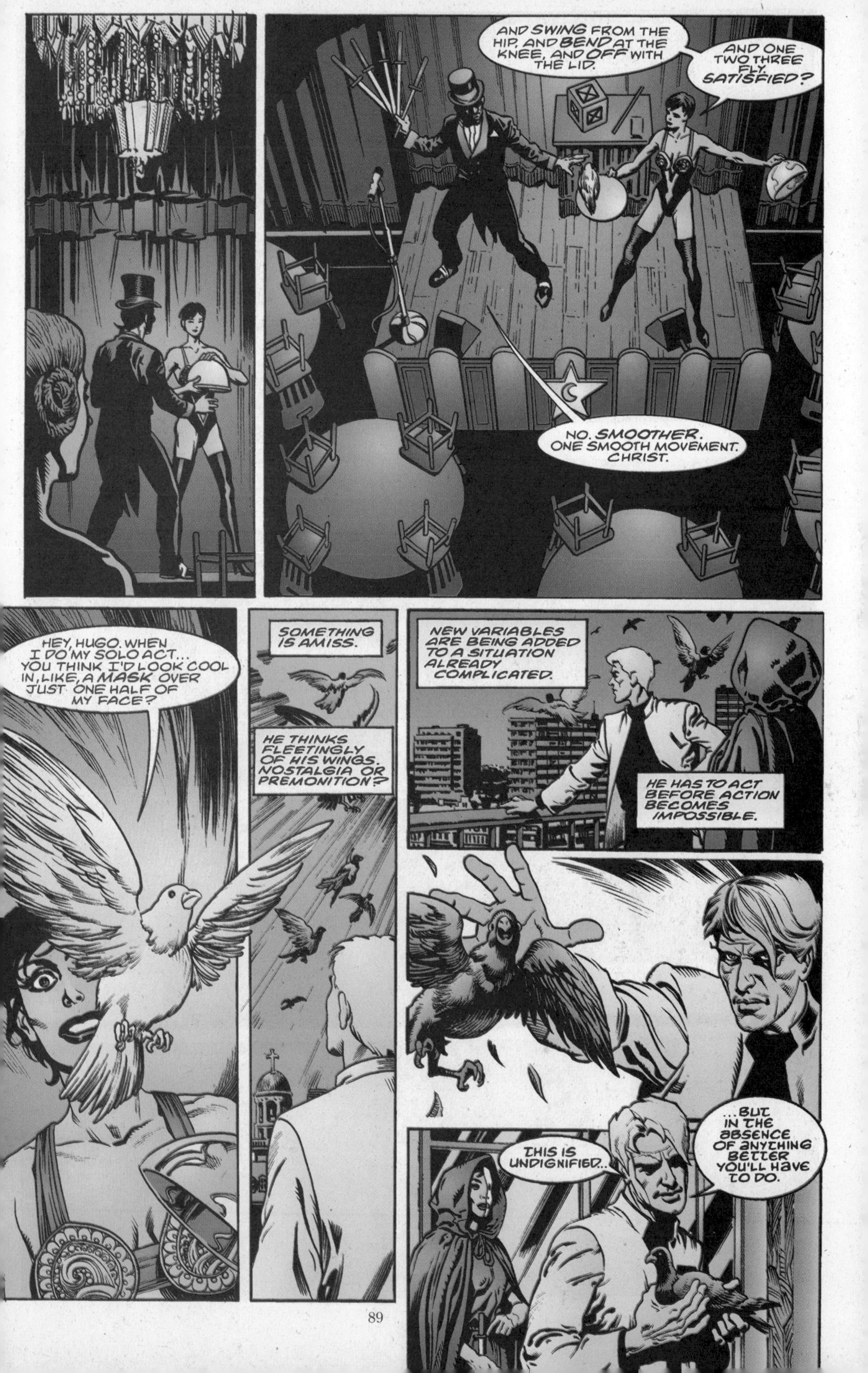
AND SWING FROM THE HIP, AND BEND AT THE KNEE, AND OFF WITH THE LID.
AND ONE TWO THREE FLY. SATISFIED?
NO. SMOOTHER. ONE SMOOTH MOVEMENT. CHRIST.
HEY, HUGO. WHEN I DO MY SOLO ACT... YOU THINK I'D LOOK COOL IN, LIKE, A MASK OVER JUST ONE HALF OF MY FACE?
SOMETHING IS AMISS.
HE THINKS FLEETINGLY OF HIS WINGS. NOSTALGIA OR PREMONITION?
NEW VARIABLES ARE BEING ADDED TO A SITUATION ALREADY COMPLICATED.
HE HAS TO ACT BEFORE ACTION BECOMES IMPOSSIBLE.
THIS IS UNDIGNIFIED...
...BUT IN THE ABSENCE OF ANYTHING BETTER YOU'LL HAVE TO DO.

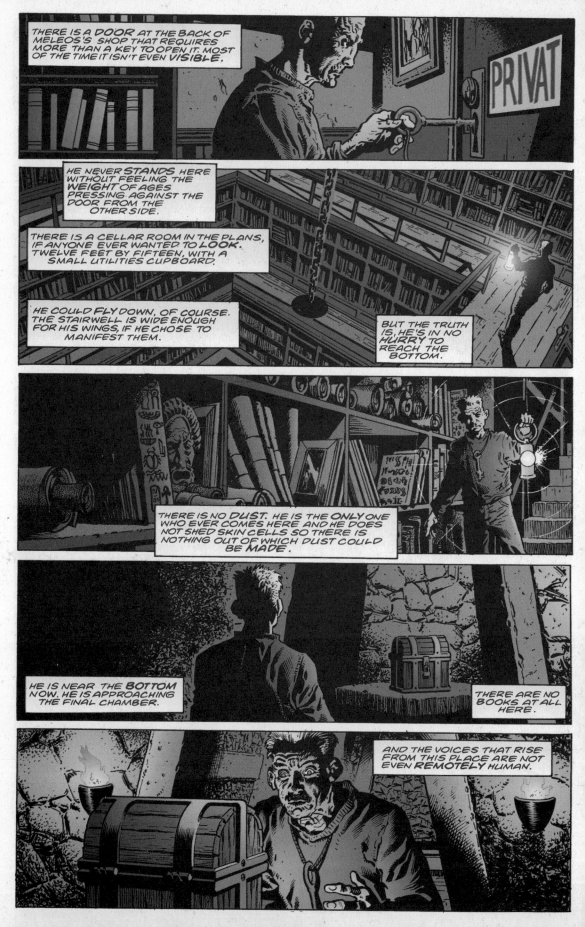

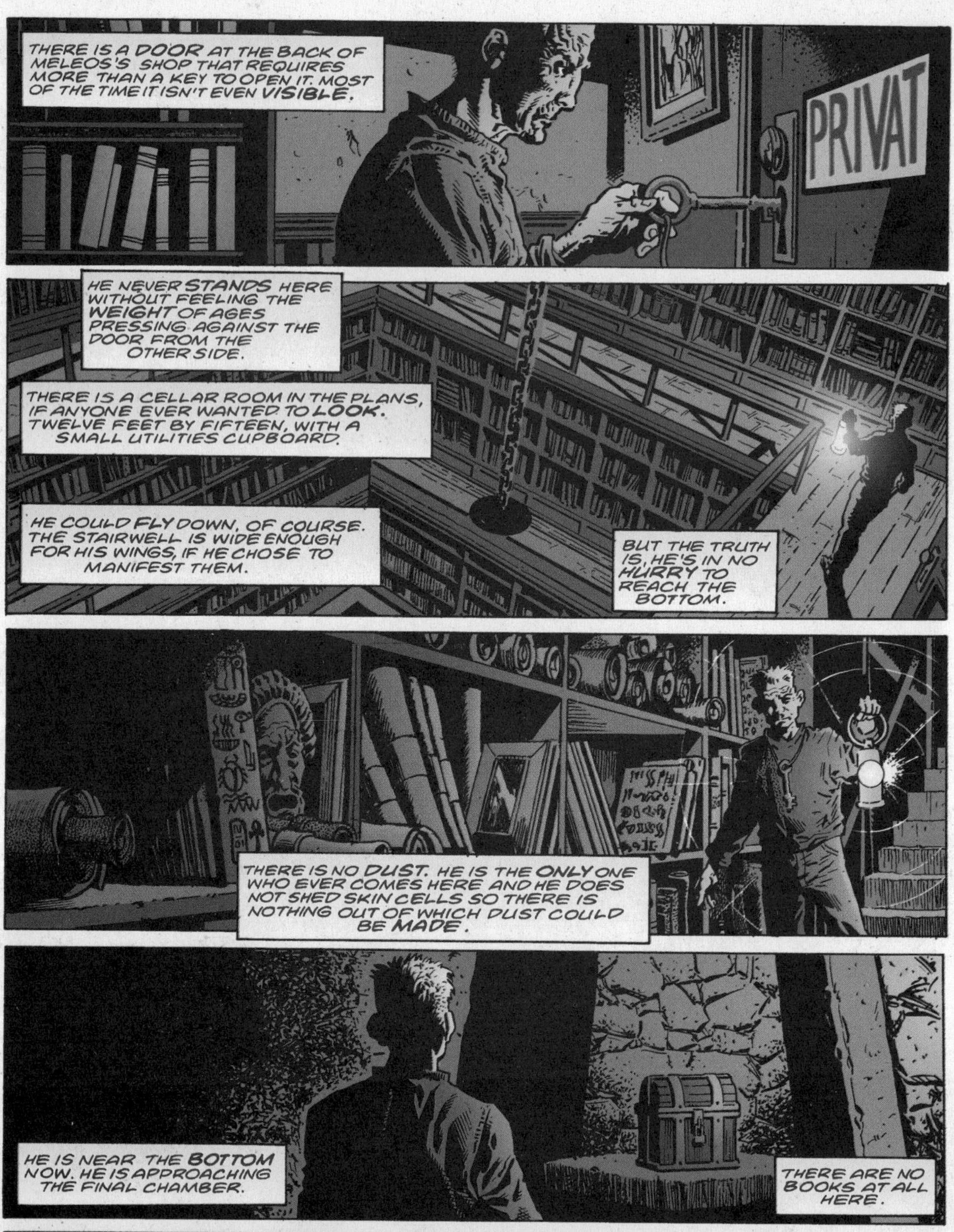
THERE IS A DOOR AT THE BACK OF MELEOS'S SHOP THAT REQUIRES MORE THAN A KEY TO OPEN IT. MOST OF THE TIME IT ISN'T EVEN VISIBLE.
PRIVAT
HE NEVER STANDS HERE WITHOUT FEELING THE WEIGHT OF AGES PRESSING AGAINST THE DOOR FROM THE OTHER SIDE.
THERE IS A CELLAR ROOM IN THE PLANS, IF ANYONE EVER WANTED TO LOOK. TWELVE FEET BY FIFTEEN, WITH A SMALL UTILITIES CUPBOARD.
HE COULD FLY DOWN, OF COURSE. THE STAIRWELL IS WIDE ENOUGH FOR HIS WINGS, IF HE CHOSE TO MANIFEST THEM.
BUT THE TRUTH IS, HE'S IN NO HURRY TO REACH THE BOTTOM.
THERE IS NO DUST. HE IS THE ONLY ONE WHO EVER COMES HERE AND HE DOES NOT SHED SKIN CELLS SO THERE IS NOTHING OUT OF WHICH DUST COULD BE MADE.
HE IS NEAR THE BOTTOM NOW. HE IS APPROACHING THE FINAL CHAMBER.
THERE ARE NO BOOKS AT ALL HERE.
AND THE VOICES THAT RISE FROM THIS PLACE ARE NOT EVEN REMOTELY HUMAN.

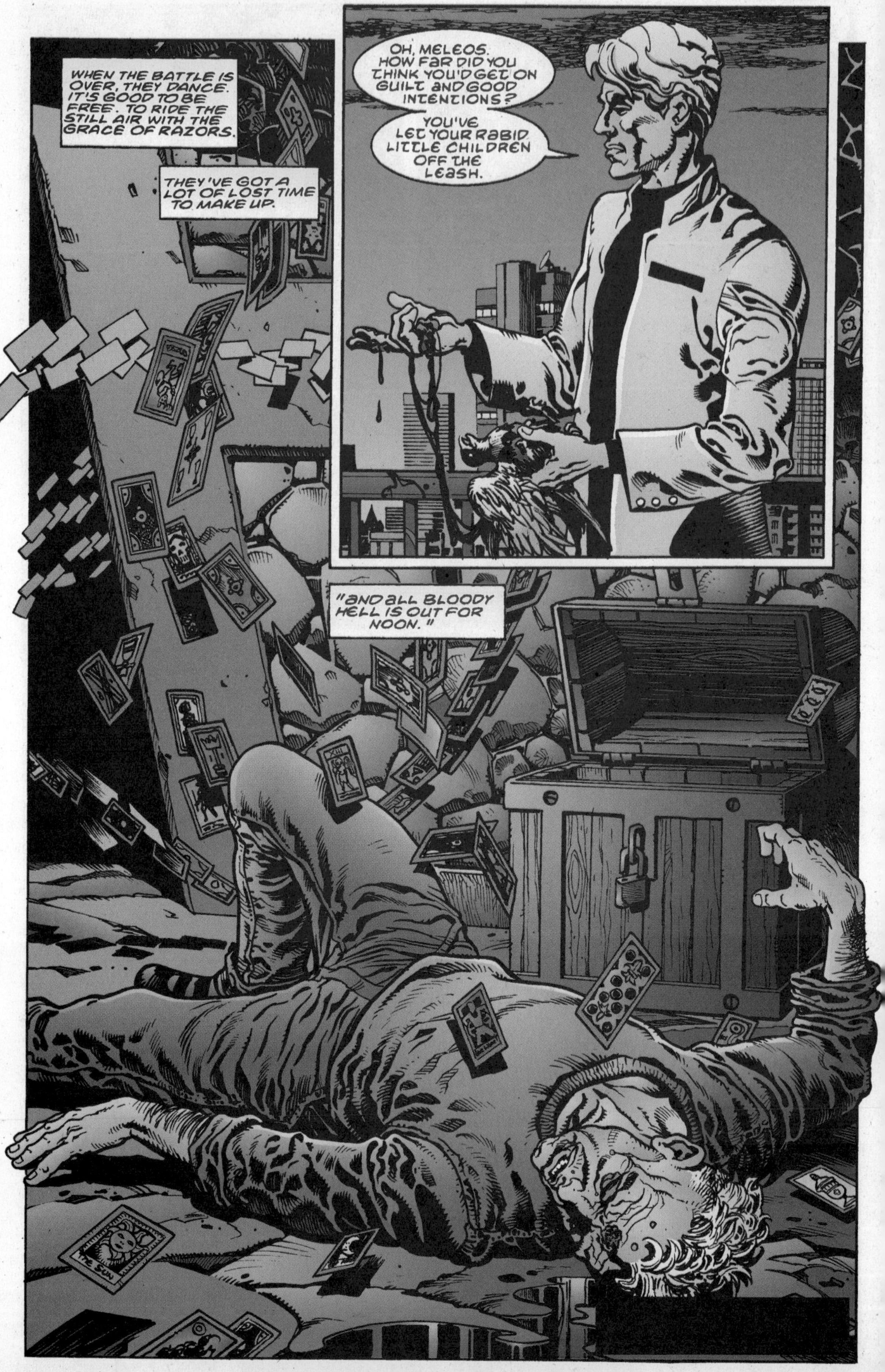
WHEN THE BATTLE IS OVER, THEY DANCE. IT'S GOOD TO BE FREE. TO RIDE THE STILL AIR WITH THE GRACE OF RAZORS.
THEY'VE GOT A LOT OF LOST TIME TO MAKE UP.
OH, MELEOS. HOW FAR DID YOU THINK YOU'D GET ON GUILT AND GOOD INTENTIONS?
YOU'VE LET YOUR RABID LITTLE CHILDREN OFF THE LEASH.
"AND ALL BLOODY HELL IS OUT FOR NOON."
THE SUN

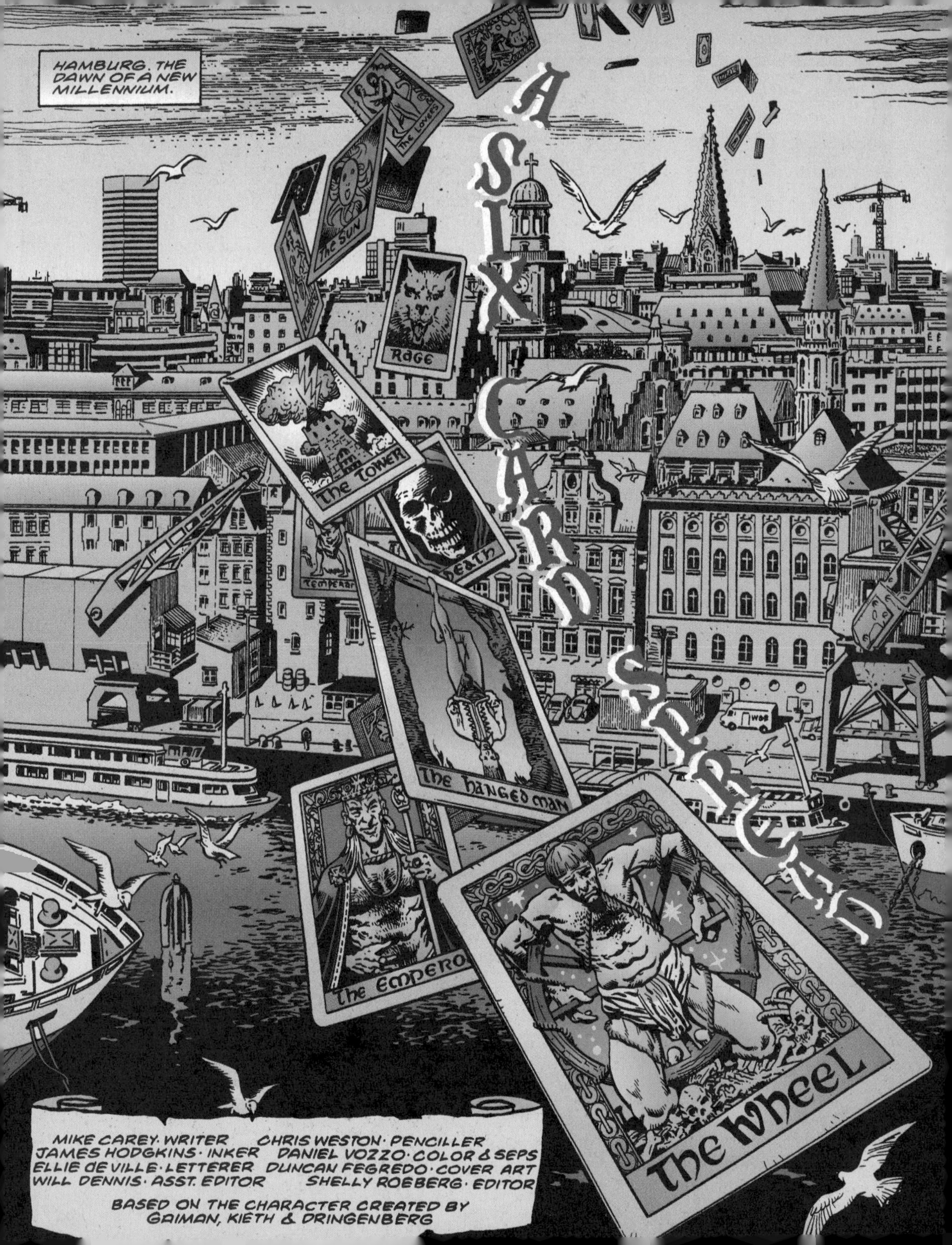

HAMBURG. THE DAWN OF A NEW MILLENNIUM.
A SIX CARD SPREAD
The Moon
The Lovers
The Sun
Rage
The Tower
Death
Temperance
The Hanged Man
The Emperor
The Wheel
MIKE CAREY · WRITER
CHRIS WESTON · PENCILLER
JAMES HODGKINS · INKER
DANIEL VOZZO · COLOR & SEPS
ELLIE DE VILLE · LETTERER
DUNCAN FEGREDO · COVER ART
WILL DENNIS · ASST. EDITOR
SHELLY ROEBERG · EDITOR
BASED ON THE CHARACTER CREATED BY GAIMAN, KIETH & DRINGENBERG

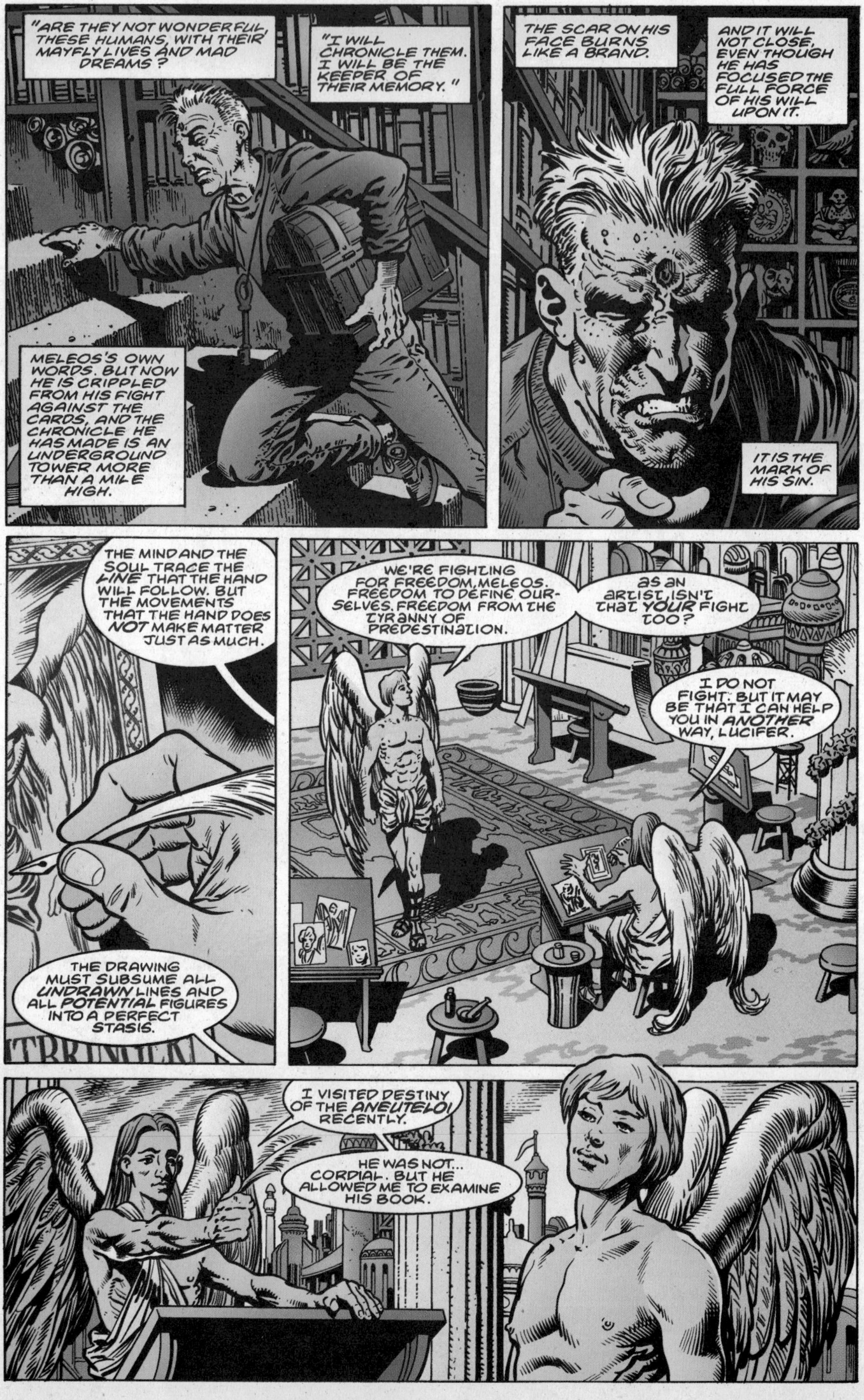
"ARE THEY NOT WONDERFUL, THESE HUMANS, WITH THEIR MAYFLY LIVES AND MAD DREAMS?
"I WILL CHRONICLE THEM. I WILL BE THE KEEPER OF THEIR MEMORY."
MELEOS'S OWN WORDS. BUT NOW HE IS CRIPPLED FROM HIS FIGHT AGAINST THE CARDS, AND THE CHRONICLE HE HAS MADE IS AN UNDERGROUND TOWER MORE THAN A MILE HIGH.
THE SCAR ON HIS FACE BURNS LIKE A BRAND.
AND IT WILL NOT CLOSE, EVEN THOUGH HE HAS FOCUSED THE FULL FORCE OF HIS WILL UPON IT.
IT IS THE MARK OF HIS SIN.
THE MIND AND THE SOUL TRACE THE LINE THAT THE HAND WILL FOLLOW. BUT THE MOVEMENTS THAT THE HAND DOES NOT MAKE MATTER JUST AS MUCH.
THE DRAWING MUST SUBSUME ALL UNDRAWN LINES AND ALL POTENTIAL FIGURES INTO A PERFECT STASIS.
WE'RE FIGHTING FOR FREEDOM, MELEOS. FREEDOM TO DEFINE OURSELVES. FREEDOM FROM THE TYRANNY OF PREDESTINATION.
AS AN ARTIST, ISN'T THAT YOUR FIGHT TOO?
I DO NOT FIGHT. BUT IT MAY BE THAT I CAN HELP YOU IN ANOTHER WAY, LUCIFER.
I VISITED DESTINY OF THE ANEUTELOI RECENTLY.
HE WAS NOT... CORDIAL. BUT HE ALLOWED ME TO EXAMINE HIS BOOK.

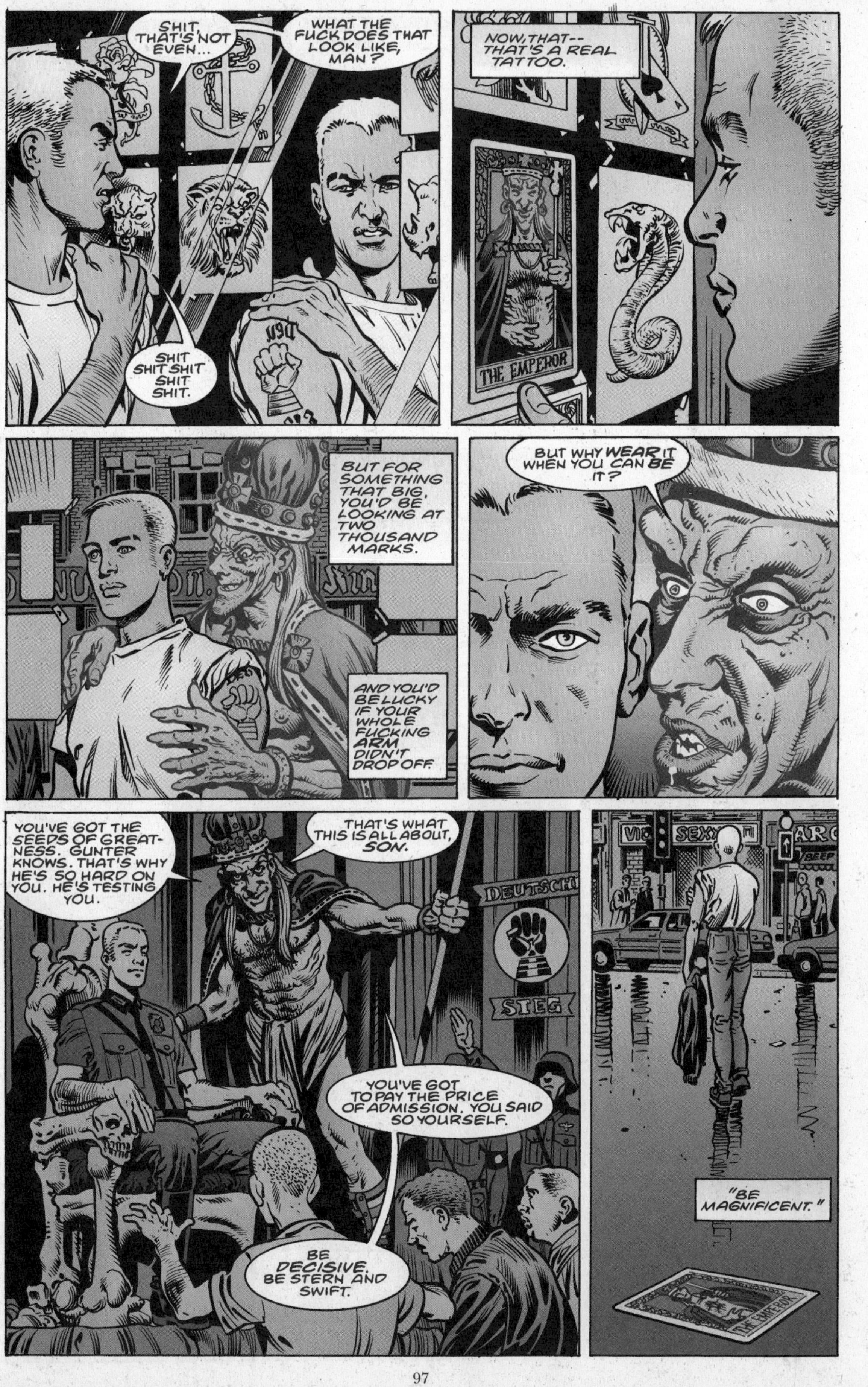
SHIT, THAT'S NOT EVEN...
WHAT THE FUCK DOES THAT LOOK LIKE, MAN?
SHIT SHIT SHIT SHIT SHIT.
NOW, THAT-- THAT'S A REAL TATTOO.
THE EMPEROR
BUT FOR SOMETHING THAT BIG, YOU'D BE LOOKING AT TWO THOUSAND MARKS.
AND YOU'D BE LUCKY IF YOUR WHOLE FUCKING ARM DIDN'T DROP OFF.
BUT WHY WEAR IT WHEN YOU CAN BE IT?
YOU'VE GOT THE SEEDS OF GREATNESS. GUNTER KNOWS. THAT'S WHY HE'S SO HARD ON YOU. HE'S TESTING YOU.
THAT'S WHAT THIS IS ALL ABOUT, SON.
DEUTSCH
SIEG
YOU'VE GOT TO PAY THE PRICE OF ADMISSION. YOU SAID SO YOURSELF.
BE DECISIVE. BE STERN AND SWIFT.
SEXY
BEEP
"BE MAGNIFICENT."
THE EMPEROR

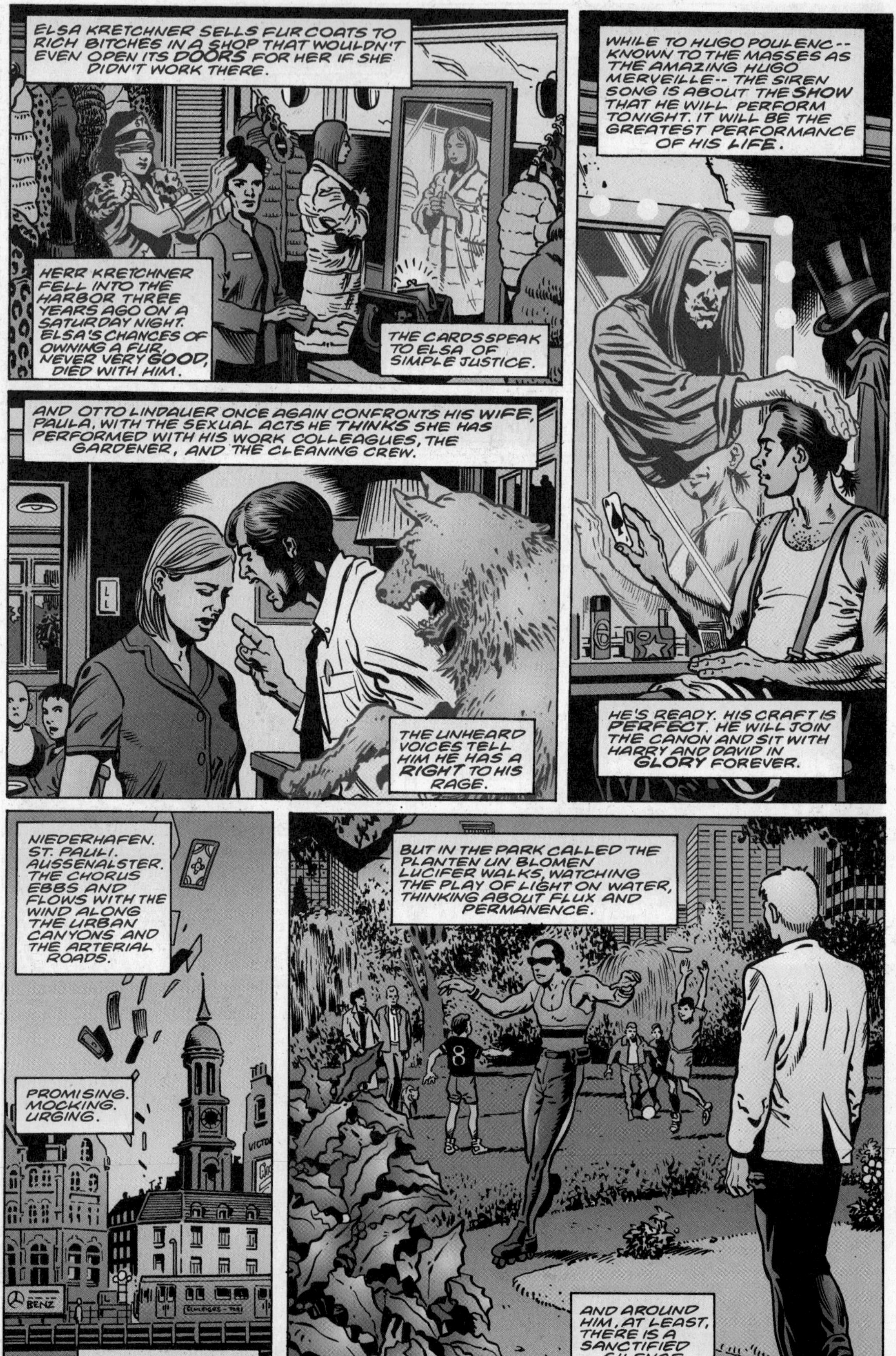
ELSA KRETCHNER SELLS FUR COATS TO RICH BITCHES IN A SHOP THAT WOULDN'T EVEN OPEN ITS DOORS FOR HER IF SHE DIDN'T WORK THERE.
HERR KRETCHNER FELL INTO THE HARBOR THREE YEARS AGO ON A SATURDAY NIGHT. ELSA'S CHANCES OF OWNING A FUR, NEVER VERY GOOD, DIED WITH HIM.
THE CARDS SPEAK TO ELSA OF SIMPLE JUSTICE.
WHILE TO HUGO POULENC -- KNOWN TO THE MASSES AS THE AMAZING HUGO MERVEILLE -- THE SIREN SONG IS ABOUT THE SHOW THAT HE WILL PERFORM TONIGHT. IT WILL BE THE GREATEST PERFORMANCE OF HIS LIFE.
AND OTTO LINDAUER ONCE AGAIN CONFRONTS HIS WIFE, PAULA, WITH THE SEXUAL ACTS HE THINKS SHE HAS PERFORMED WITH HIS WORK COLLEAGUES, THE GARDENER, AND THE CLEANING CREW.
THE UNHEARD VOICES TELL HIM HE HAS A RIGHT TO HIS RAGE.
HE'S READY. HIS CRAFT IS PERFECT. HE WILL JOIN THE CANON AND SIT WITH HARRY AND DAVID IN GLORY FOREVER.
NIEDERHAFEN. ST. PAULI. AUSSENALSTER. THE CHORUS EBBS AND FLOWS WITH THE WIND ALONG THE URBAN CANYONS AND THE ARTERIAL ROADS.
PROMISING. MOCKING. URGING.
BENZ
PLAYING THE GAME OF THE BASANOS WITH HUMANKIND.
BUT IN THE PARK CALLED THE PLANTEN UN BLOMEN LUCIFER WALKS, WATCHING THE PLAY OF LIGHT ON WATER, THINKING ABOUT FLUX AND PERMANENCE.
AND AROUND HIM, AT LEAST, THERE IS A SANCTIFIED SILENCE.

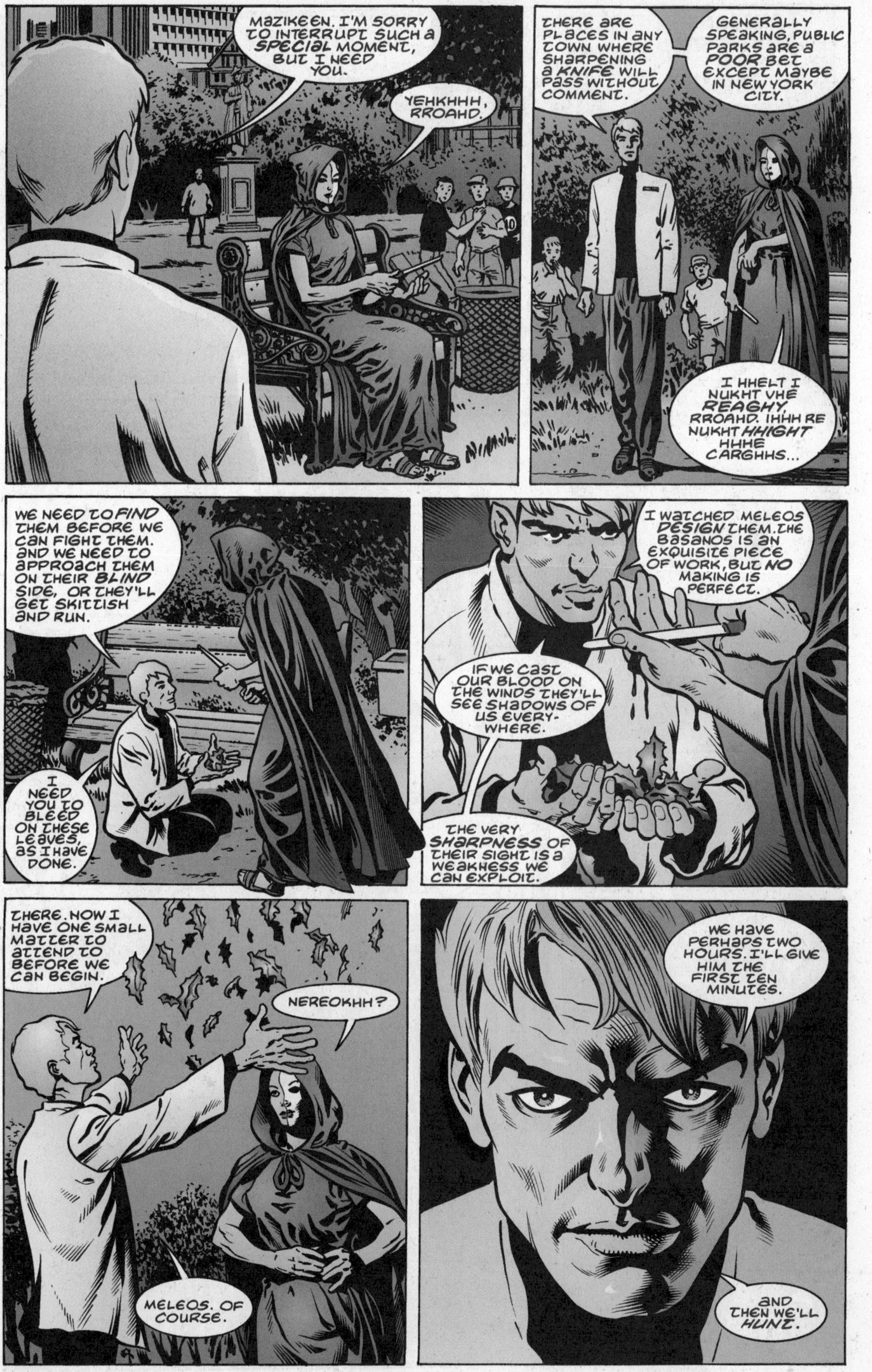
MAZIKEEN. I'M SORRY TO INTERRUPT SUCH A SPECIAL MOMENT, BUT I NEED YOU.
YEHKHHH, RROAHD.
THERE ARE PLACES IN ANY TOWN WHERE SHARPENING A KNIFE WILL PASS WITHOUT COMMENT.
GENERALLY SPEAKING, PUBLIC PARKS ARE A POOR BET EXCEPT MAYBE IN NEW YORK CITY.
I HHELT I NUKHT VHE REAGHY, RROAHD. IHHH RE NUKHT HHIGHT HHHE CARGHHS...
WE NEED TO FIND THEM BEFORE WE CAN FIGHT THEM. AND WE NEED TO APPROACH THEM ON THEIR BLIND SIDE, OR THEY'LL GET SKITTISH AND RUN.
I NEED YOU TO BLEED ON THESE LEAVES, AS I HAVE DONE.
I WATCHED MELEOS DESIGN THEM. THE BASANOS IS AN EXQUISITE PIECE OF WORK, BUT NO MAKING IS PERFECT.
IF WE CAST OUR BLOOD ON THE WINDS THEY'LL SEE SHADOWS OF US EVERY-WHERE.
THE VERY SHARPNESS OF THEIR SIGHT IS A WEAKNESS WE CAN EXPLOIT.
THERE. NOW I HAVE ONE SMALL MATTER TO ATTEND TO BEFORE WE CAN BEGIN.
NEREOKHH?
MELEOS. OF COURSE.
WE HAVE PERHAPS TWO HOURS. I'LL GIVE HIM THE FIRST TEN MINUTES.
AND THEN WE'LL HUNT.

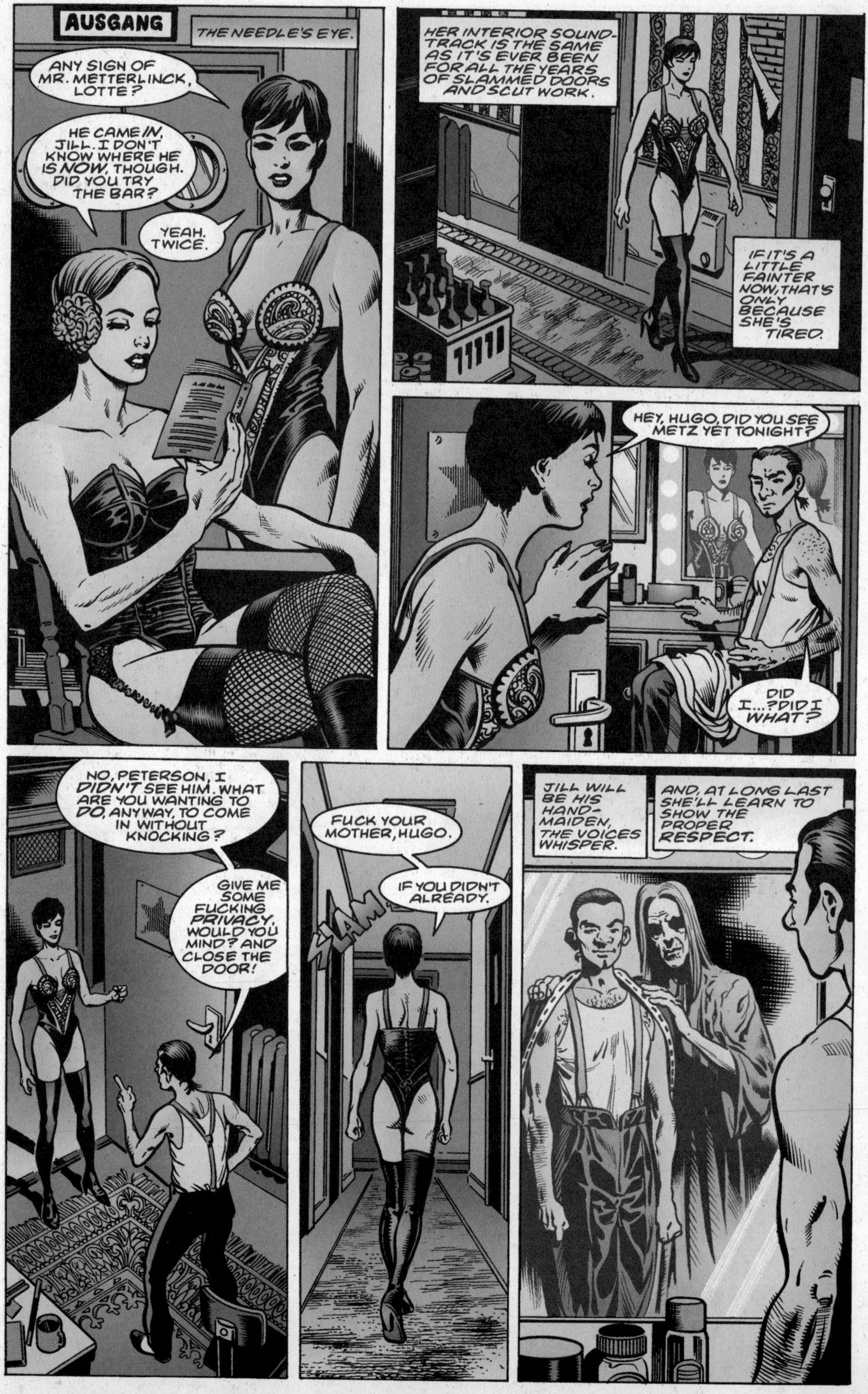
AUSGANG
THE NEEDLE'S EYE.
ANY SIGN OF MR. METTERLINCK, LOTTE?
HE CAME IN, JILL. I DON'T KNOW WHERE HE IS NOW, THOUGH. DID YOU TRY THE BAR?
YEAH. TWICE.
HER INTERIOR SOUNDTRACK IS THE SAME AS IT'S EVER BEEN FOR ALL THE YEARS OF SLAMMED DOORS AND SCUT WORK.
IF IT'S A LITTLE FAINTER NOW, THAT'S ONLY BECAUSE SHE'S TIRED.
HEY, HUGO, DID YOU SEE METZ YET TONIGHT?
DID I...? DID I WHAT?
NO, PETERSON, I DIDN'T SEE HIM. WHAT ARE YOU WANTING TO DO, ANYWAY, TO COME IN WITHOUT KNOCKING?
GIVE ME SOME FUCKING PRIVACY, WOULD YOU MIND? AND CLOSE THE DOOR!
FUCK YOUR MOTHER, HUGO.
IF YOU DIDN'T ALREADY.
SLAM
JILL WILL BE HIS HANDMAIDEN, THE VOICES WHISPER.
AND, AT LONG LAST SHE'LL LEARN TO SHOW THE PROPER RESPECT.

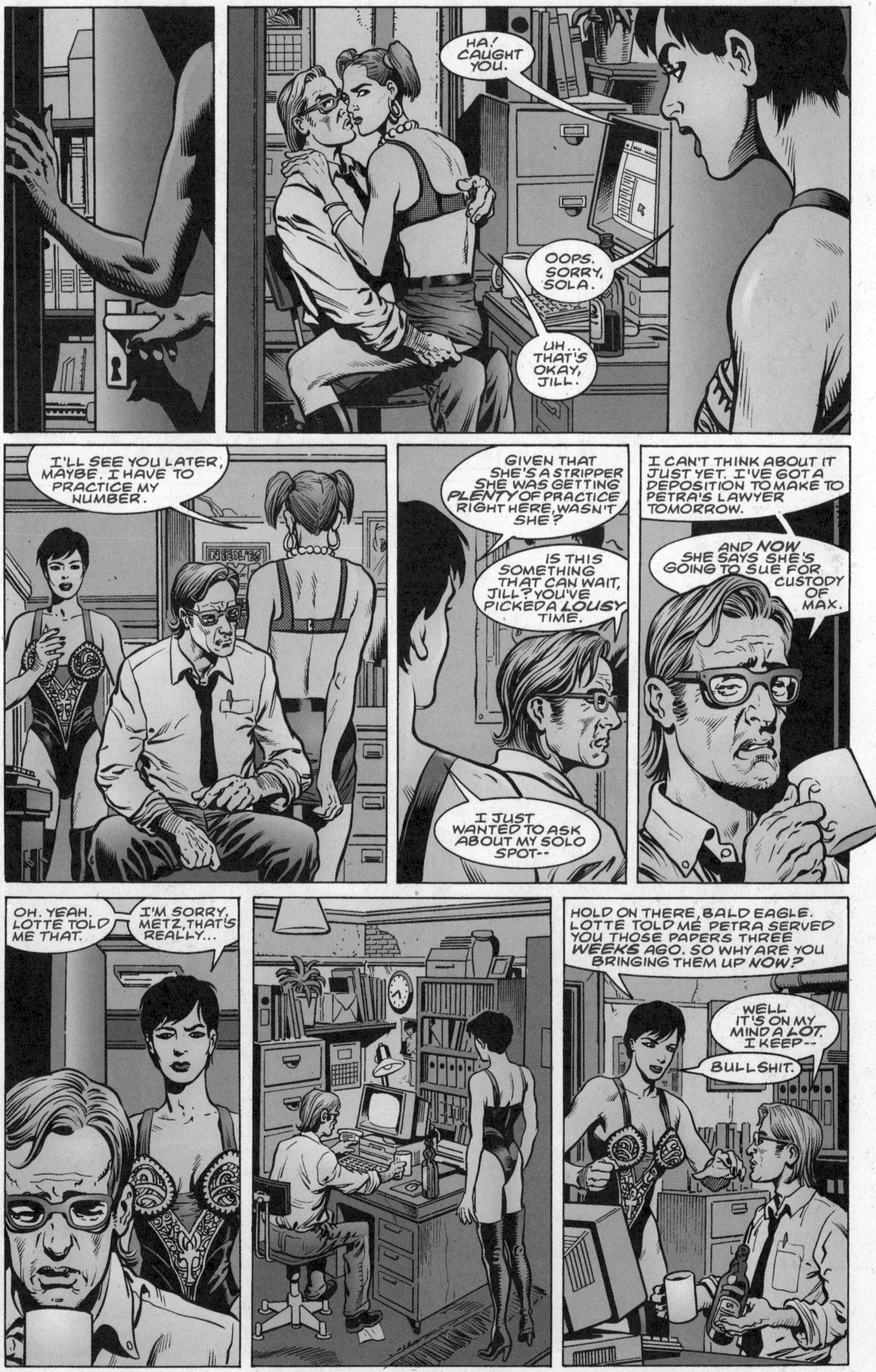
HA! CAUGHT YOU.
OOPS. SORRY, SOLA.
UH... THAT'S OKAY, JILL.
I'LL SEE YOU LATER, MAYBE. I HAVE TO PRACTICE MY NUMBER.
GIVEN THAT SHE'S A STRIPPER SHE WAS GETTING PLENTY OF PRACTICE RIGHT HERE, WASN'T SHE?
IS THIS SOMETHING THAT CAN WAIT, JILL? YOU'VE PICKED A LOUSY TIME.
I JUST WANTED TO ASK ABOUT MY SOLO SPOT--
I CAN'T THINK ABOUT IT JUST YET. I'VE GOT A DEPOSITION TO MAKE TO PETRA'S LAWYER TOMORROW.
AND NOW SHE SAYS SHE'S GOING TO SUE FOR CUSTODY OF MAX.
OH. YEAH. LOTTE TOLD ME THAT.
I'M SORRY, METZ, THAT'S REALLY...
HOLD ON THERE, BALD EAGLE. LOTTE TOLD ME PETRA SERVED YOU THOSE PAPERS THREE WEEKS AGO. SO WHY ARE YOU BRINGING THEM UP NOW?
WELL IT'S ON MY MIND A LOT. I KEEP--
BULLSHIT.

YOU USED YOUR *PRIVATE* LIFE TO CHANGE THE SUBJECT ON ME, METZ. FOR ABOUT THE *FIFTH* TIME.

NOW GIVE ME A *STRAIGHT* ANSWER.

OKAY, JILL. THE *STRAIGHT* ANSWER.

YOU'RE NOT *UP* TO IT. YOU *SING* OKAY, BUT YOUR *MOVES* ARE AWKWARD AND YOU DON'T *PRO-JECT* YOUR *PERSONALITY* ALL THAT WELL.

MY MOVES? SONOFABITCH! WHAT ABOUT *YOUR* MOVES? YOU ONLY GAVE SOLA HER BIG CAGE ROUTINE BECAUSE SHE WENT DOWN ON YOU!

ON SECOND THOUGHT, YOU PROJECT JUST *FINE*-- YOU COME ACROSS AS *LOUD* AND *COARSE.*

COARSE? YOU WANNA SEE *COARSE*?

GIMME MY COAT, LOTTE. I NEED A DRINK.

JUST WAIT UNTIL I FINISH THIS PARA-GRAPH--

HIS WIFE DIES OF LEUKEMIA AND HE MARRIES THE NURSE, OKAY?

YOU'RE ON AT TEN THIRTY, YOU KNOW. I COULD GET YOU A DRINK FROM THE BAR.

THEN THE NURSE *DIVORCES* HIM AND HE SPENDS THE REST OF HIS BEER-BELLIED LIFE *FUCKING* EIGHTEEN-YEAR-OLD STRIPPERS.

IT'S BASED ON A TRUE STORY. RIGHT METZ?

--GO INTO THE OFFICE AND TYPE UP A *TERMINATION* LETTER.

LOTTE--

"AND LEAVE SOME SPACES FOR *ADJECTIVES.*"

103

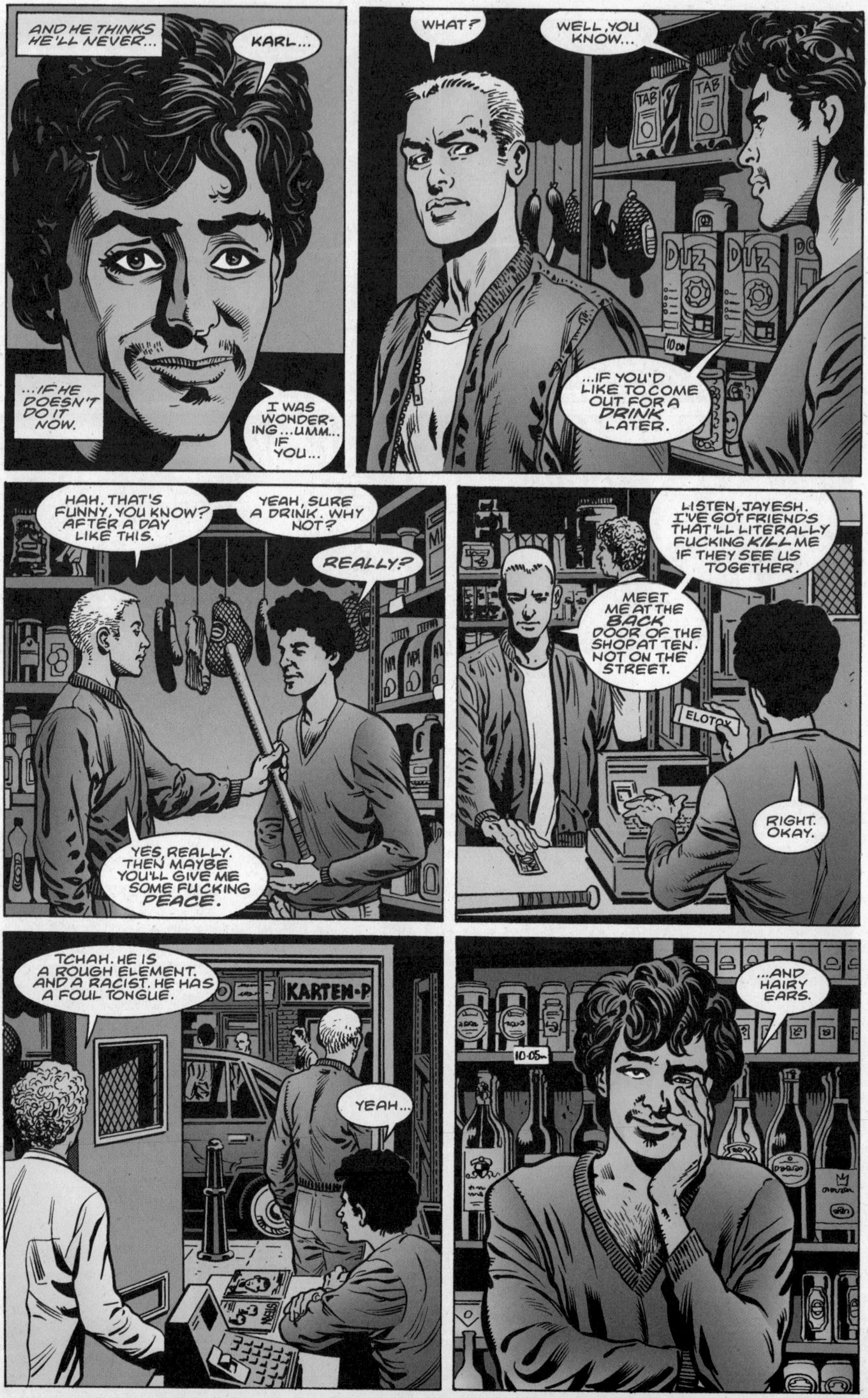
AND HE THINKS HE'LL NEVER...
KARL...
...IF HE DOESN'T DO IT NOW.
I WAS WONDERING...UMM... IF YOU...
WHAT?
WELL, YOU KNOW...
TAB
TAB
DUZ
DUZ
...IF YOU'D LIKE TO COME OUT FOR A DRINK LATER.
HAH. THAT'S FUNNY, YOU KNOW? AFTER A DAY LIKE THIS.
YEAH, SURE A DRINK. WHY NOT?
REALLY?
YES, REALLY. THEN MAYBE YOU'LL GIVE ME SOME FUCKING PEACE.
LISTEN, JAYESH. I'VE GOT FRIENDS THAT'LL LITERALLY FUCKING KILL ME IF THEY SEE US TOGETHER.
MEET ME AT THE BACK DOOR OF THE SHOPAT TEN. NOT ON THE STREET.
ELOTOX
RIGHT. OKAY.
TCHAH. HE IS A ROUGH ELEMENT. AND A RACIST. HE HAS A FOUL TONGUE.
KARTEN-P
YEAH...
STERN
...AND HAIRY EARS.

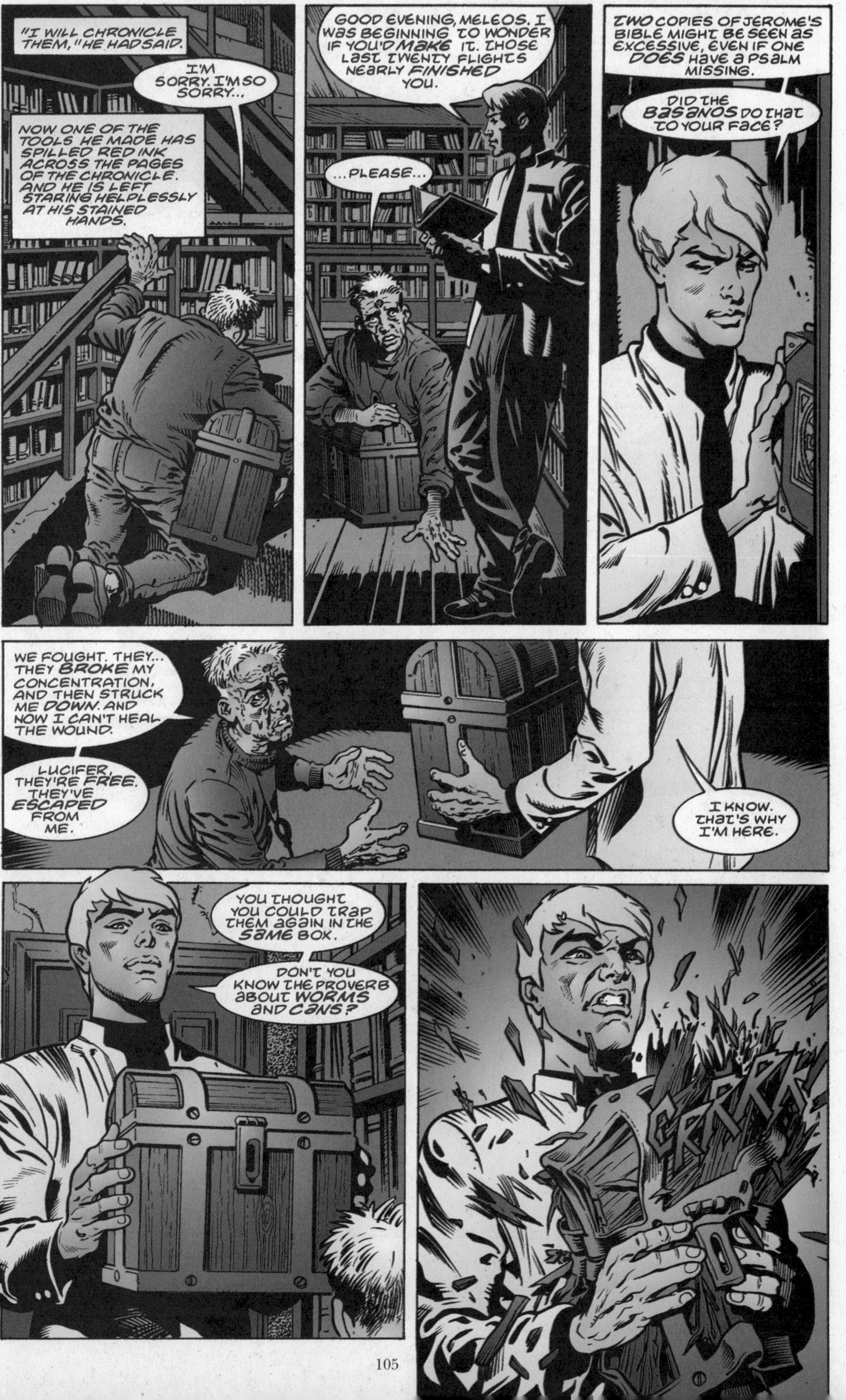
"I WILL CHRONICLE THEM," HE HAD SAID.
I'M SORRY. I'M SO SORRY...
NOW ONE OF THE TOOLS HE MADE HAS SPILLED RED INK ACROSS THE PAGES OF THE CHRONICLE. AND HE IS LEFT STARING HELPLESSLY AT HIS STAINED HANDS.
GOOD EVENING, MELEOS. I WAS BEGINNING TO WONDER IF YOU'D MAKE IT. THOSE LAST TWENTY FLIGHTS NEARLY FINISHED YOU.
...PLEASE...
TWO COPIES OF JEROME'S BIBLE MIGHT BE SEEN AS EXCESSIVE, EVEN IF ONE DOES HAVE A PSALM MISSING.
DID THE BASANOS DO THAT TO YOUR FACE?
WE FOUGHT. THEY... THEY BROKE MY CONCENTRATION, AND THEN STRUCK ME DOWN. AND NOW I CAN'T HEAL THE WOUND.
LUCIFER, THEY'RE FREE. THEY'VE ESCAPED FROM ME.
I KNOW. THAT'S WHY I'M HERE.
YOU THOUGHT YOU COULD TRAP THEM AGAIN IN THE SAME BOX.
DON'T YOU KNOW THE PROVERB ABOUT WORMS AND CANS?
CRKKK

106

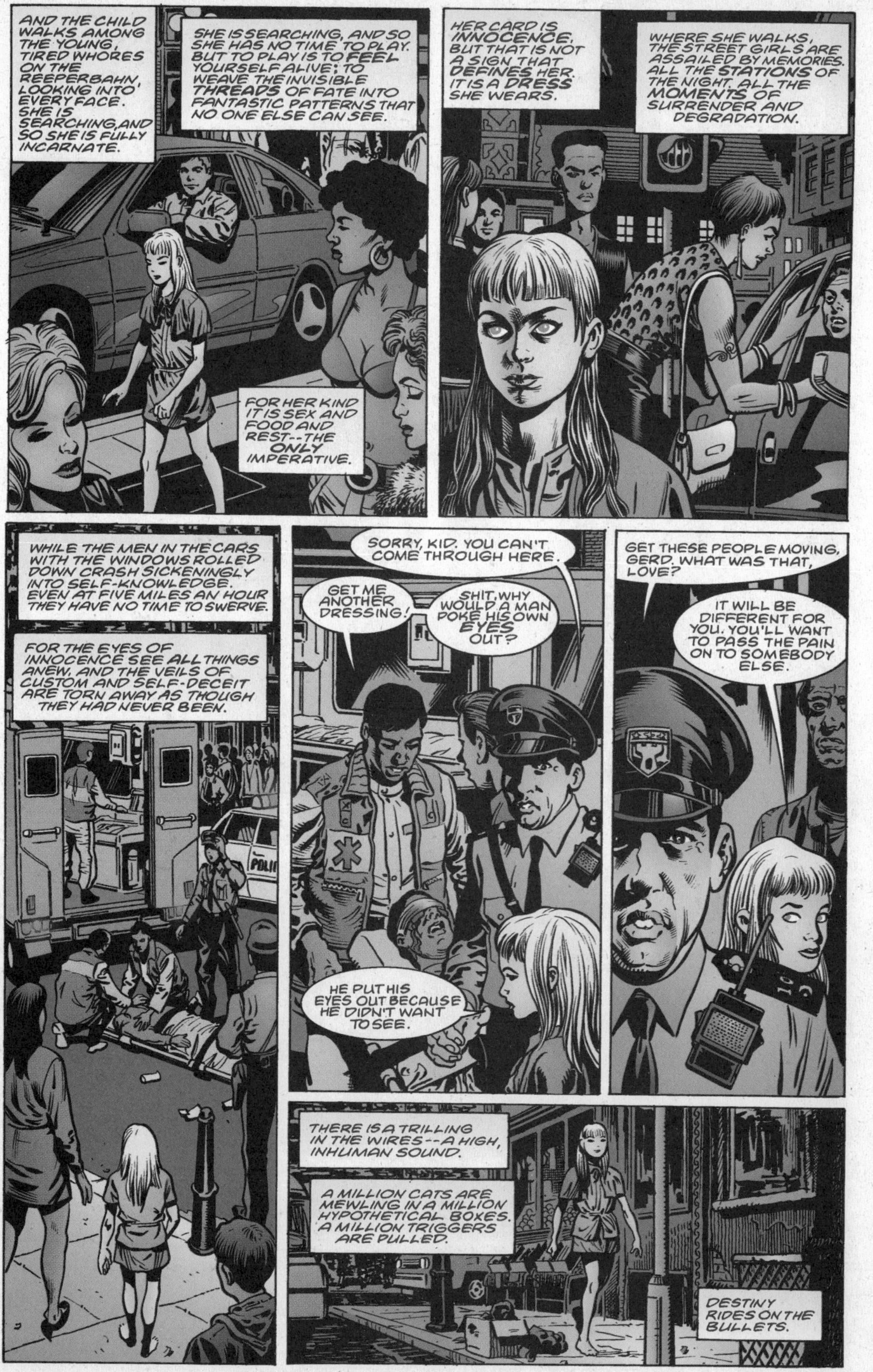

AND THE CHILD WALKS AMONG THE YOUNG, TIRED WHORES ON THE REEPERBAHN, LOOKING INTO EVERY FACE. SHE IS SEARCHING, AND SO SHE IS FULLY INCARNATE.
SHE IS SEARCHING, AND SO SHE HAS NO TIME TO PLAY. BUT TO PLAY IS TO FEEL YOURSELF ALIVE; TO WEAVE THE INVISIBLE THREADS OF FATE INTO FANTASTIC PATTERNS THAT NO ONE ELSE CAN SEE.
FOR HER KIND IT IS SEX AND FOOD AND REST--THE ONLY IMPERATIVE.
HER CARD IS INNOCENCE, BUT THAT IS NOT A SIGN THAT DEFINES HER. IT IS A DRESS SHE WEARS.
WHERE SHE WALKS, THE STREET GIRLS ARE ASSAILED BY MEMORIES. ALL THE STATIONS OF THE NIGHT. ALL THE MOMENTS OF SURRENDER AND DEGRADATION.
WHILE THE MEN IN THE CARS WITH THE WINDOWS ROLLED DOWN CRASH SICKENINGLY INTO SELF-KNOWLEDGE. EVEN AT FIVE MILES AN HOUR THEY HAVE NO TIME TO SWERVE.
FOR THE EYES OF INNOCENCE SEE ALL THINGS ANEW, AND THE VEILS OF CUSTOM AND SELF-DECEIT ARE TORN AWAY AS THOUGH THEY HAD NEVER BEEN.
POLI
SORRY, KID. YOU CAN'T COME THROUGH HERE.
GET ME ANOTHER DRESSING!
SHIT, WHY WOULD A MAN POKE HIS OWN EYES OUT?
HE PUT HIS EYES OUT BECAUSE HE DIDN'T WANT TO SEE.
GET THESE PEOPLE MOVING, GERD. WHAT WAS THAT, LOVE?
IT WILL BE DIFFERENT FOR YOU. YOU'LL WANT TO PASS THE PAIN ON TO SOMEBODY ELSE.
THERE IS A TRILLING IN THE WIRES--A HIGH, INHUMAN SOUND.
A MILLION CATS ARE MEWLING IN A MILLION HYPOTHETICAL BOXES. A MILLION TRIGGERS ARE PULLED.
DESTINY RIDES ON THE BULLETS.

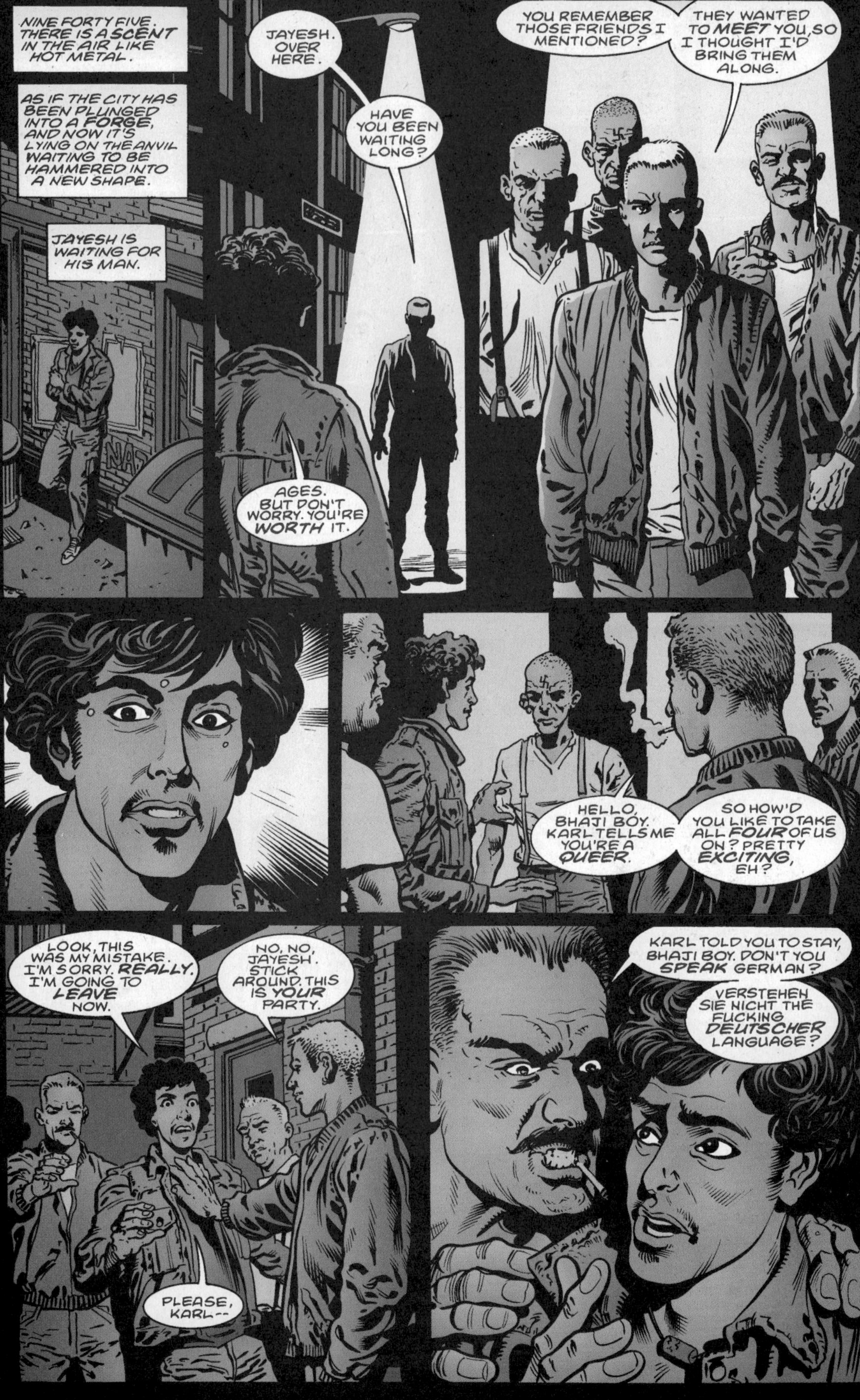
NINE FORTY FIVE. THERE IS A SCENT IN THE AIR LIKE HOT METAL.
AS IF THE CITY HAS BEEN PLUNGED INTO A FORGE, AND NOW IT'S LYING ON THE ANVIL WAITING TO BE HAMMERED INTO A NEW SHAPE.
JAYESH IS WAITING FOR HIS MAN.
JAYESH. OVER HERE.
HAVE YOU BEEN WAITING LONG?
AGES. BUT DON'T WORRY. YOU'RE WORTH IT.
YOU REMEMBER THOSE FRIENDS I MENTIONED?
THEY WANTED TO MEET YOU, SO I THOUGHT I'D BRING THEM ALONG.
HELLO, BHAJI BOY. KARL TELLS ME YOU'RE A QUEER.
SO HOW'D YOU LIKE TO TAKE ALL FOUR OF US ON? PRETTY EXCITING, EH?
LOOK, THIS WAS MY MISTAKE. I'M SORRY. REALLY. I'M GOING TO LEAVE NOW.
NO, NO, JAYESH. STICK AROUND. THIS IS YOUR PARTY.
PLEASE, KARL--
KARL TOLD YOU TO STAY, BHAJI BOY. DON'T YOU SPEAK GERMAN?
VERSTEHEN SIE NICHT THE FUCKING DEUTSCHER LANGUAGE?

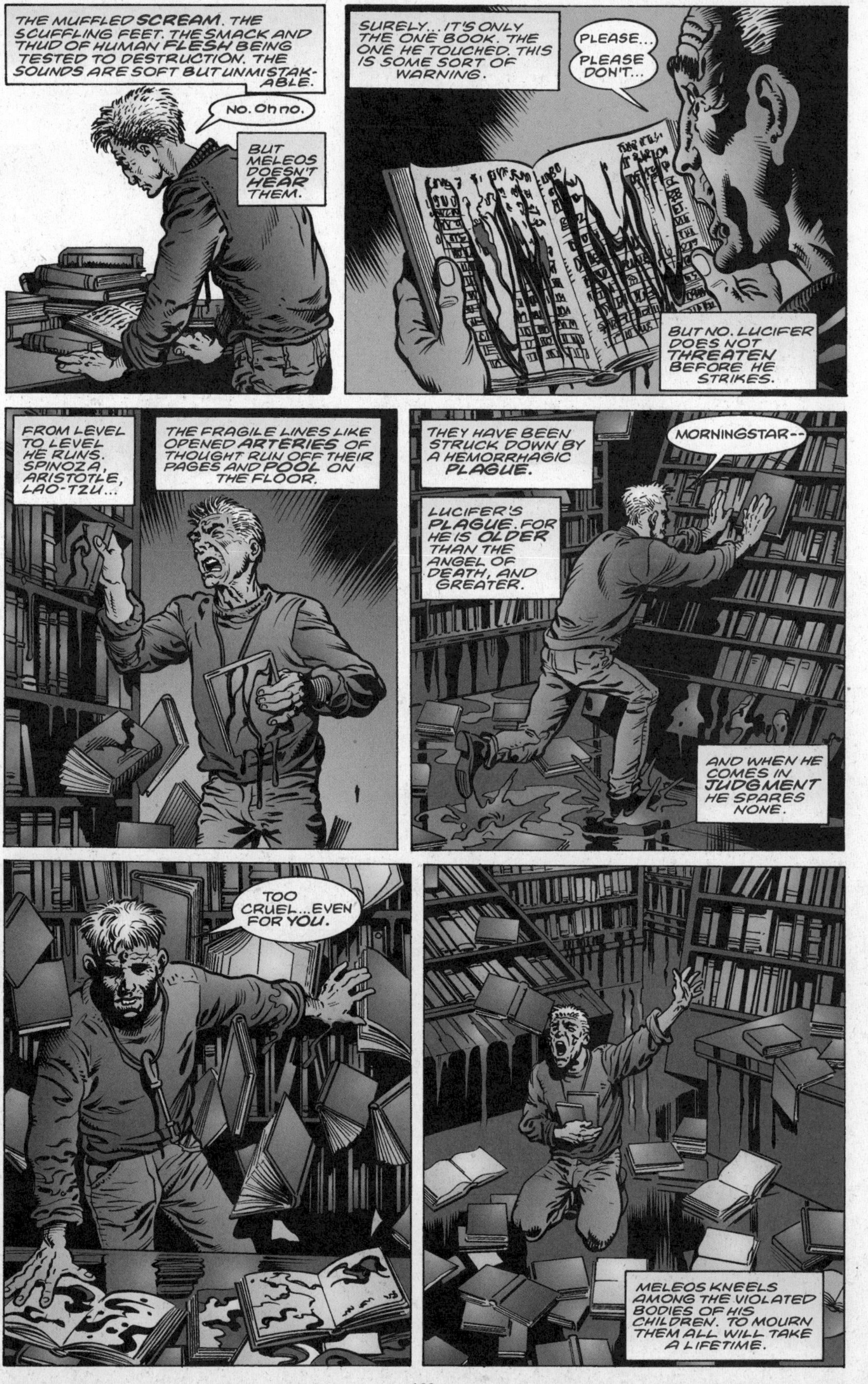
THE MUFFLED SCREAM. THE SCUFFLING FEET. THE SMACK AND THUD OF HUMAN FLESH BEING TESTED TO DESTRUCTION. THE SOUNDS ARE SOFT BUT UNMISTAKABLE.
No. Oh no.
BUT MELEOS DOESN'T HEAR THEM.
SURELY... IT'S ONLY THE ONE BOOK. THE ONE HE TOUCHED. THIS IS SOME SORT OF WARNING.
PLEASE... PLEASE DON'T...
BUT NO. LUCIFER DOES NOT THREATEN BEFORE HE STRIKES.
FROM LEVEL TO LEVEL HE RUNS. SPINOZA, ARISTOTLE, LAO-TZU...
THE FRAGILE LINES LIKE OPENED ARTERIES OF THOUGHT RUN OFF THEIR PAGES AND POOL ON THE FLOOR.
THEY HAVE BEEN STRUCK DOWN BY A HEMORRHAGIC PLAGUE.
MORNINGSTAR--
LUCIFER'S PLAGUE. FOR HE IS OLDER THAN THE ANGEL OF DEATH, AND GREATER.
AND WHEN HE COMES IN JUDGMENT HE SPARES NONE.
TOO CRUEL... EVEN FOR YOU.
MELEOS KNEELS AMONG THE VIOLATED BODIES OF HIS CHILDREN. TO MOURN THEM ALL WILL TAKE A LIFETIME.

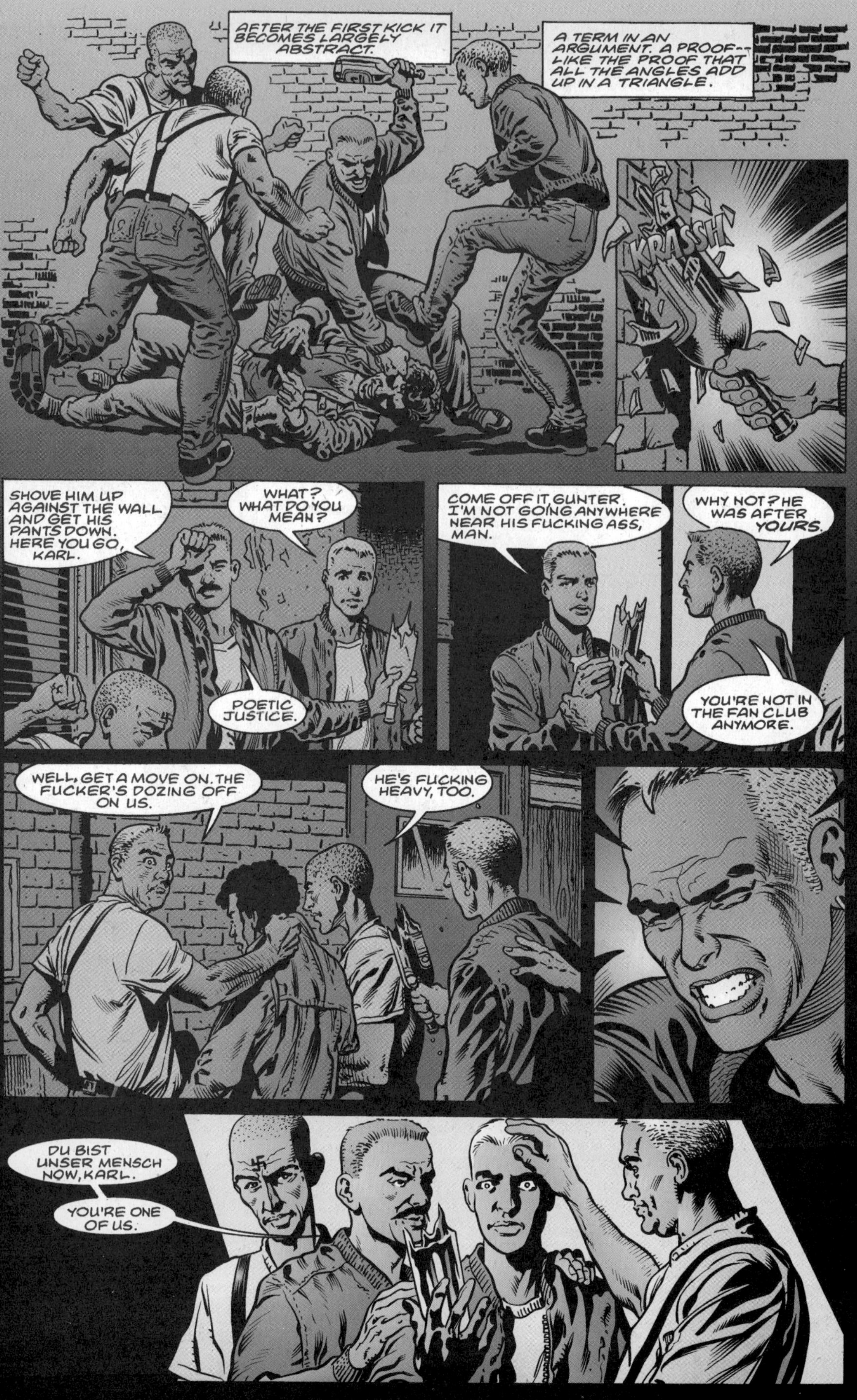
AFTER THE FIRST KICK IT BECOMES LARGELY ABSTRACT.
A TERM IN AN ARGUMENT. A PROOF-- LIKE THE PROOF THAT ALL THE ANGLES ADD UP IN A TRIANGLE.
KRASSH
SHOVE HIM UP AGAINST THE WALL AND GET HIS PANTS DOWN. HERE YOU GO, KARL.
WHAT? WHAT DO YOU MEAN?
POETIC JUSTICE.
COME OFF IT, GUNTER. I'M NOT GOING ANYWHERE NEAR HIS FUCKING ASS, MAN.
WHY NOT? HE WAS AFTER YOURS.
YOU'RE NOT IN THE FAN CLUB ANYMORE.
WELL, GET A MOVE ON. THE FUCKER'S DOZING OFF ON US.
HE'S FUCKING HEAVY, TOO.
DU BIST UNSER MENSCH NOW, KARL.
YOU'RE ONE OF US.

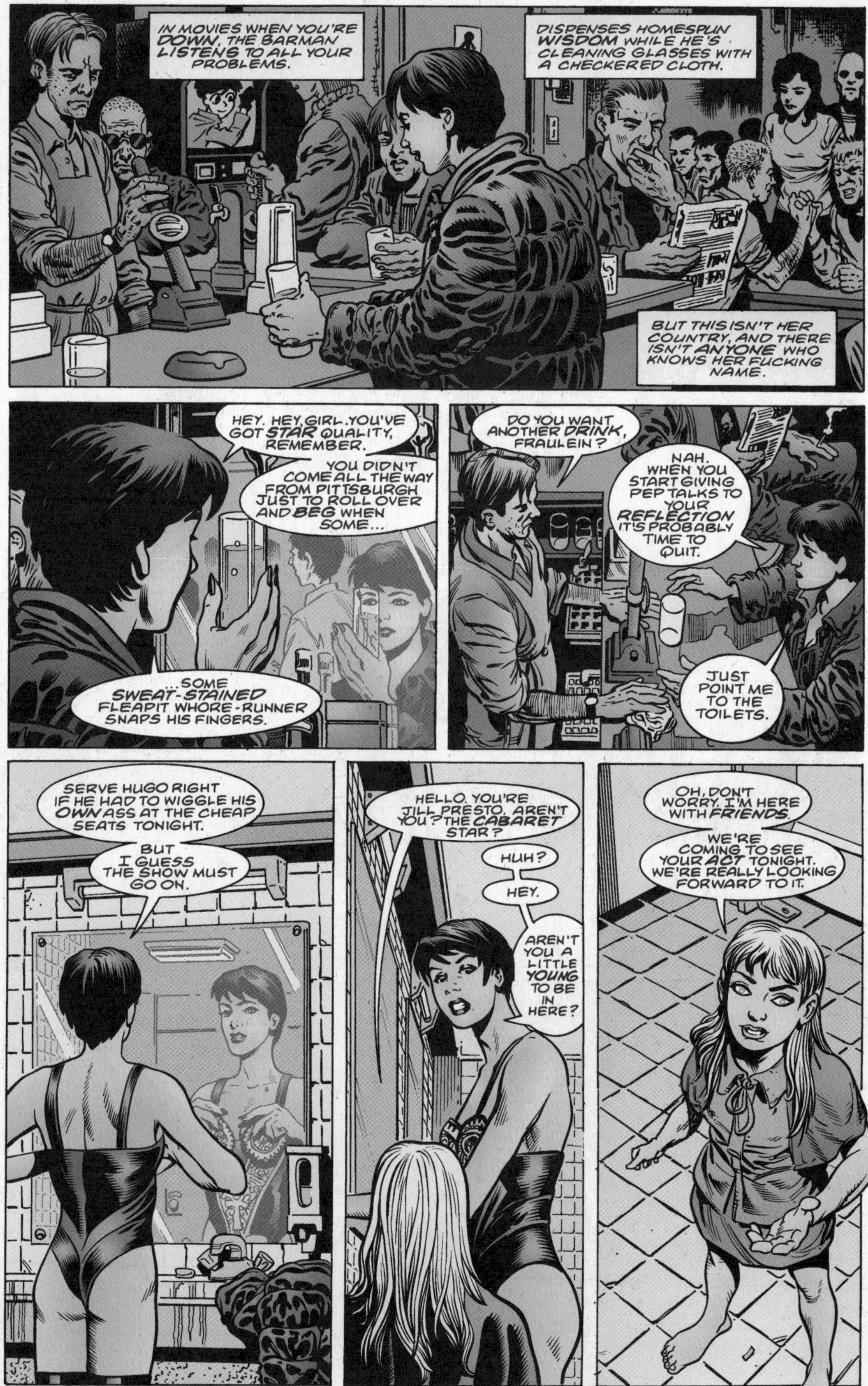
IN MOVIES WHEN YOU'RE DOWN, THE BARMAN LISTENS TO ALL YOUR PROBLEMS.
DISPENSES HOMESPUN WISDOM WHILE HE'S CLEANING GLASSES WITH A CHECKERED CLOTH.
BUT THIS ISN'T HER COUNTRY, AND THERE ISN'T ANYONE WHO KNOWS HER FUCKING NAME.
HEY. HEY, GIRL. YOU'VE GOT STAR QUALITY, REMEMBER.
YOU DIDN'T COME ALL THE WAY FROM PITTSBURGH JUST TO ROLL OVER AND BEG WHEN SOME...
...SOME SWEAT-STAINED FLEAPIT WHORE-RUNNER SNAPS HIS FINGERS.
DO YOU WANT ANOTHER DRINK, FRAULEIN?
NAH. WHEN YOU START GIVING PEP TALKS TO YOUR REFLECTION IT'S PROBABLY TIME TO QUIT.
JUST POINT ME TO THE TOILETS.
SERVE HUGO RIGHT IF HE HAD TO WIGGLE HIS OWN ASS AT THE CHEAP SEATS TONIGHT.
BUT I GUESS THE SHOW MUST GO ON.
HELLO. YOU'RE JILL PRESTO, AREN'T YOU? THE CABARET STAR?
HUH?
HEY.
AREN'T YOU A LITTLE YOUNG TO BE IN HERE?
OH, DON'T WORRY. I'M HERE WITH FRIENDS.
WE'RE COMING TO SEE YOUR ACT TONIGHT. WE'RE REALLY LOOKING FORWARD TO IT.

WELL THAT'S VERY *FLATTERING*, KIDDO, BUT THE NEEDLE'S EYE IS ADULTS ONLY.

GOD-- I CAN'T BELIEVE YOU KNOW MY STUFF.

WE KNOW *EVERYTHING* ABOUT YOU, JILL. YOU SEE, WE'VE SORT OF BEEN AUDITIONING. LOOKING FOR SOMEONE TO *WORK* WITH.

YEAH? WHAT SORT OF ACT?

YOU MEAN AN *M.C.*? THAT REALLY DOESN'T SOUND LIKE MY *LINE*.

UMMM... WHAT AM I MEANT TO BE *LOOKING* AT?

YOUR *FUTURE*. YOUR *PAST*. YOUR *DESTINY*. CAN'T YOU *SEE*?

VARIETY. *LIMITLESS* VARIETY. ALL WE NEED IS A *HOST*. TAKE A LOOK.

CUTE, BUT WEIRD. ARE YOU A LITTLE *CULT* KID? DO YOUR FOLKS SELL *FLOWERS* AT MAJOR AIRPORTS? LOOK, YOU CAN *KEEP* THE CARDS. I'M NOT INTERESTED.

YOU'VE ALREADY *ACCEPTED* THEM, JILL. DON'T BE AFRAID--THE *DEATH* CARD STANDS FOR *CHANGE* AND *REBIRTH*. IT'S A GOOD OMEN.

WHAT *DIES* IS JUST THE PART OF YOU YOU DON'T *NEED* ANYMORE.

112

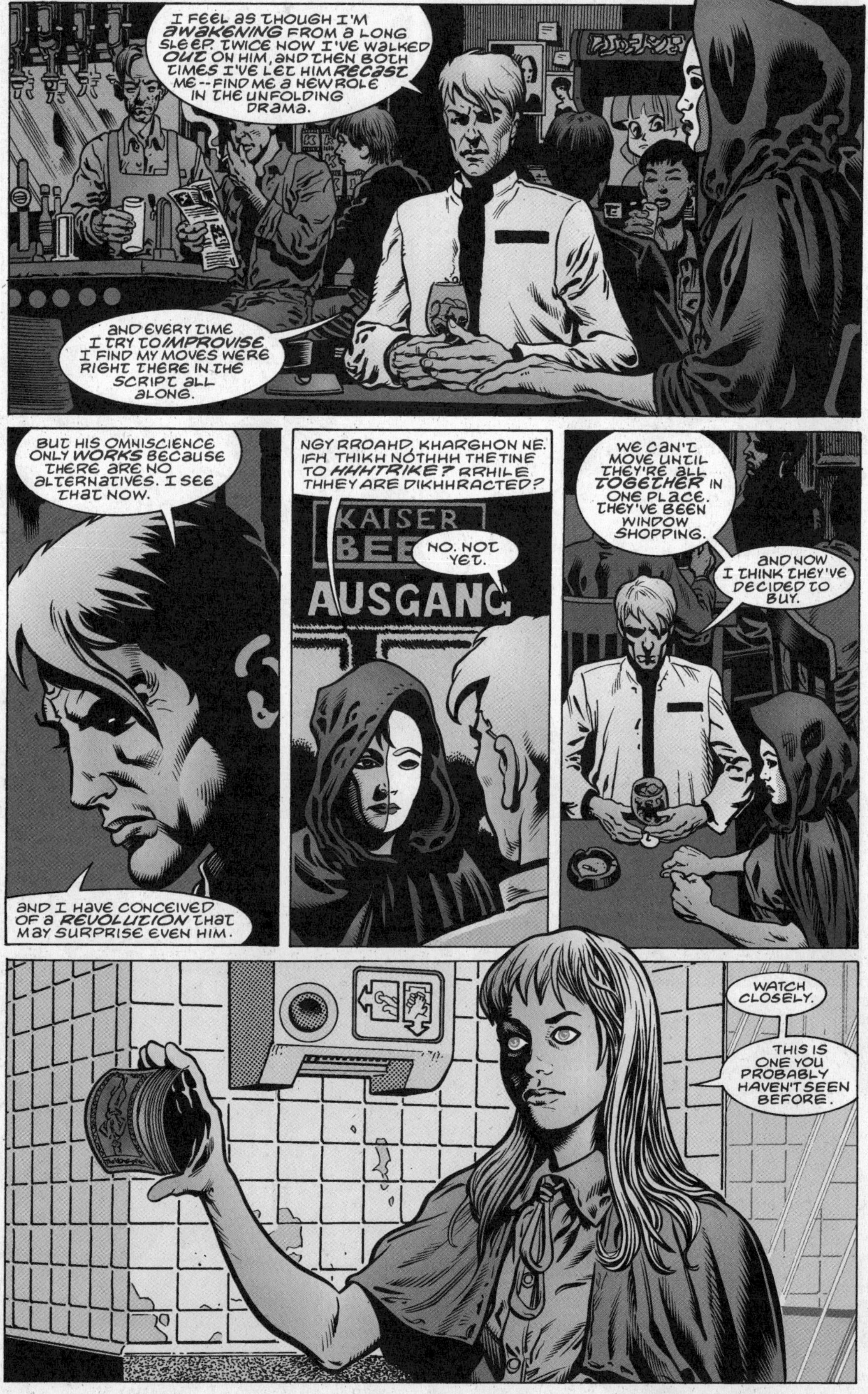
I FEEL AS THOUGH I'M AWAKENING FROM A LONG SLEEP. TWICE NOW I'VE WALKED OUT ON HIM, AND THEN BOTH TIMES I'VE LET HIM RECAST ME -- FIND ME A NEW ROLE IN THE UNFOLDING DRAMA.
AND EVERY TIME I TRY TO IMPROVISE, I FIND MY MOVES WERE RIGHT THERE IN THE SCRIPT ALL ALONG.
BUT HIS OMNISCIENCE ONLY WORKS BECAUSE THERE ARE NO ALTERNATIVES. I SEE THAT NOW.
AND I HAVE CONCEIVED OF A REVOLUTION THAT MAY SURPRISE EVEN HIM.
NGY RROAHD, KHARGHON NE. IFH THIKH NÓTHHH THE TINE TO HHHTRIKE? RRHILE THHEY ARE DIKHHRACTED?
KAISER BEE
NO. NOT YET.
AUSGANG
WE CAN'T MOVE UNTIL THEY'RE ALL TOGETHER IN ONE PLACE. THEY'VE BEEN WINDOW SHOPPING.
AND NOW I THINK THEY'VE DECIDED TO BUY.
WATCH CLOSELY.
THIS IS ONE YOU PROBABLY HAVEN'T SEEN BEFORE.

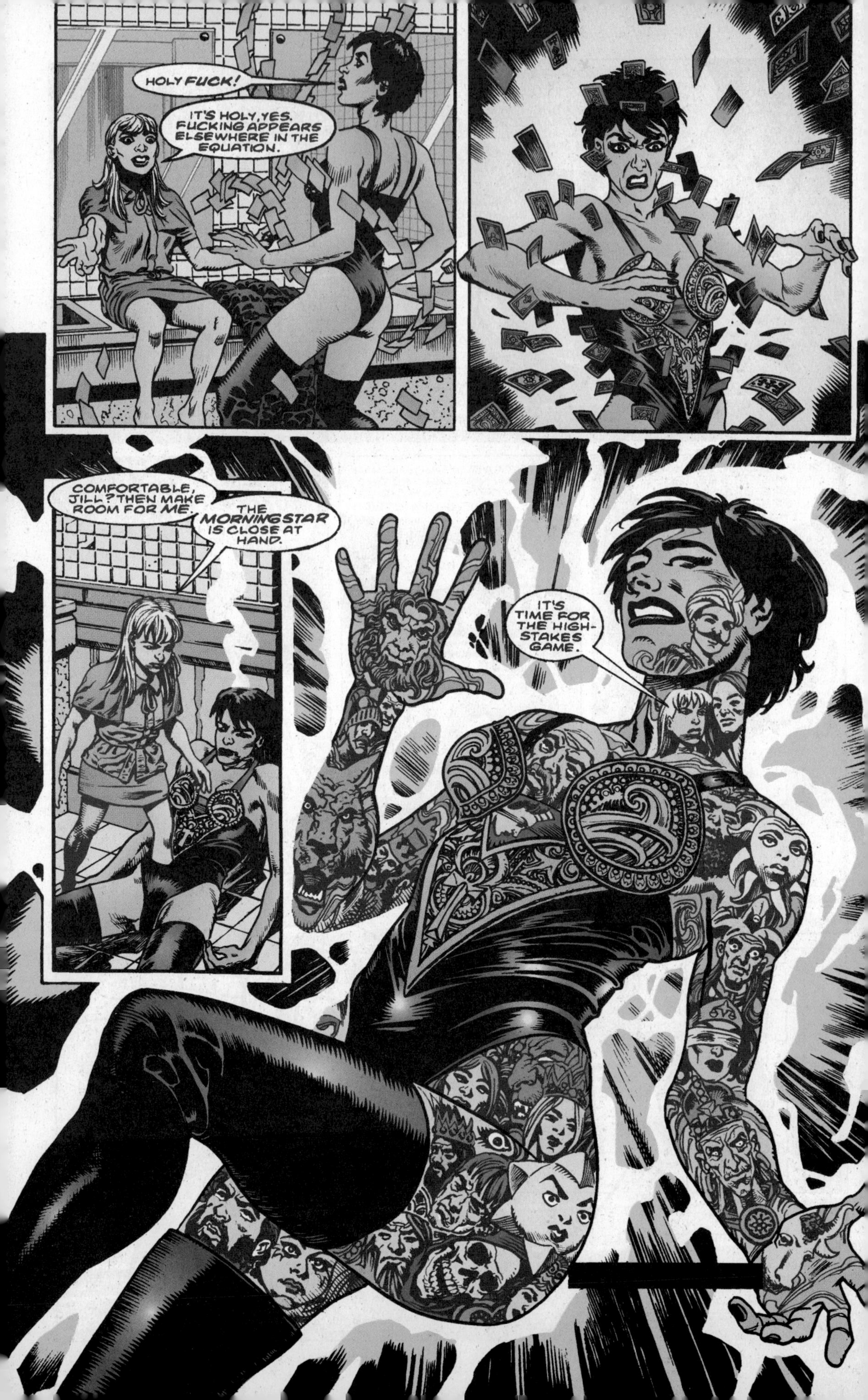
HOLY FUCK!
IT'S HOLY, YES. FUCKING APPEARS ELSEWHERE IN THE EQUATION.
COMFORTABLE, JILL? THEN MAKE ROOM FOR ME.
THE MORNINGSTAR IS CLOSE AT HAND.
IT'S TIME FOR THE HIGH-STAKES GAME.

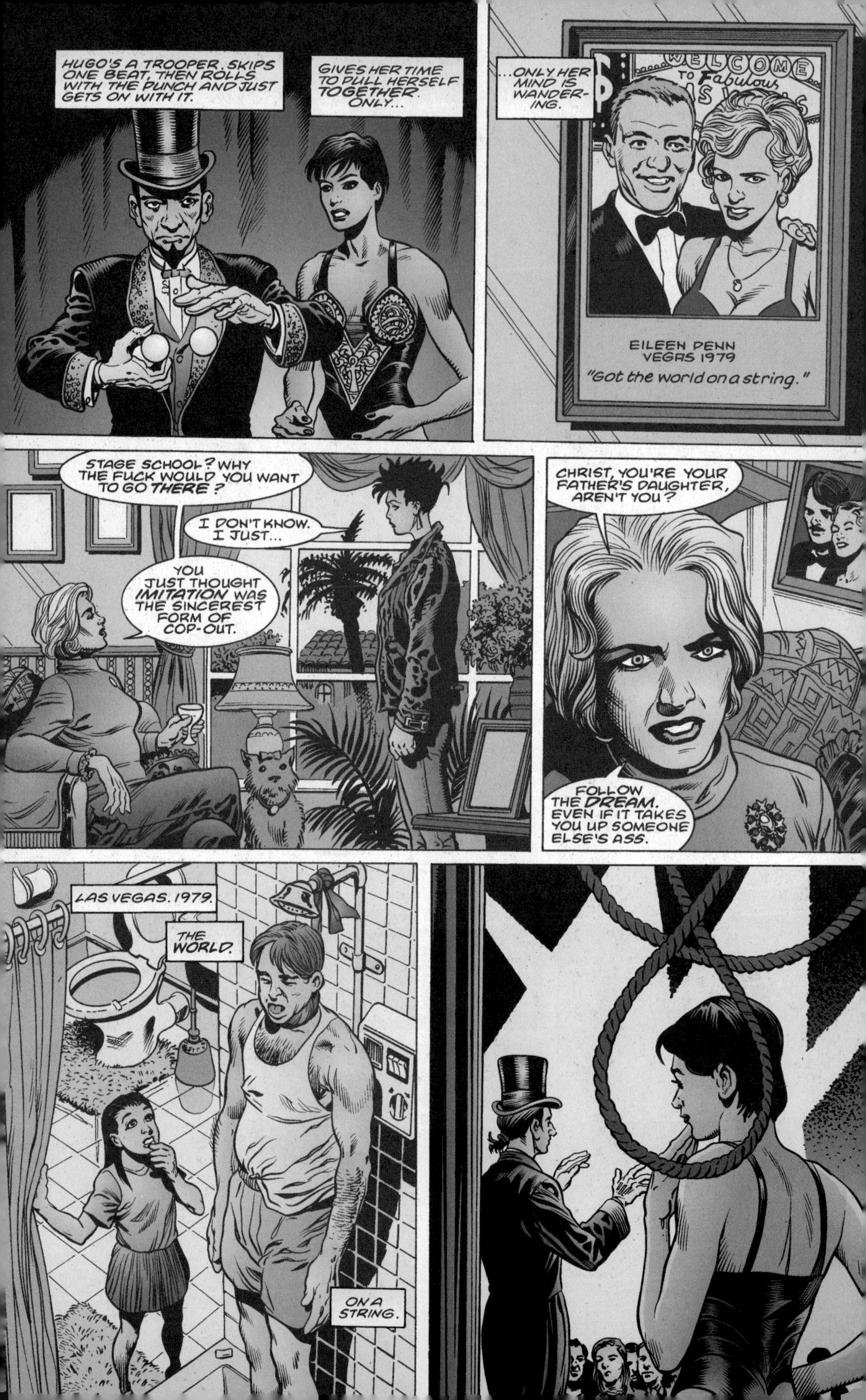
HUGO'S A TROOPER. SKIPS ONE BEAT, THEN ROLLS WITH THE PUNCH AND JUST GETS ON WITH IT.
GIVES HER TIME TO PULL HERSELF TOGETHER. ONLY...
...ONLY HER MIND IS WANDER-ING.
WELCOME TO Fabulous
EILEEN PENN
VEGAS 1979
"Got the world on a string."
STAGE SCHOOL? WHY THE FUCK WOULD YOU WANT TO GO THERE?
I DON'T KNOW. I JUST...
YOU JUST THOUGHT IMITATION WAS THE SINCEREST FORM OF COP-OUT.
CHRIST, YOU'RE YOUR FATHER'S DAUGHTER, AREN'T YOU?
FOLLOW THE DREAM. EVEN IF IT TAKES YOU UP SOMEONE ELSE'S ASS.
LAS VEGAS. 1979.
THE WORLD.
ON A STRING.

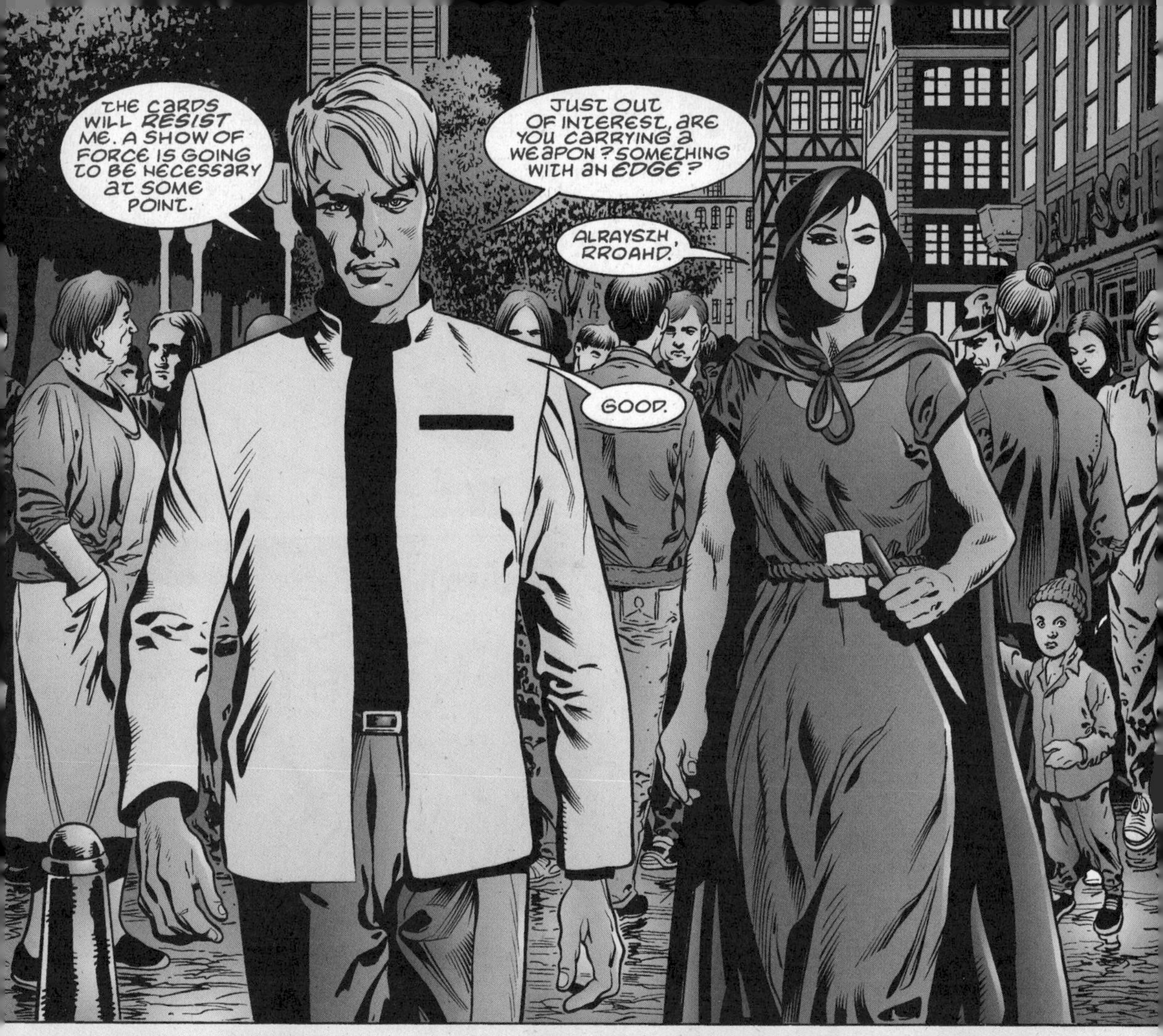
THE CARDS WILL RESIST ME. A SHOW OF FORCE IS GOING TO BE NECESSARY AT SOME POINT.
JUST OUT OF INTEREST, ARE YOU CARRYING A WEAPON? SOMETHING WITH AN EDGE?
ALRAYSZH, RROAHD.
GOOD.
DEUTSCH

A SIX-CARD SPREAD

MIKE CAREY · WRITER CHRIS WESTON · PENCILLER + INKER PPS. 14, 17-19, 21 JAMES HODGKINS · INKER PPS. 1-13, 15-16, 20, 22 DANIEL VOZZO · COLOR + SEPS ELLIE DE VILLE · LETTERER DUNCAN FEGREDO · COVER ART WILL DENNIS · ASST EDITOR SHELLY ROEBERG · EDITOR
BASED ON THE CHARACTER CREATED BY GAIMAN, KIETH AND DRINGENBERG

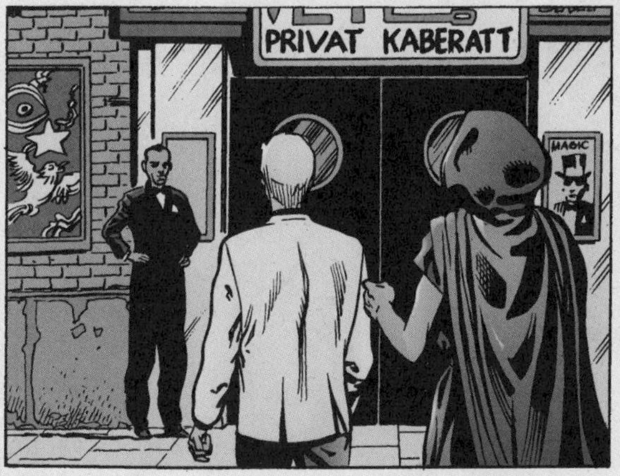
PRIVAT KABERATT
MAGIC

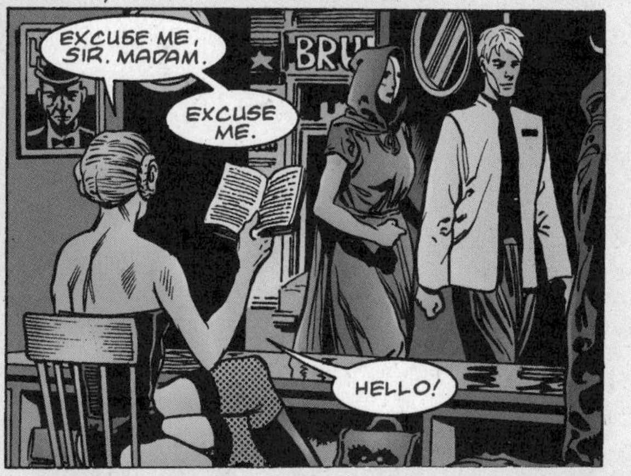
EXCUSE ME, SIR. MADAM.
EXCUSE ME.
HELLO!

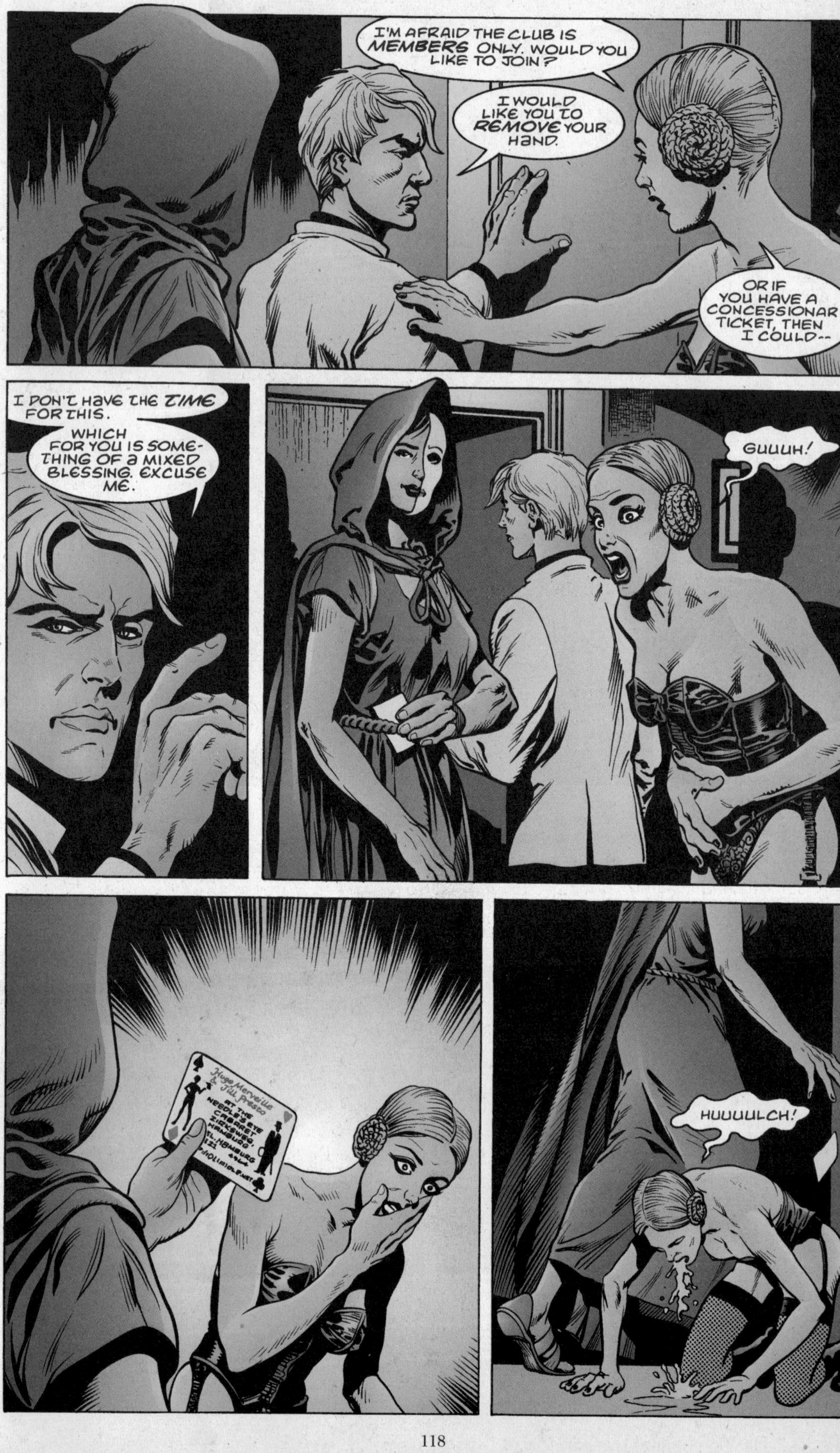
I'M AFRAID THE CLUB IS MEMBERS ONLY. WOULD YOU LIKE TO JOIN?
I WOULD LIKE YOU TO REMOVE YOUR HAND.
OR IF YOU HAVE A CONCESSIONARY TICKET, THEN I COULD--
I DON'T HAVE THE TIME FOR THIS.
WHICH FOR YOU IS SOMETHING OF A MIXED BLESSING. EXCUSE ME.
GUUUH!
Hugo Merveille & Jill Presto
AT THE NEEDLE'S EYE CABARET
ZIRKSWEG, HAMBURG
HUUUULCH!

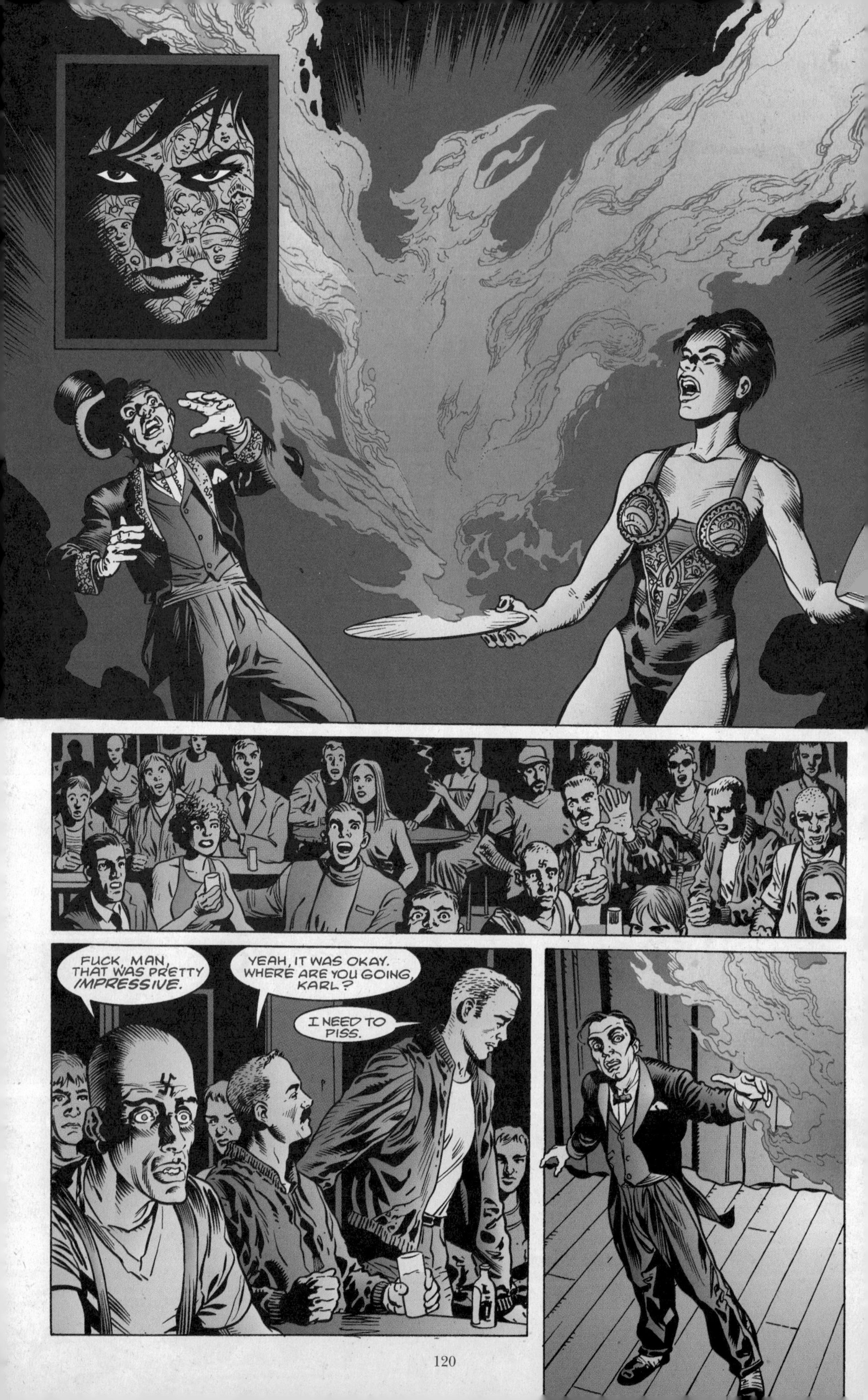
FUCK, MAN, THAT WAS PRETTY IMPRESSIVE.
YEAH, IT WAS OKAY. WHERE ARE YOU GOING, KARL?
I NEED TO PISS.

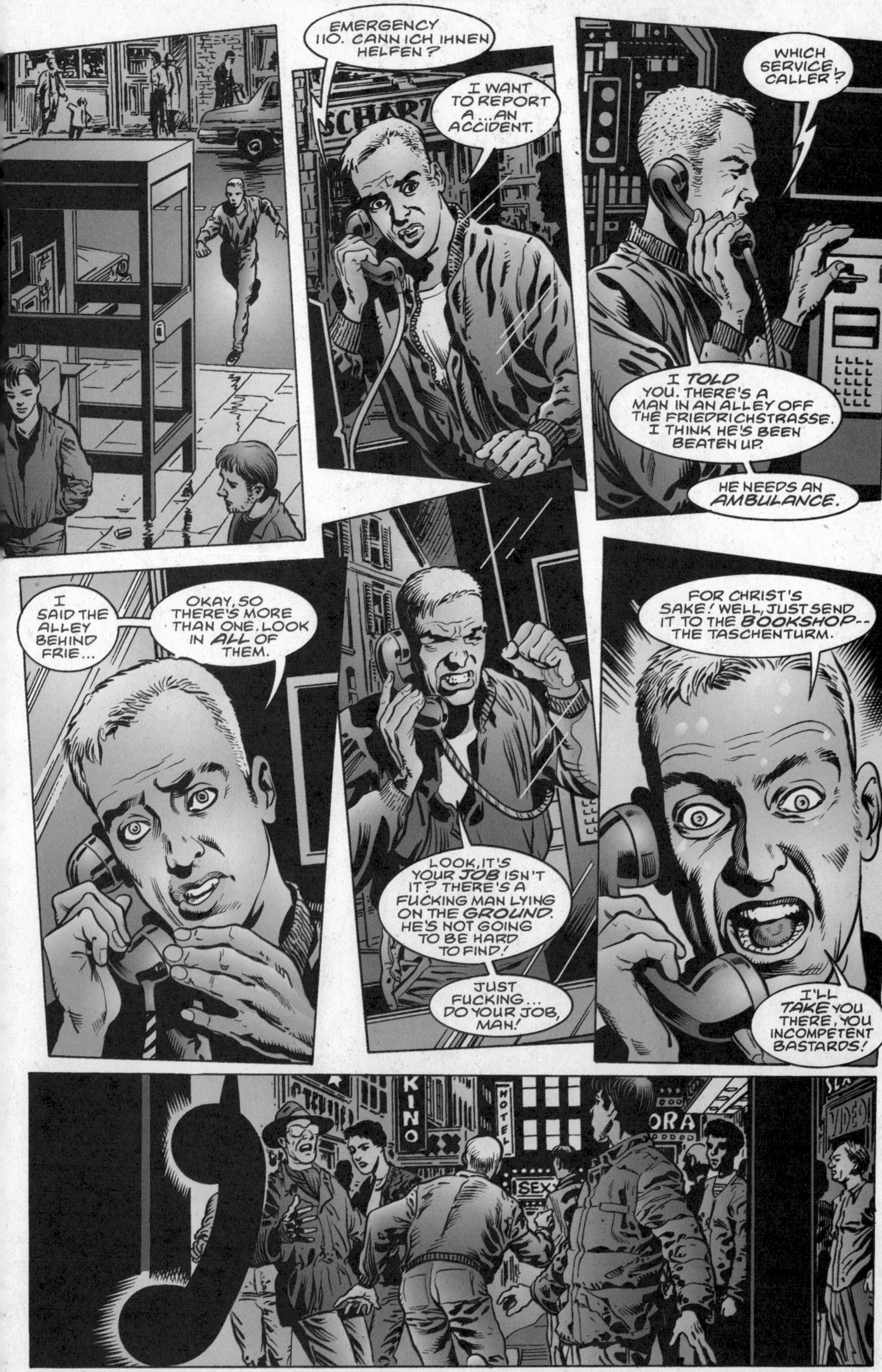
EMERGENCY 110. CANN ICH IHNEN HELFEN?
I WANT TO REPORT A...AN ACCIDENT.
WHICH SERVICE, CALLER?
I TOLD YOU. THERE'S A MAN IN AN ALLEY OFF THE FRIEDRICHSTRASSE. I THINK HE'S BEEN BEATEN UP.
HE NEEDS AN AMBULANCE.
I SAID THE ALLEY BEHIND FRIE...
OKAY, SO THERE'S MORE THAN ONE. LOOK IN ALL OF THEM.
LOOK, IT'S YOUR JOB ISN'T IT? THERE'S A FUCKING MAN LYING ON THE GROUND. HE'S NOT GOING TO BE HARD TO FIND!
JUST FUCKING... DO YOUR JOB, MAN!
FOR CHRIST'S SAKE! WELL, JUST SEND IT TO THE BOOKSHOP-- THE TASCHENTURM.
I'LL TAKE YOU THERE, YOU INCOMPETENT BASTARDS!
KINO
HOTEL
SEX
VIDEO

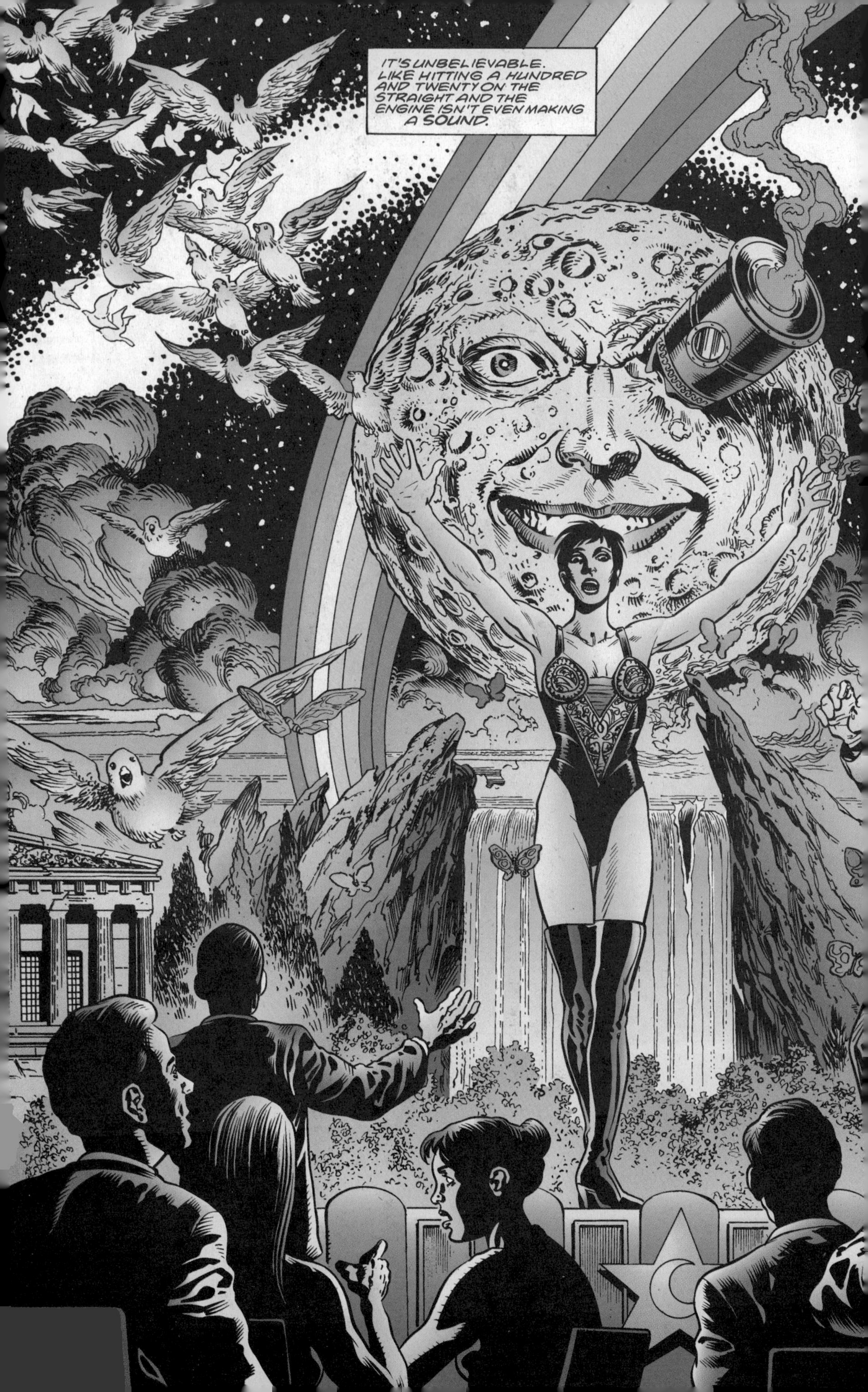
IT'S UNBELIEVABLE. LIKE HITTING A HUNDRED AND TWENTY ON THE STRAIGHT AND THE ENGINE ISN'T EVEN MAKING A SOUND.

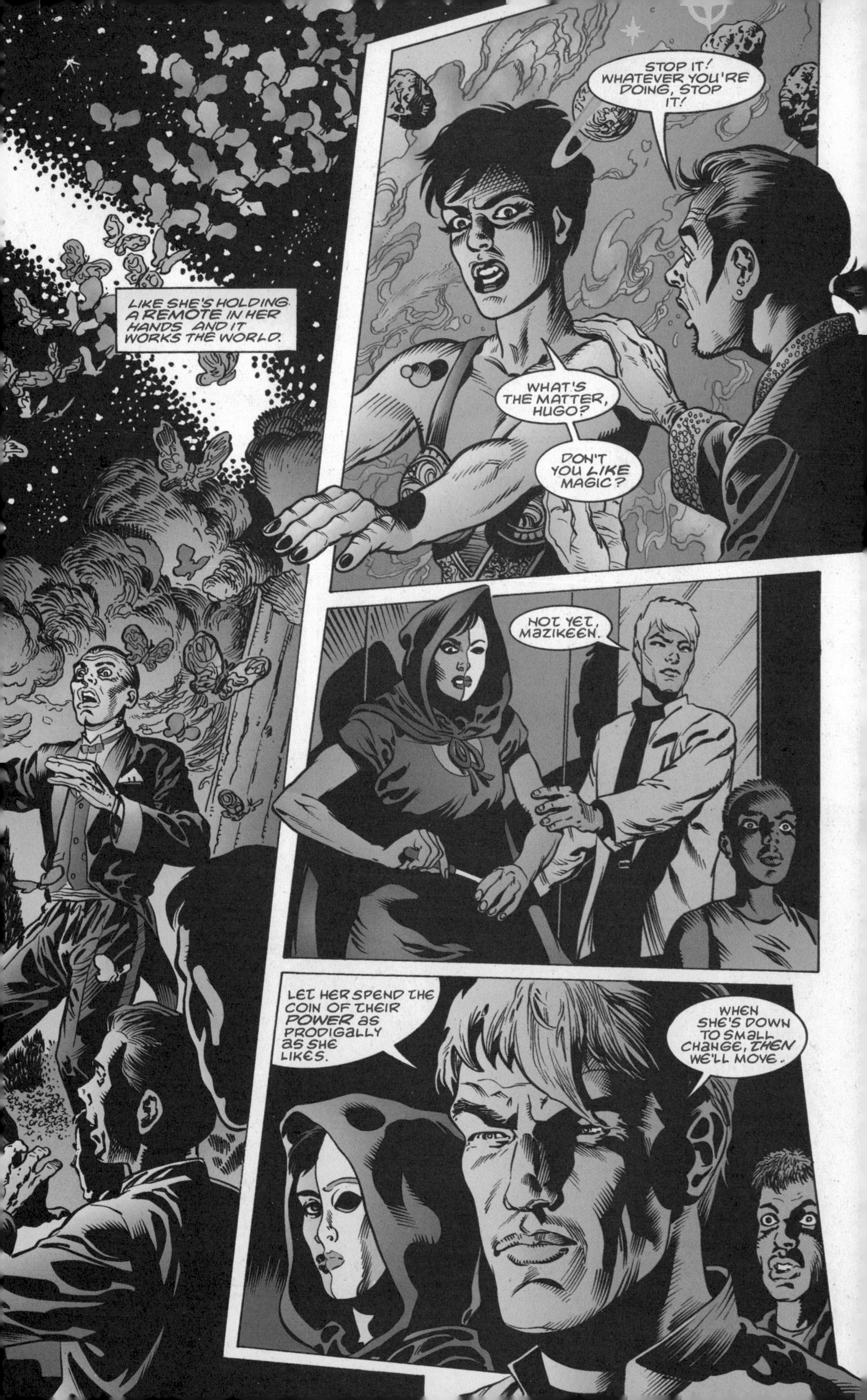
LIKE SHE'S HOLDING A REMOTE IN HER HANDS AND IT WORKS THE WORLD.
STOP IT! WHATEVER YOU'RE DOING, STOP IT!
WHAT'S THE MATTER, HUGO?
DON'T YOU LIKE MAGIC?
NOT YET, MAZIKEEN.
LET HER SPEND THE COIN OF THEIR POWER AS PRODIGALLY AS SHE LIKES.
WHEN SHE'S DOWN TO SMALL CHANGE, THEN WE'LL MOVE.

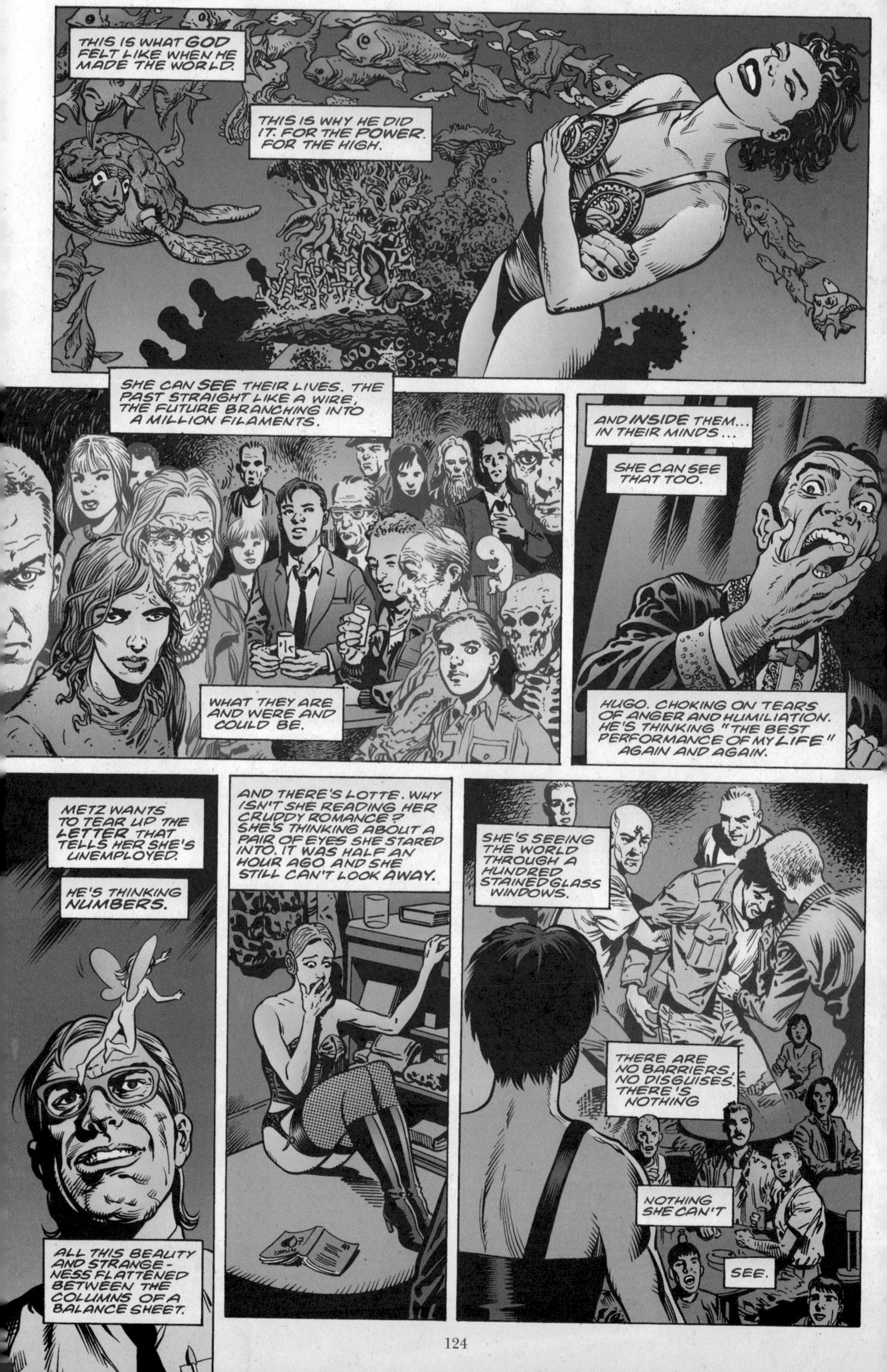
THIS IS WHAT GOD FELT LIKE WHEN HE MADE THE WORLD.
THIS IS WHY HE DID IT. FOR THE POWER. FOR THE HIGH.
SHE CAN SEE THEIR LIVES. THE PAST STRAIGHT LIKE A WIRE, THE FUTURE BRANCHING INTO A MILLION FILAMENTS.
WHAT THEY ARE AND WERE AND COULD BE.
AND INSIDE THEM... IN THEIR MINDS...
SHE CAN SEE THAT TOO.
HUGO. CHOKING ON TEARS OF ANGER AND HUMILIATION. HE'S THINKING "THE BEST PERFORMANCE OF MY LIFE" AGAIN AND AGAIN.
METZ WANTS TO TEAR UP THE LETTER THAT TELLS HER SHE'S UNEMPLOYED.
HE'S THINKING NUMBERS.
ALL THIS BEAUTY AND STRANGE-NESS FLATTENED BETWEEN THE COLUMNS OF A BALANCE SHEET.
AND THERE'S LOTTE. WHY ISN'T SHE READING HER CRUDDY ROMANCE? SHE'S THINKING ABOUT A PAIR OF EYES SHE STARED INTO. IT WAS HALF AN HOUR AGO AND SHE STILL CAN'T LOOK AWAY.
SHE'S SEEING THE WORLD THROUGH A HUNDRED STAINED GLASS WINDOWS.
THERE ARE NO BARRIERS, NO DISGUISES. THERE'S NOTHING
NOTHING SHE CAN'T
SEE.

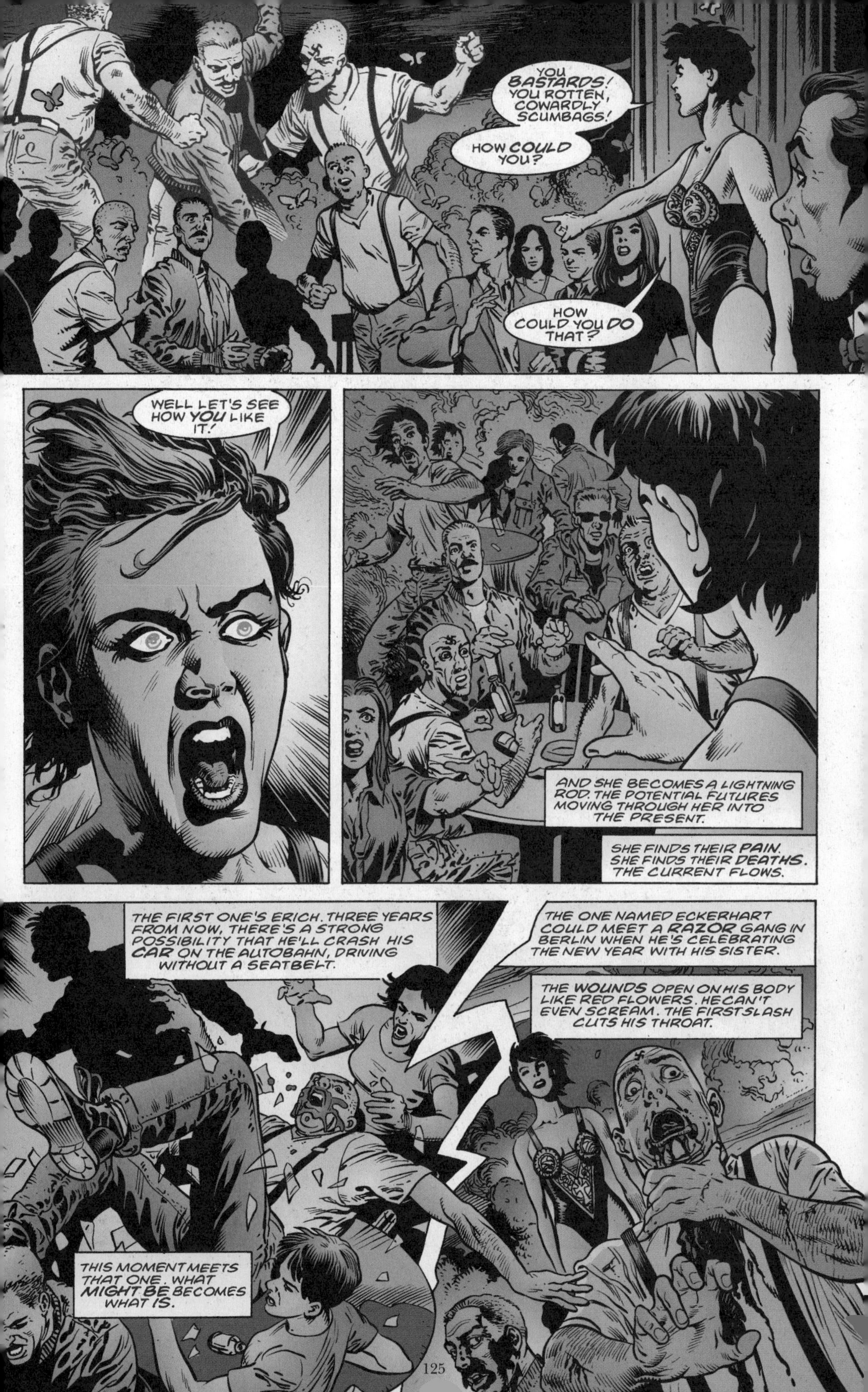
YOU BASTARDS! YOU ROTTEN, COWARDLY SCUMBAGS!
HOW COULD YOU?
HOW COULD YOU DO THAT?
WELL LET'S SEE HOW YOU LIKE IT!
AND SHE BECOMES A LIGHTNING ROD. THE POTENTIAL FUTURES MOVING THROUGH HER INTO THE PRESENT.
SHE FINDS THEIR PAIN. SHE FINDS THEIR DEATHS. THE CURRENT FLOWS.
THE FIRST ONE'S ERICH. THREE YEARS FROM NOW, THERE'S A STRONG POSSIBILITY THAT HE'LL CRASH HIS CAR ON THE AUTOBAHN, DRIVING WITHOUT A SEATBELT.
THE ONE NAMED ECKERHART COULD MEET A RAZOR GANG IN BERLIN WHEN HE'S CELEBRATING THE NEW YEAR WITH HIS SISTER.
THE WOUNDS OPEN ON HIS BODY LIKE RED FLOWERS. HE CAN'T EVEN SCREAM. THE FIRST SLASH CUTS HIS THROAT.
THIS MOMENT MEETS THAT ONE. WHAT MIGHT BE BECOMES WHAT IS.

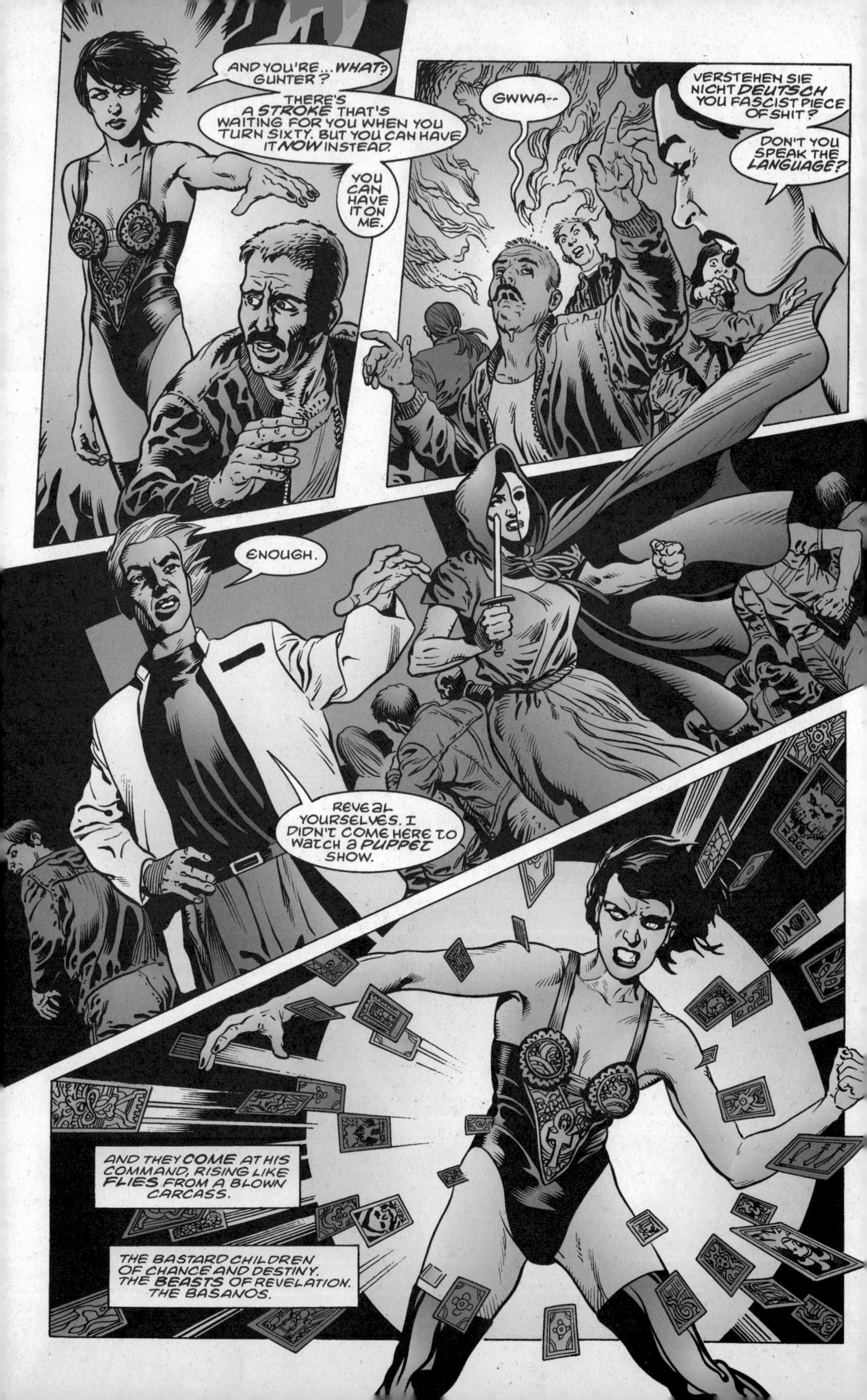
AND YOU'RE... WHAT? GUNTER?
THERE'S A STROKE THAT'S WAITING FOR YOU WHEN YOU TURN SIXTY. BUT YOU CAN HAVE IT NOW INSTEAD.
YOU CAN HAVE IT ON ME.
GWWA--
VERSTEHEN SIE NICHT DEUTSCH YOU FASCIST PIECE OF SHIT?
DON'T YOU SPEAK THE LANGUAGE?
ENOUGH.
REVEAL YOURSELVES. I DIDN'T COME HERE TO WATCH A PUPPET SHOW.
RAGE
AND THEY COME AT HIS COMMAND, RISING LIKE FLIES FROM A BLOWN CARCASS.
THE BASTARD CHILDREN OF CHANCE AND DESTINY. THE BEASTS OF REVELATION. THE BASANOS.

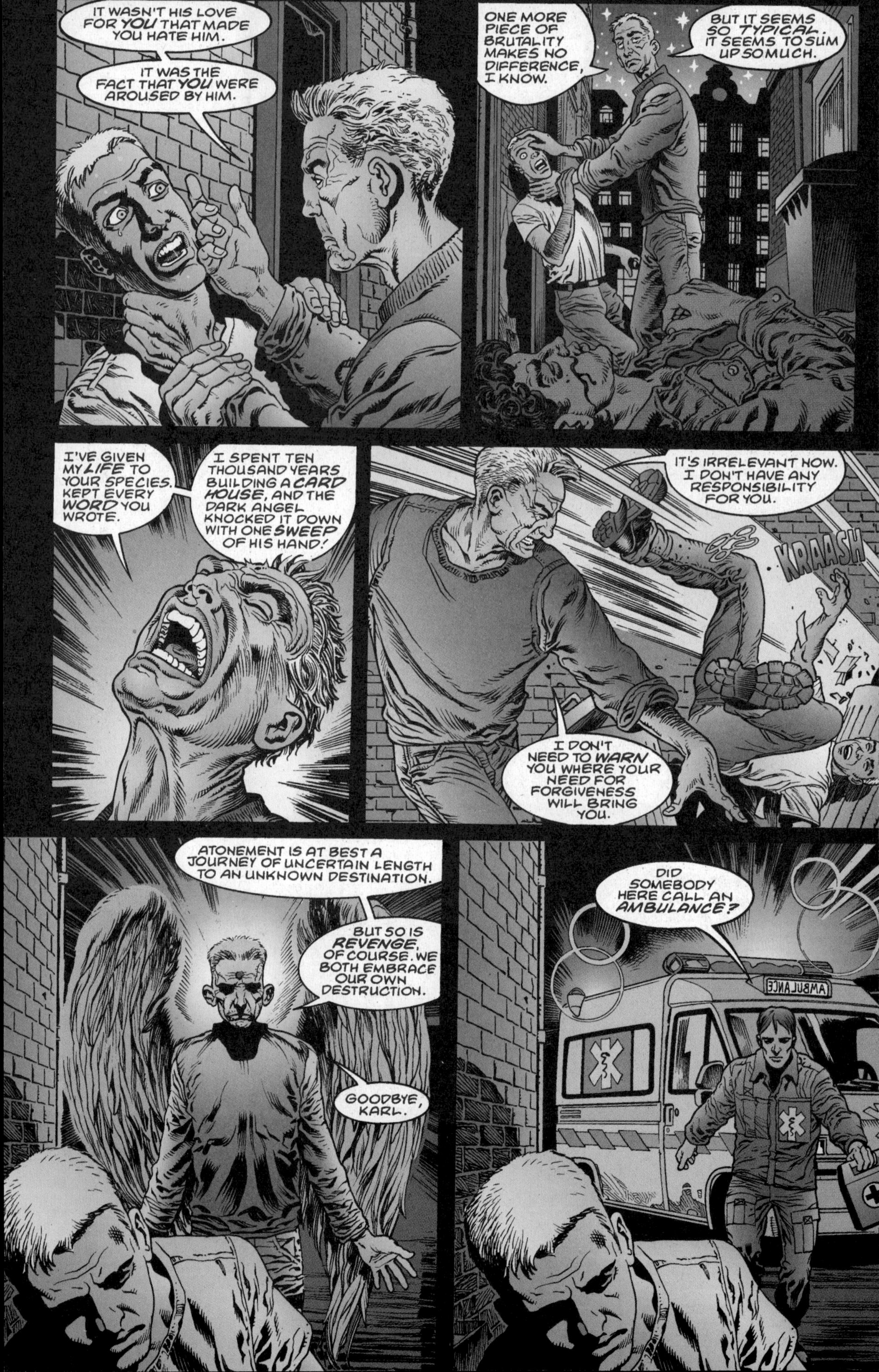
IT WASN'T HIS LOVE FOR YOU THAT MADE YOU HATE HIM.
IT WAS THE FACT THAT YOU WERE AROUSED BY HIM.
ONE MORE PIECE OF BRUTALITY MAKES NO DIFFERENCE, I KNOW.
BUT IT SEEMS SO TYPICAL. IT SEEMS TO SUM UP SO MUCH.
I'VE GIVEN MY LIFE TO YOUR SPECIES. KEPT EVERY WORD YOU WROTE.
I SPENT TEN THOUSAND YEARS BUILDING A CARD HOUSE, AND THE DARK ANGEL KNOCKED IT DOWN WITH ONE SWEEP OF HIS HAND!
IT'S IRRELEVANT NOW. I DON'T HAVE ANY RESPONSIBILITY FOR YOU.
KRAASH
I DON'T NEED TO WARN YOU WHERE YOUR NEED FOR FORGIVENESS WILL BRING YOU.
ATONEMENT IS AT BEST A JOURNEY OF UNCERTAIN LENGTH TO AN UNKNOWN DESTINATION.
BUT SO IS REVENGE, OF COURSE. WE BOTH EMBRACE OUR OWN DESTRUCTION.
GOODBYE, KARL.
DID SOMEBODY HERE CALL AN AMBULANCE?
AMBULANCE

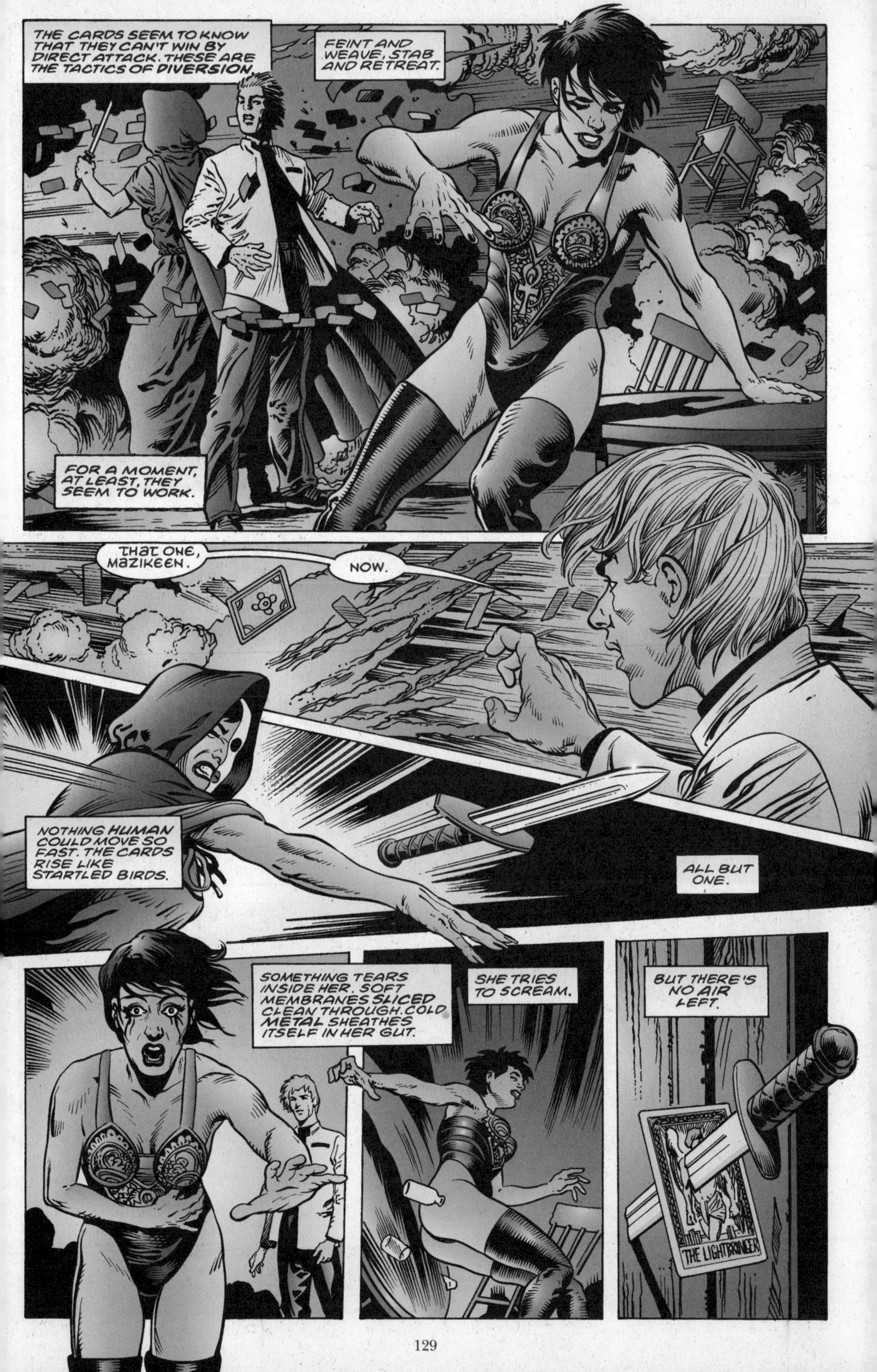
THE CARDS SEEM TO KNOW THAT THEY CAN'T WIN BY DIRECT ATTACK. THESE ARE THE TACTICS OF DIVERSION.
FEINT AND WEAVE, STAB AND RETREAT.
FOR A MOMENT, AT LEAST, THEY SEEM TO WORK.
THAT ONE, MAZIKEEN.
NOW.
NOTHING HUMAN COULD MOVE SO FAST. THE CARDS RISE LIKE STARTLED BIRDS.
ALL BUT ONE.
SOMETHING TEARS INSIDE HER. SOFT MEMBRANES SLICED CLEAN THROUGH. COLD METAL SHEATHES ITSELF IN HER GUT.
SHE TRIES TO SCREAM.
BUT THERE'S NO AIR LEFT.
THE LIGHTBRINGER

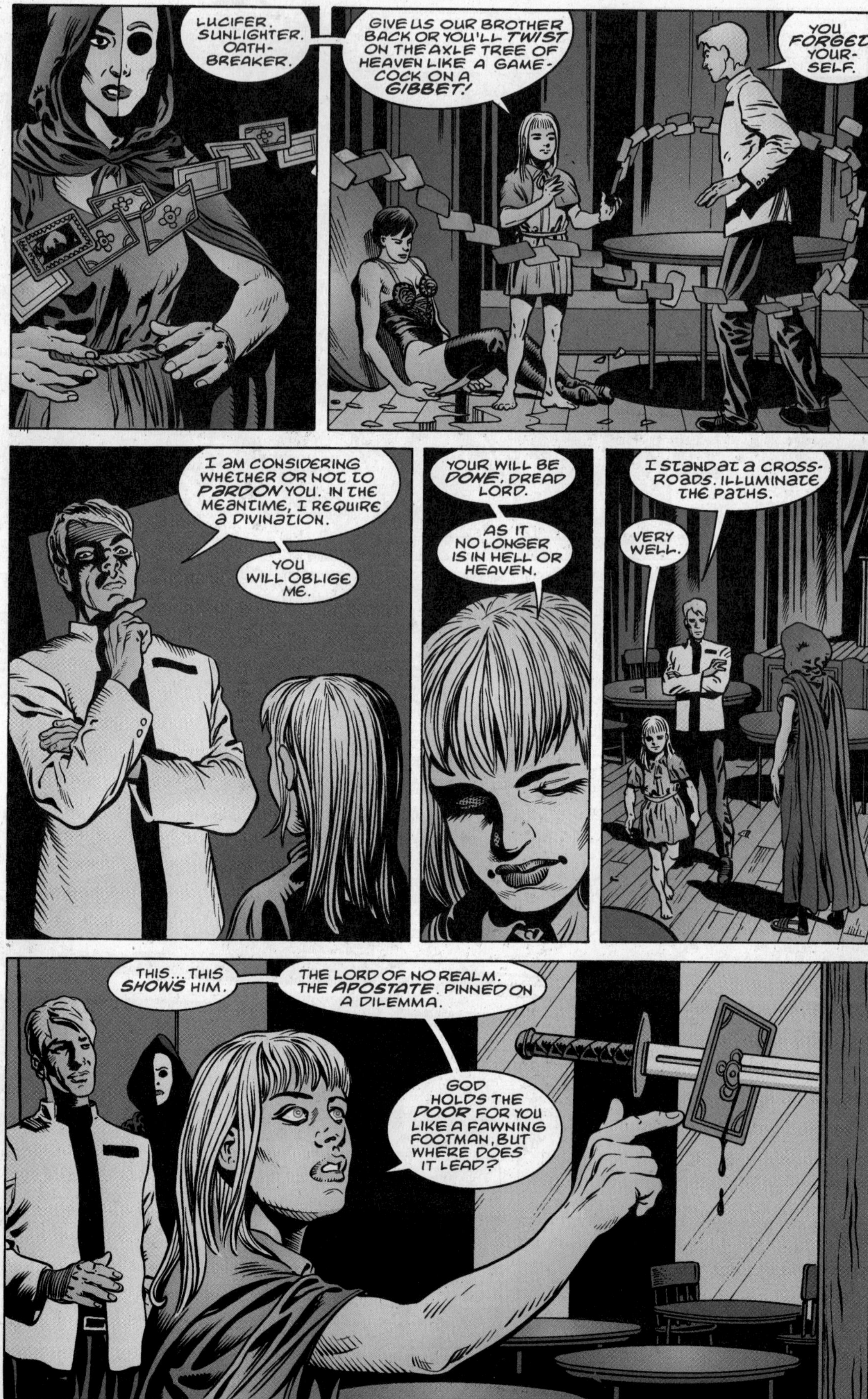
LUCIFER. SUNLIGHTER. OATH-BREAKER.
GIVE US OUR BROTHER BACK OR YOU'LL TWIST ON THE AXLE TREE OF HEAVEN LIKE A GAME-COCK ON A GIBBET!
YOU FORGET YOURSELF.
I AM CONSIDERING WHETHER OR NOT TO PARDON YOU. IN THE MEANTIME, I REQUIRE A DIVINATION.
YOU WILL OBLIGE ME.
YOUR WILL BE DONE, DREAD LORD.
AS IT NO LONGER IS IN HELL OR HEAVEN.
I STAND AT A CROSS-ROADS. ILLUMINATE THE PATHS.
VERY WELL.
THIS... THIS SHOWS HIM.
THE LORD OF NO REALM. THE APOSTATE. PINNED ON A DILEMMA.
GOD HOLDS THE DOOR FOR YOU LIKE A FAWNING FOOTMAN, BUT WHERE DOES IT LEAD?

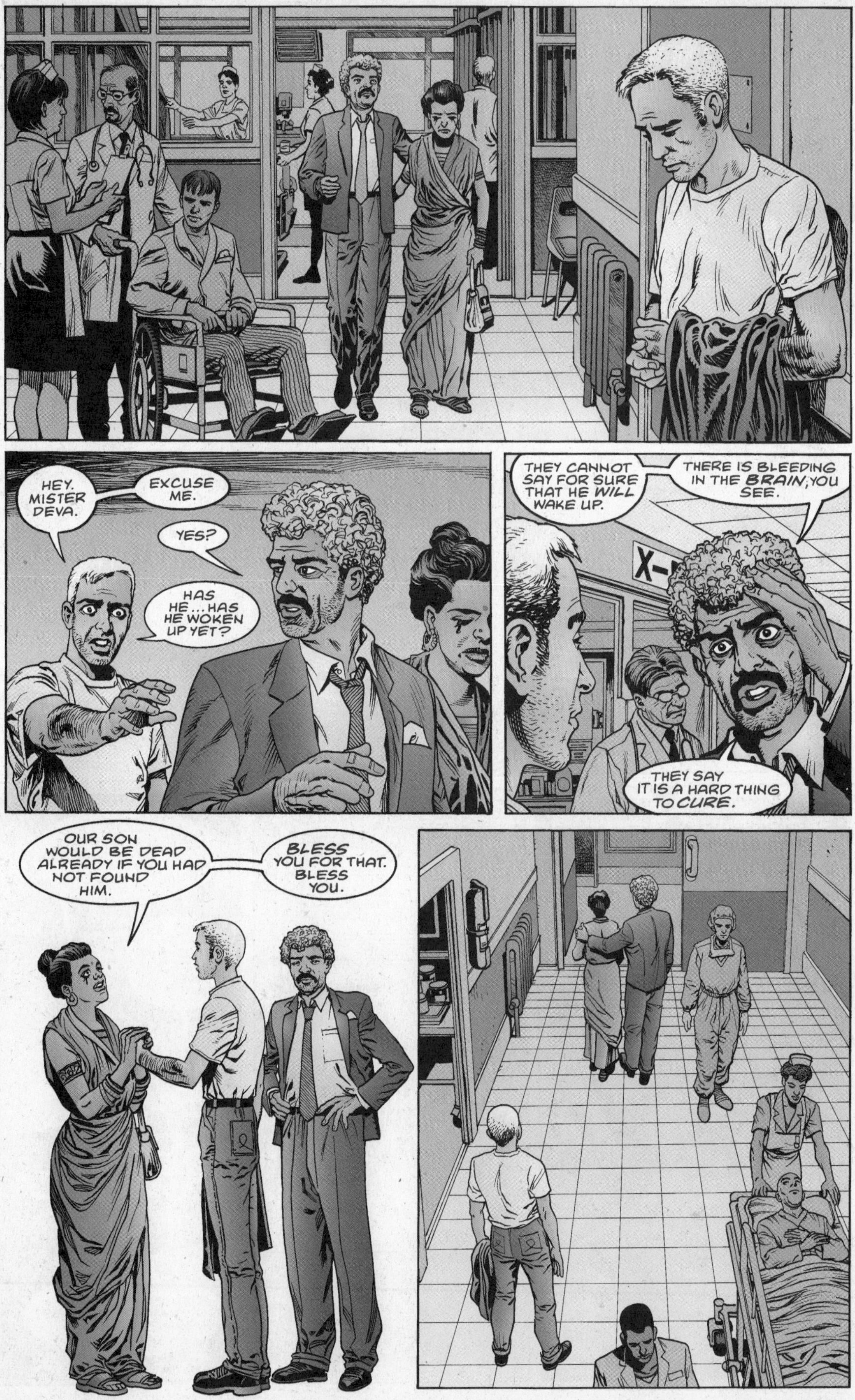
HEY. MISTER DEVA.
EXCUSE ME.
YES?
HAS HE... HAS HE WOKEN UP YET?
THEY CANNOT SAY FOR SURE THAT HE WILL WAKE UP.
THERE IS BLEEDING IN THE BRAIN, YOU SEE.
X-
THEY SAY IT IS A HARD THING TO CURE.
OUR SON WOULD BE DEAD ALREADY IF YOU HAD NOT FOUND HIM.
BLESS YOU FOR THAT. BLESS YOU.

134

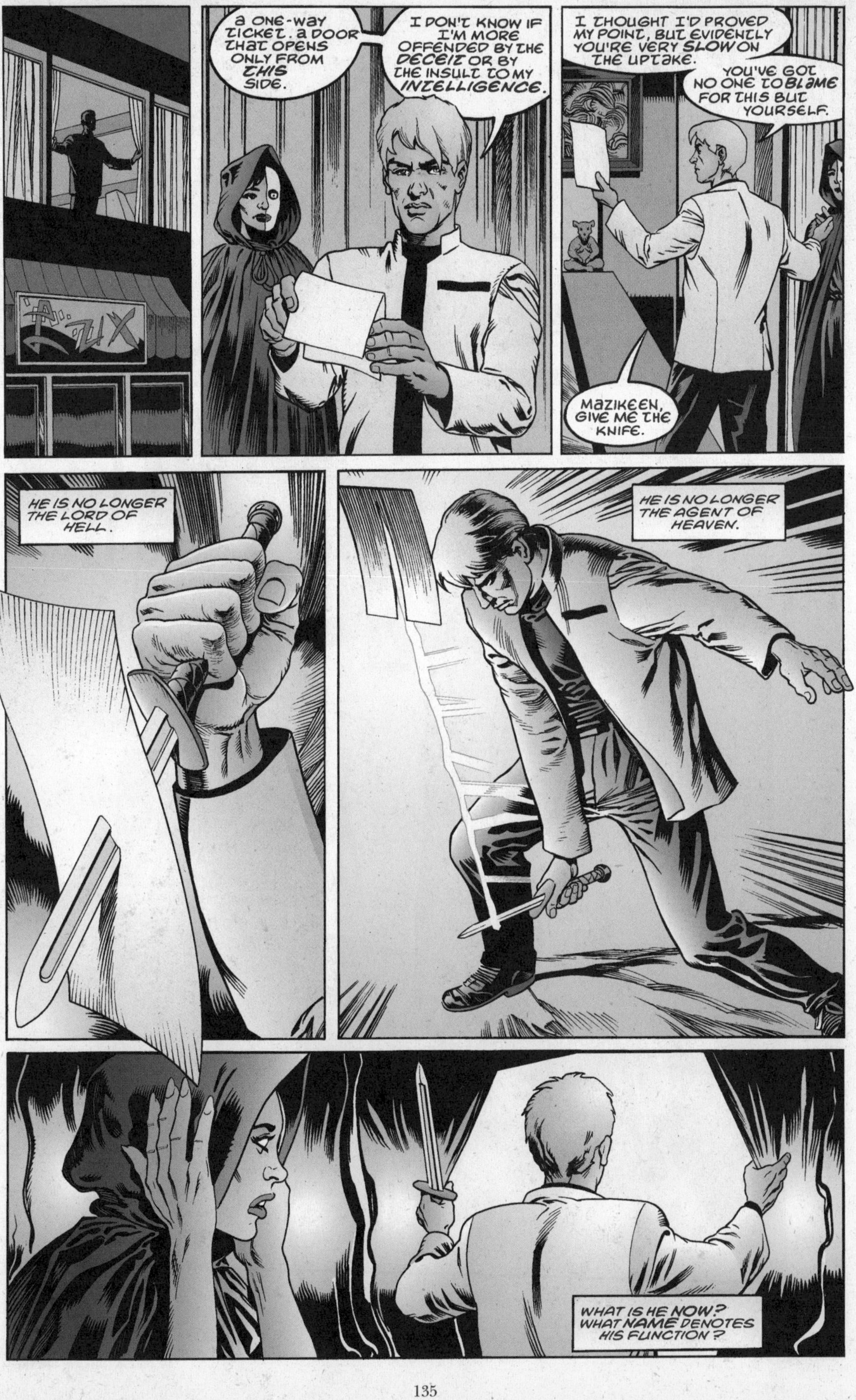
A ONE-WAY TICKET. A DOOR THAT OPENS ONLY FROM THIS SIDE.
I DON'T KNOW IF I'M MORE OFFENDED BY THE DECEIT OR BY THE INSULT TO MY INTELLIGENCE.
I THOUGHT I'D PROVED MY POINT, BUT EVIDENTLY YOU'RE VERY SLOW ON THE UPTAKE.
YOU'VE GOT NO ONE TO BLAME FOR THIS BUT YOURSELF.
MAZIKEEN, GIVE ME THE KNIFE.
HE IS NO LONGER THE LORD OF HELL.
HE IS NO LONGER THE AGENT OF HEAVEN.
WHAT IS HE NOW? WHAT NAME DENOTES HIS FUNCTION?

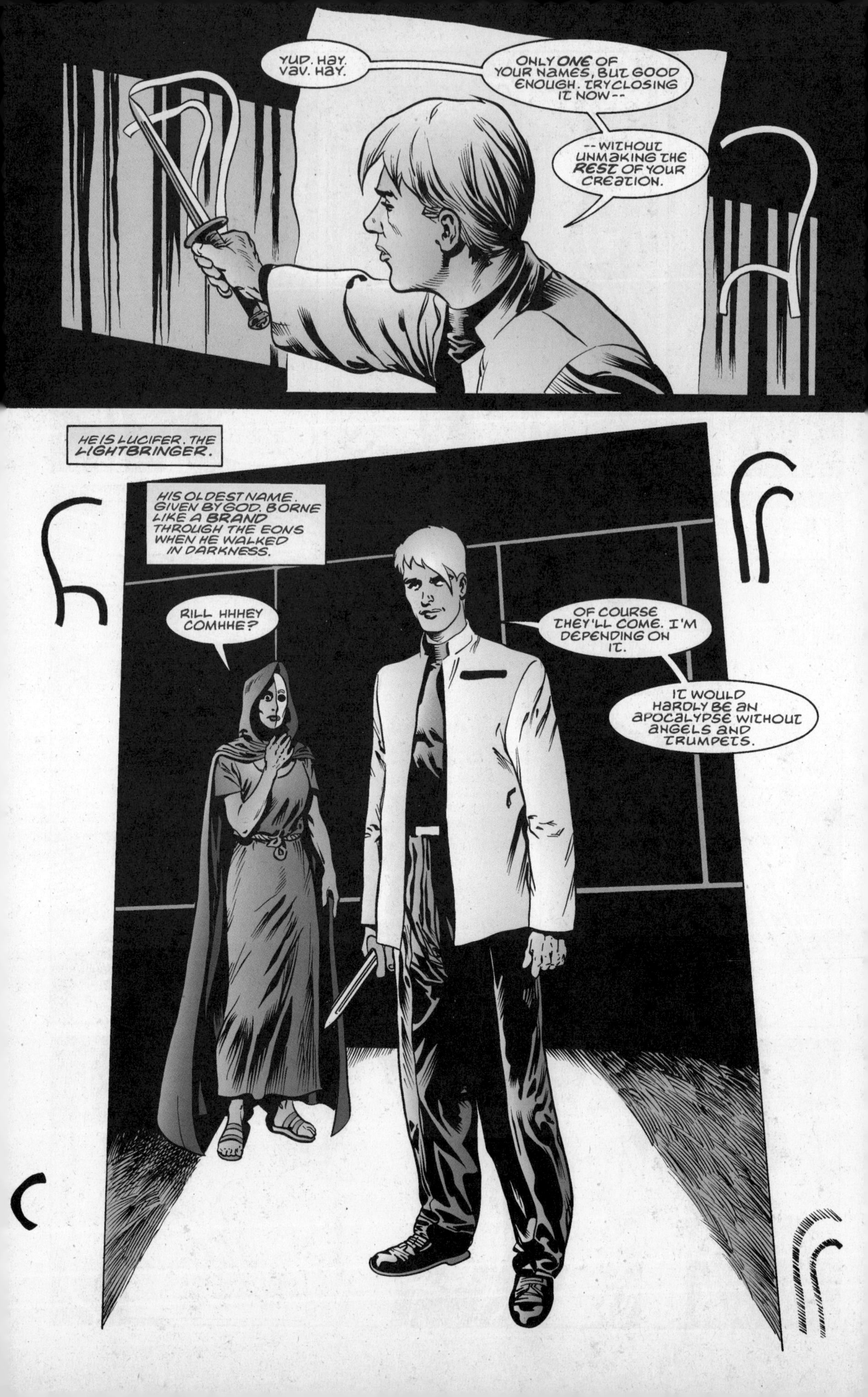
YUD. HAY. VAV. HAY.
ONLY ONE OF YOUR NAMES, BUT GOOD ENOUGH. TRY CLOSING IT NOW--
--WITHOUT UNMAKING THE REST OF YOUR CREATION.
HE IS LUCIFER. THE LIGHTBRINGER.
HIS OLDEST NAME. GIVEN BY GOD. BORNE LIKE A BRAND THROUGH THE EONS WHEN HE WALKED IN DARKNESS.
RILL HHHEY COMHHE?
OF COURSE THEY'LL COME. I'M DEPENDING ON IT.
IT WOULD HARDLY BE AN APOCALYPSE WITHOUT ANGELS AND TRUMPETS.

138

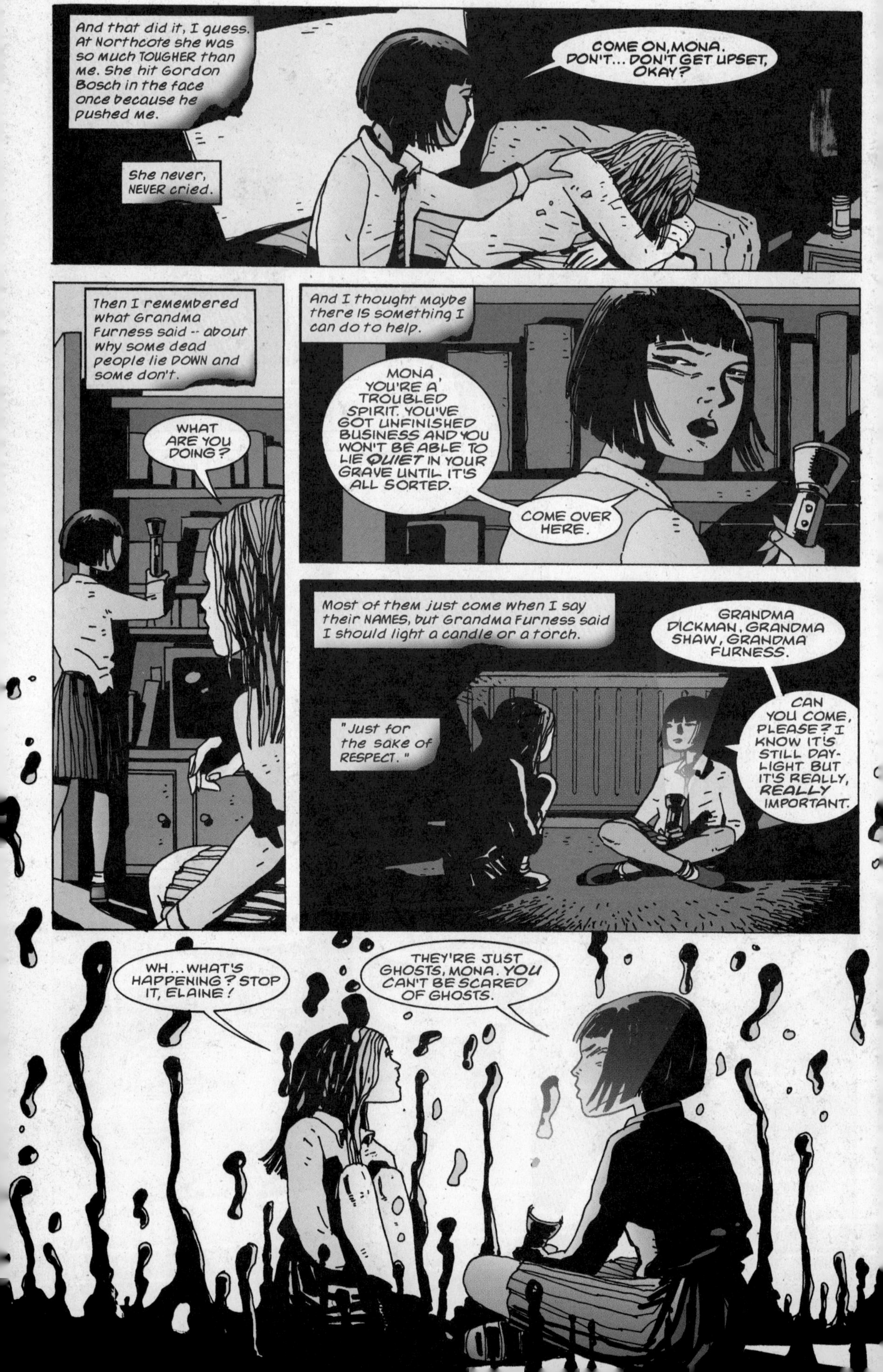
And that did it, I guess. At Northcote she was so much TOUGHER than me. She hit Gordon Bosch in the face once because he pushed me.
COME ON, MONA. DON'T... DON'T GET UPSET, OKAY?
She never, NEVER cried.
Then I remembered what Grandma Furness said -- about why some dead people lie DOWN and some don't.
WHAT ARE YOU DOING?
And I thought maybe there IS something I can do to help.
MONA, YOU'RE A TROUBLED SPIRIT. YOU'VE GOT UNFINISHED BUSINESS AND YOU WON'T BE ABLE TO LIE QUIET IN YOUR GRAVE UNTIL IT'S ALL SORTED.
COME OVER HERE.
Most of them just come when I say their NAMES, but Grandma Furness said I should light a candle or a torch.
GRANDMA DICKMAN, GRANDMA SHAW, GRANDMA FURNESS.
"Just for the sake of RESPECT."
CAN YOU COME, PLEASE? I KNOW IT'S STILL DAY-LIGHT BUT IT'S REALLY, REALLY IMPORTANT.
WH... WHAT'S HAPPENING? STOP IT, ELAINE!
THEY'RE JUST GHOSTS, MONA. YOU CAN'T BE SCARED OF GHOSTS.

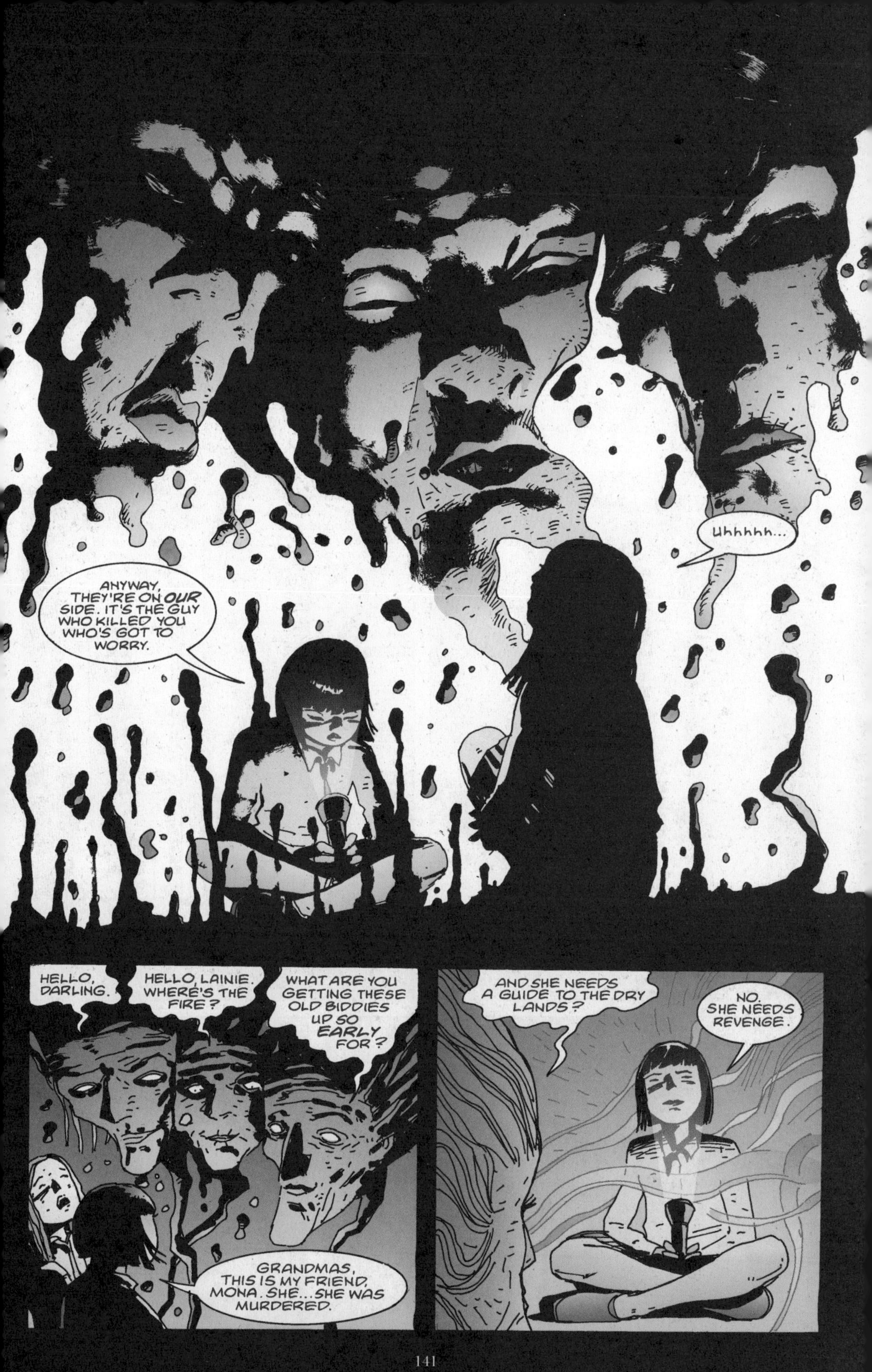
Uhhhhh...
ANYWAY, THEY'RE ON OUR SIDE. IT'S THE GUY WHO KILLED YOU WHO'S GOT TO WORRY.
HELLO, DARLING.
HELLO, LAINIE. WHERE'S THE FIRE?
WHAT ARE YOU GETTING THESE OLD BIDDIES UP SO EARLY FOR?
GRANDMAS, THIS IS MY FRIEND, MONA. SHE... SHE WAS MURDERED.
AND SHE NEEDS A GUIDE TO THE DRY LANDS?
NO. SHE NEEDS REVENGE.

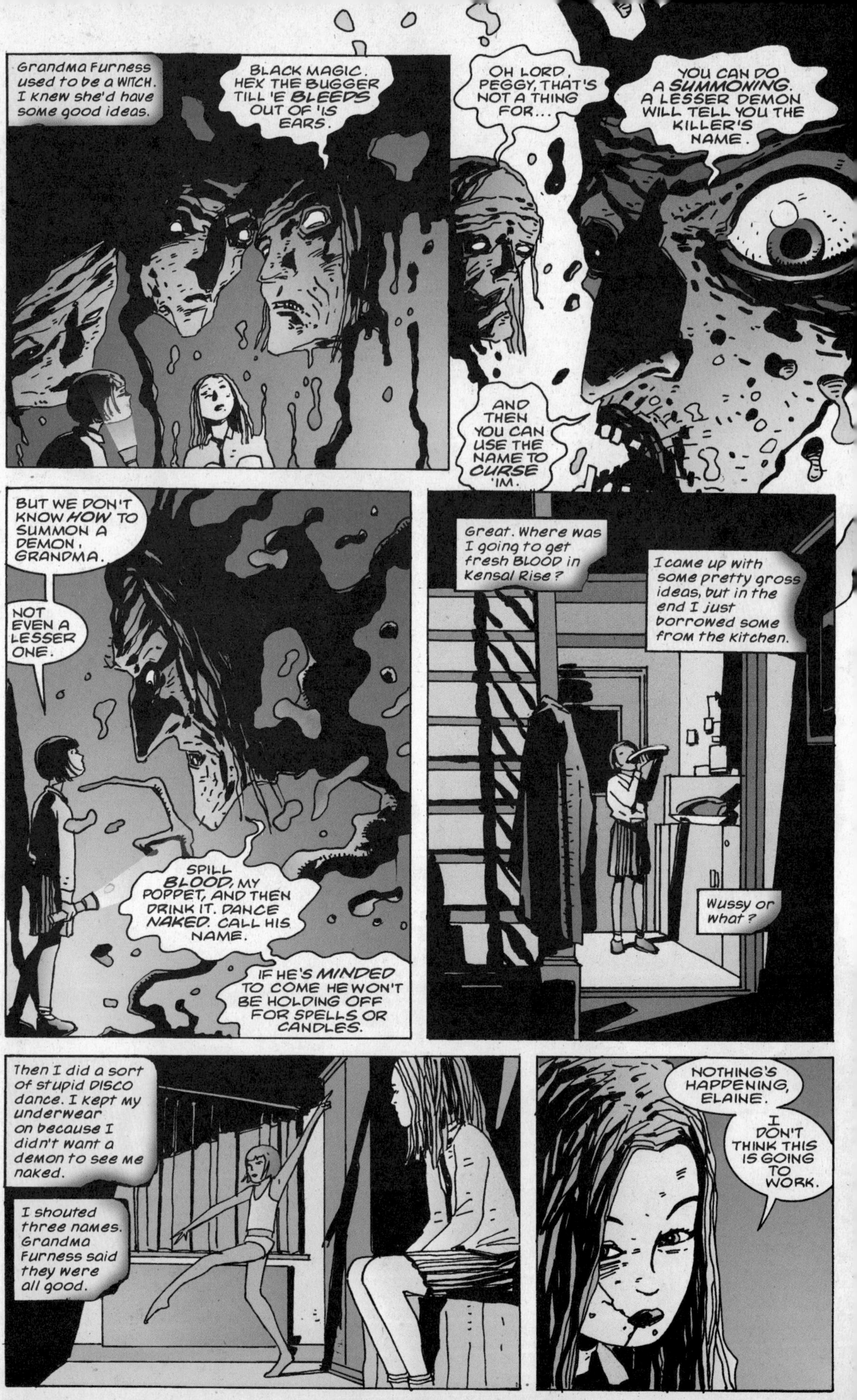

Grandma Furness used to be a WITCH. I knew she'd have some good ideas.
BLACK MAGIC. HEX THE BUGGER TILL 'E BLEEDS OUT OF 'IS EARS.
OH LORD, PEGGY, THAT'S NOT A THING FOR...
YOU CAN DO A SUMMONING. A LESSER DEMON WILL TELL YOU THE KILLER'S NAME.
AND THEN YOU CAN USE THE NAME TO CURSE 'IM.
BUT WE DON'T KNOW HOW TO SUMMON A DEMON, GRANDMA.
NOT EVEN A LESSER ONE.
SPILL BLOOD, MY POPPET, AND THEN DRINK IT. DANCE NAKED. CALL HIS NAME.
IF HE'S MINDED TO COME HE WON'T BE HOLDING OFF FOR SPELLS OR CANDLES.
Great. Where was I going to get fresh BLOOD in Kensal Rise?
I came up with some pretty gross ideas, but in the end I just borrowed some from the kitchen.
Wussy or what?
Then I did a sort of stupid DISCO dance. I kept my underwear on because I didn't want a demon to see me naked.
I shouted three names. Grandma Furness said they were all good.
NOTHING'S HAPPENING, ELAINE.
I DON'T THINK THIS IS GOING TO WORK.

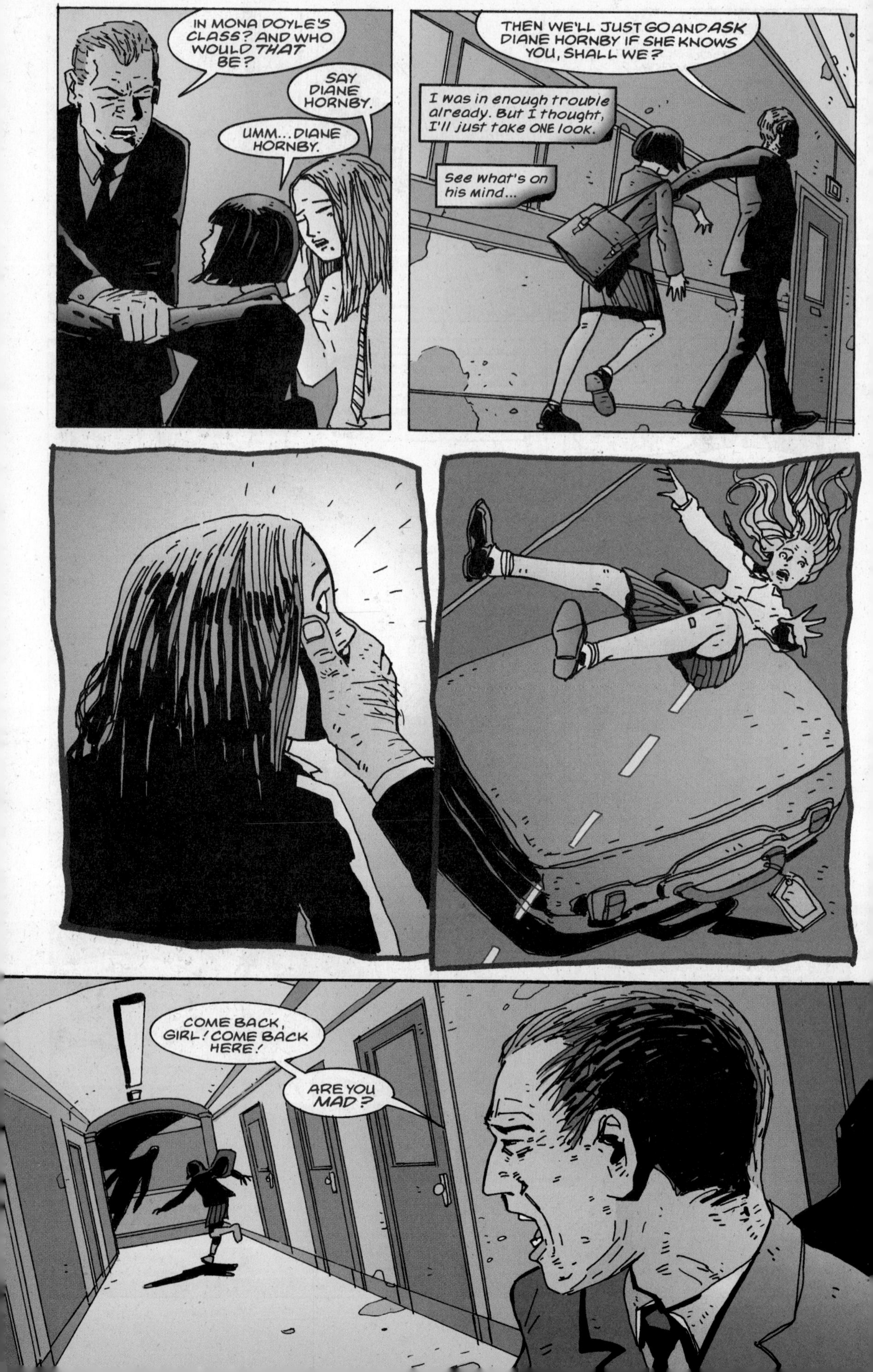
IN MONA DOYLE'S CLASS? AND WHO WOULD THAT BE?
SAY DIANE HORNBY.
UMM... DIANE HORNBY.
THEN WE'LL JUST GO AND ASK DIANE HORNBY IF SHE KNOWS YOU, SHALL WE?
I was in enough trouble already. But I thought, I'll just take ONE look.
See what's on his mind...
!
COME BACK, GIRL! COME BACK HERE!
ARE YOU MAD?

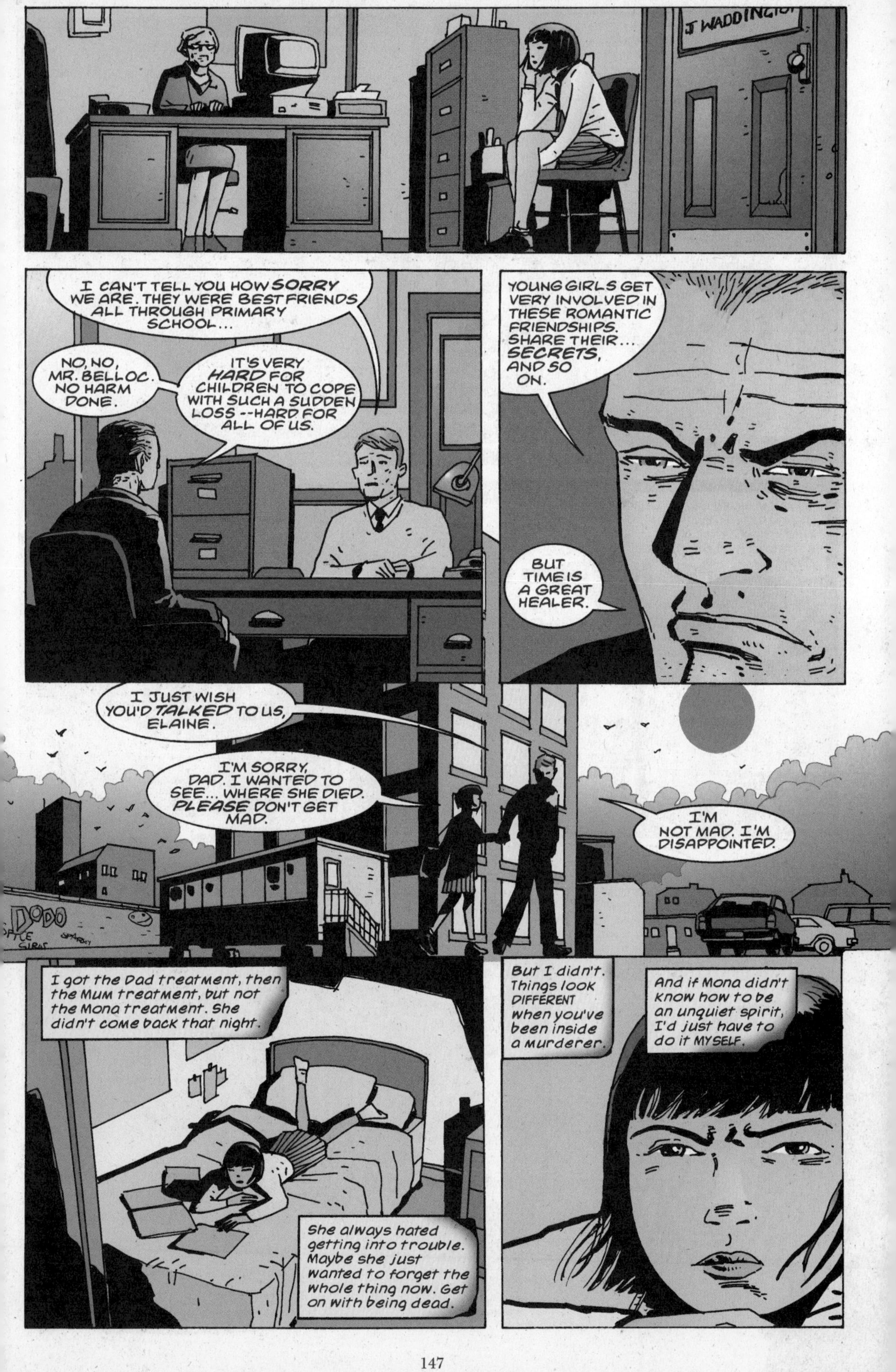
J WADDINGTON
I CAN'T TELL YOU HOW SORRY WE ARE. THEY WERE BEST FRIENDS ALL THROUGH PRIMARY SCHOOL...
NO, NO, MR. BELLOC. NO HARM DONE.
IT'S VERY HARD FOR CHILDREN TO COPE WITH SUCH A SUDDEN LOSS --HARD FOR ALL OF US.
YOUNG GIRLS GET VERY INVOLVED IN THESE ROMANTIC FRIENDSHIPS. SHARE THEIR... SECRETS, AND SO ON.
BUT TIME IS A GREAT HEALER.
I JUST WISH YOU'D TALKED TO US, ELAINE.
I'M SORRY, DAD. I WANTED TO SEE... WHERE SHE DIED. PLEASE DON'T GET MAD.
I'M NOT MAD. I'M DISAPPOINTED.
DODO
I got the Dad treatment, then the Mum treatment, but not the Mona treatment. She didn't come back that night.
She always hated getting into trouble. Maybe she just wanted to forget the whole thing now. Get on with being dead.
But I didn't. Things look DIFFERENT when you've been inside a murderer.
And if Mona didn't know how to be an unquiet spirit, I'd just have to do it MYSELF.

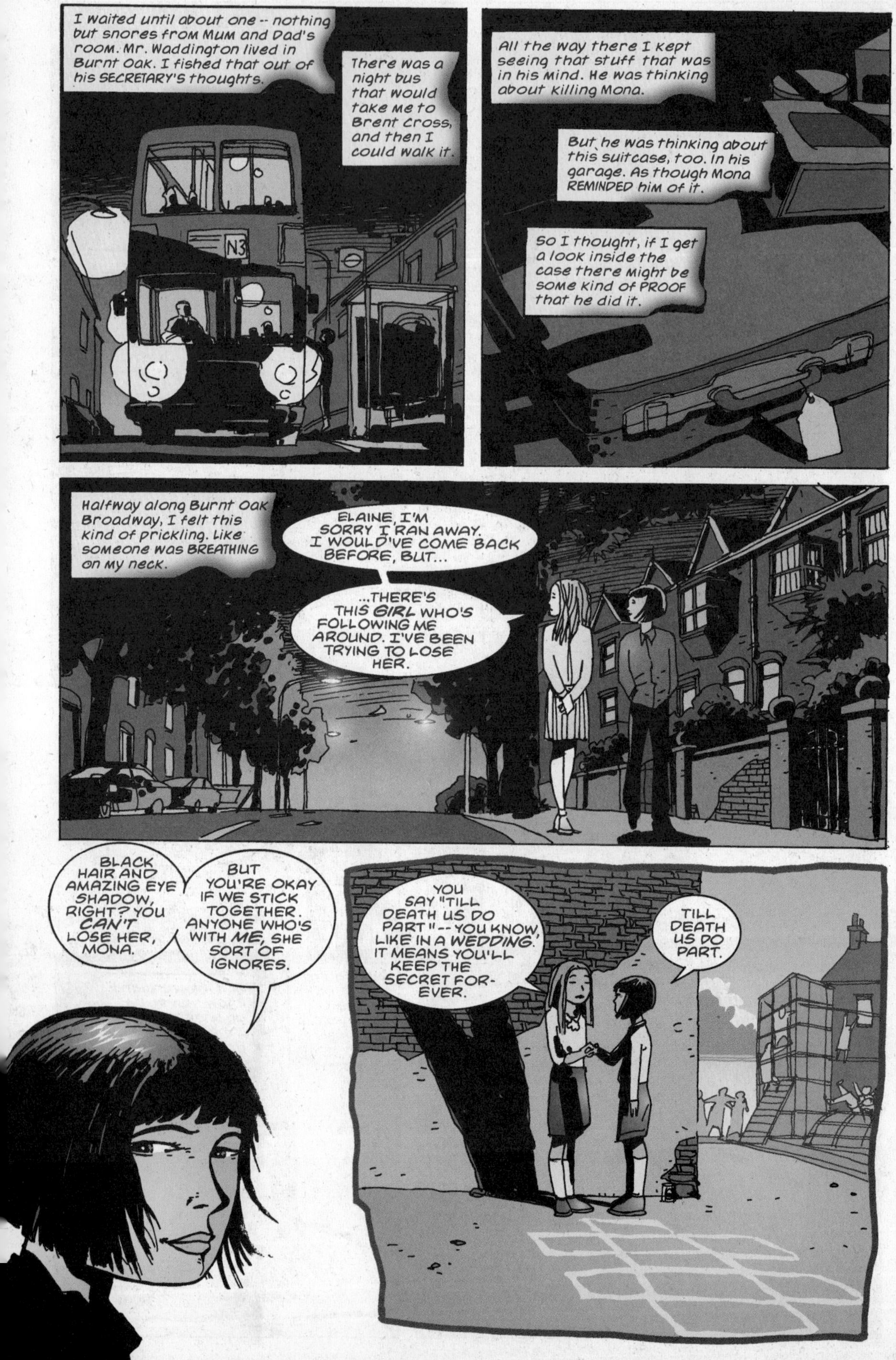

I waited until about one -- nothing but snores from Mum and Dad's room. Mr. Waddington lived in Burnt Oak. I fished that out of his SECRETARY'S thoughts.
There was a night bus that would take me to Brent Cross, and then I could walk it.
N3
All the way there I kept seeing that stuff that was in his mind. He was thinking about killing Mona.
But he was thinking about this suitcase, too. In his garage. As though Mona REMINDED him of it.
So I thought, if I get a look inside the case there might be some kind of PROOF that he did it.
Halfway along Burnt Oak Broadway, I felt this kind of prickling. Like someone was BREATHING on my neck.
ELAINE, I'M SORRY I RAN AWAY. I WOULD'VE COME BACK BEFORE, BUT...
...THERE'S THIS GIRL WHO'S FOLLOWING ME AROUND. I'VE BEEN TRYING TO LOSE HER.
BLACK HAIR AND AMAZING EYE SHADOW, RIGHT? YOU CAN'T LOSE HER, MONA.
BUT YOU'RE OKAY IF WE STICK TOGETHER. ANYONE WHO'S WITH ME, SHE SORT OF IGNORES.
YOU SAY "TILL DEATH US DO PART" -- YOU KNOW, LIKE IN A WEDDING. IT MEANS YOU'LL KEEP THE SECRET FOREVER.
TILL DEATH US DO PART.

150

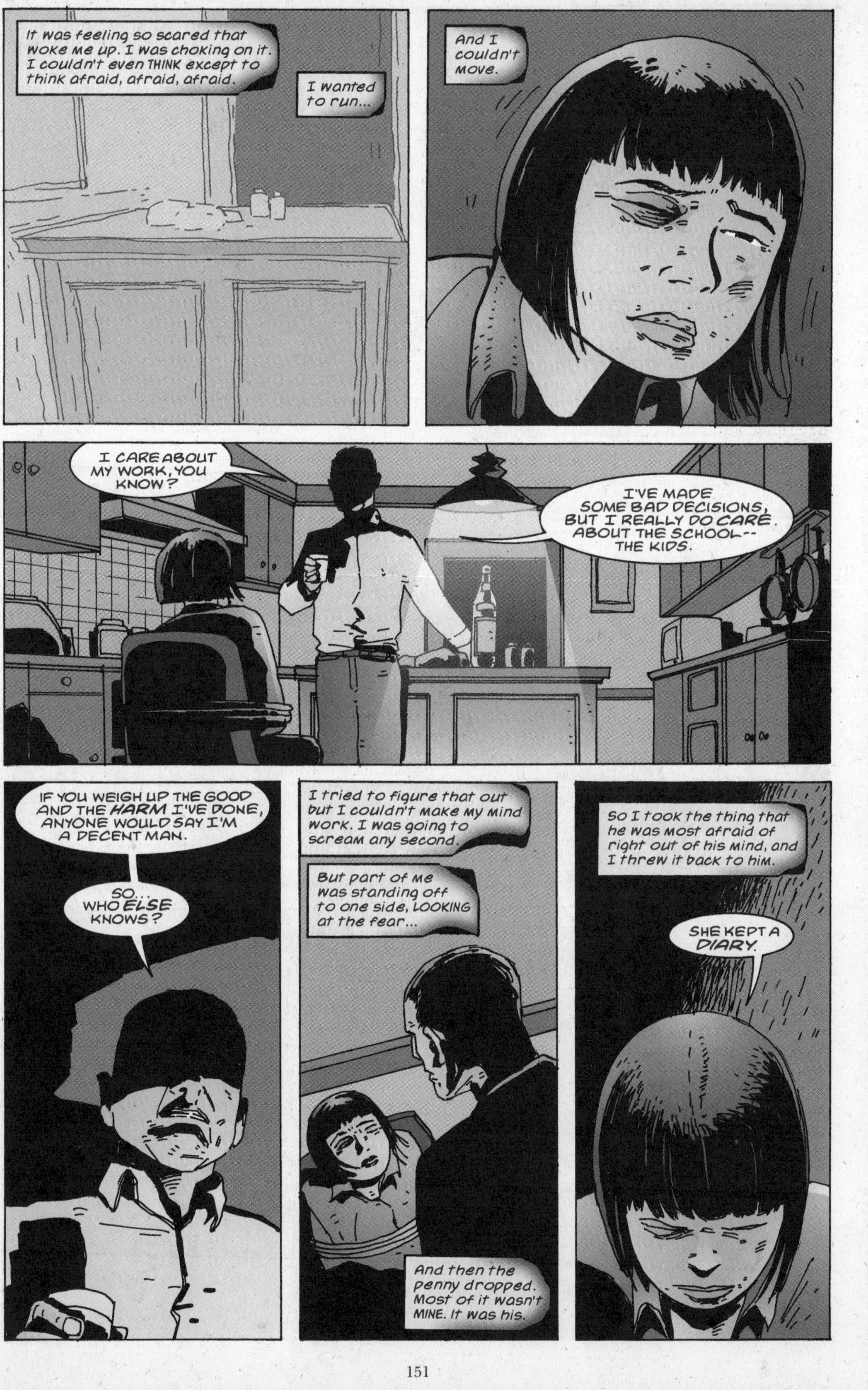
It was feeling so scared that woke me up. I was choking on it. I couldn't even THINK except to think afraid, afraid, afraid.
I wanted to run...
And I couldn't move.
I CARE ABOUT MY WORK, YOU KNOW?
I'VE MADE SOME BAD DECISIONS, BUT I REALLY DO CARE. ABOUT THE SCHOOL-- THE KIDS.
IF YOU WEIGH UP THE GOOD AND THE HARM I'VE DONE, ANYONE WOULD SAY I'M A DECENT MAN.
SO... WHO ELSE KNOWS?
I tried to figure that out but I couldn't make my mind work. I was going to scream any second.
But part of me was standing off to one side, LOOKING at the fear...
And then the penny dropped. Most of it wasn't MINE. It was his.
So I took the thing that he was most afraid of right out of his mind, and I threw it back to him.
SHE KEPT A DIARY.

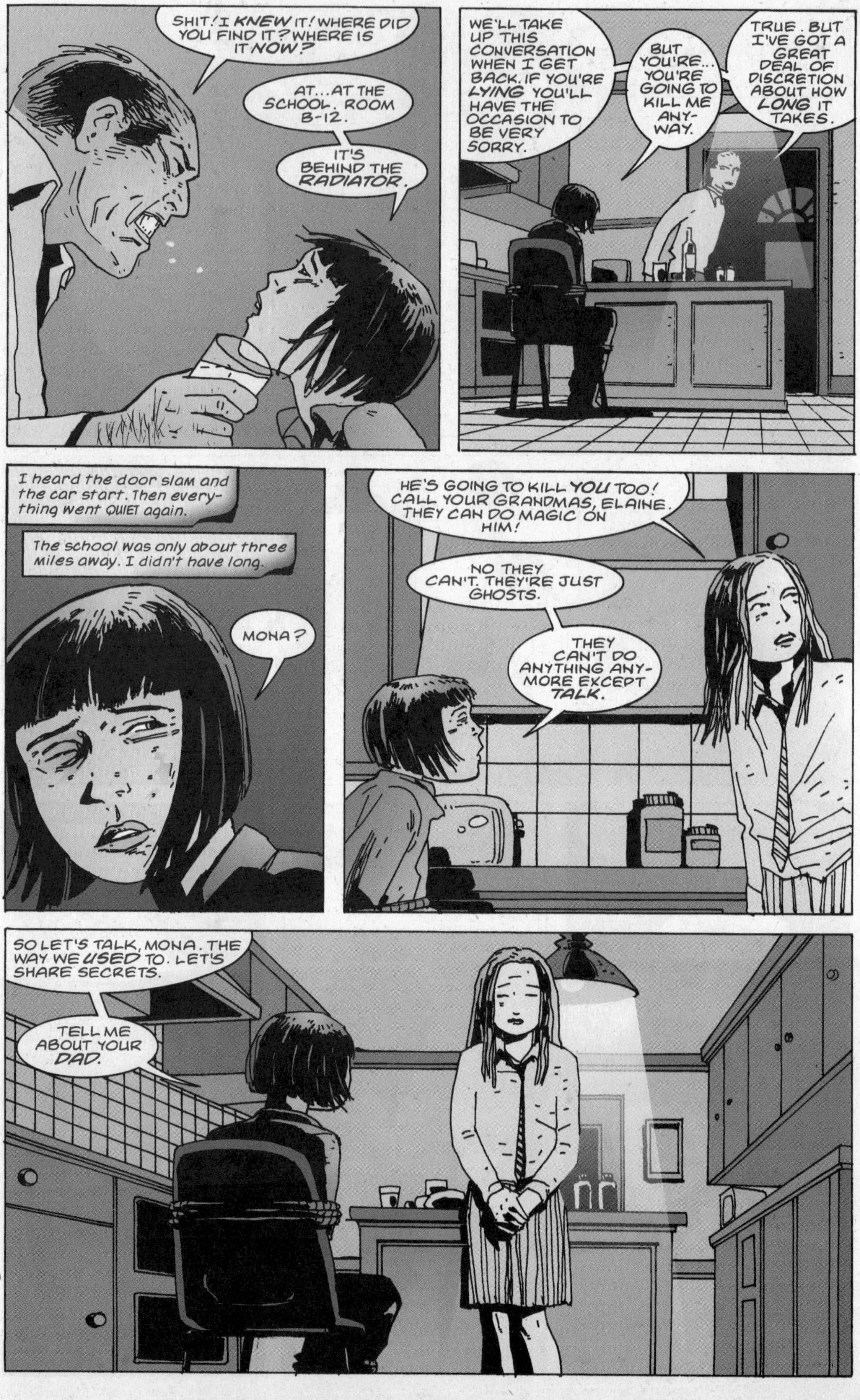

SHIT! I KNEW IT! WHERE DID YOU FIND IT? WHERE IS IT NOW?
AT... AT THE SCHOOL. ROOM B-12.
IT'S BEHIND THE RADIATOR.
WE'LL TAKE UP THIS CONVERSATION WHEN I GET BACK. IF YOU'RE LYING YOU'LL HAVE THE OCCASION TO BE VERY SORRY.
BUT YOU'RE... YOU'RE GOING TO KILL ME ANY-WAY.
TRUE. BUT I'VE GOT A GREAT DEAL OF DISCRETION ABOUT HOW LONG IT TAKES.
I heard the door slam and the car start. Then every-thing went QUIET again.
The school was only about three miles away. I didn't have long.
MONA?
HE'S GOING TO KILL YOU TOO! CALL YOUR GRANDMAS, ELAINE. THEY CAN DO MAGIC ON HIM!
NO THEY CAN'T. THEY'RE JUST GHOSTS.
THEY CAN'T DO ANYTHING ANY-MORE EXCEPT TALK.
SO LET'S TALK, MONA. THE WAY WE USED TO. LET'S SHARE SECRETS.
TELL ME ABOUT YOUR DAD.

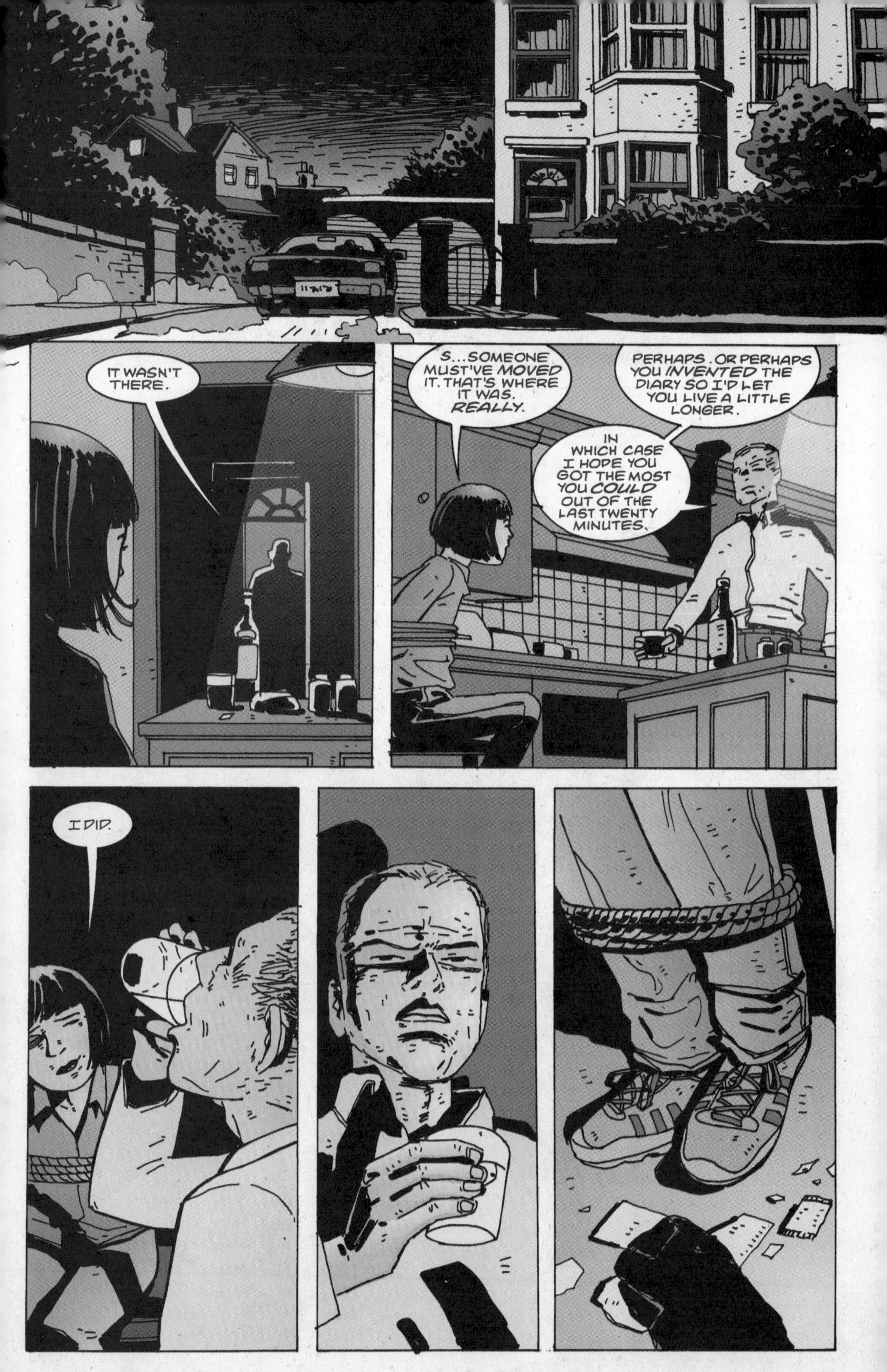
IT WASN'T THERE.
S...SOMEONE MUST'VE *MOVED* IT. THAT'S WHERE IT WAS. *REALLY*.
PERHAPS. OR PERHAPS YOU *INVENTED* THE DIARY SO I'D LET YOU LIVE A LITTLE LONGER.
IN WHICH CASE I HOPE YOU GOT THE MOST YOU *COULD* OUT OF THE LAST TWENTY MINUTES.
I DID.

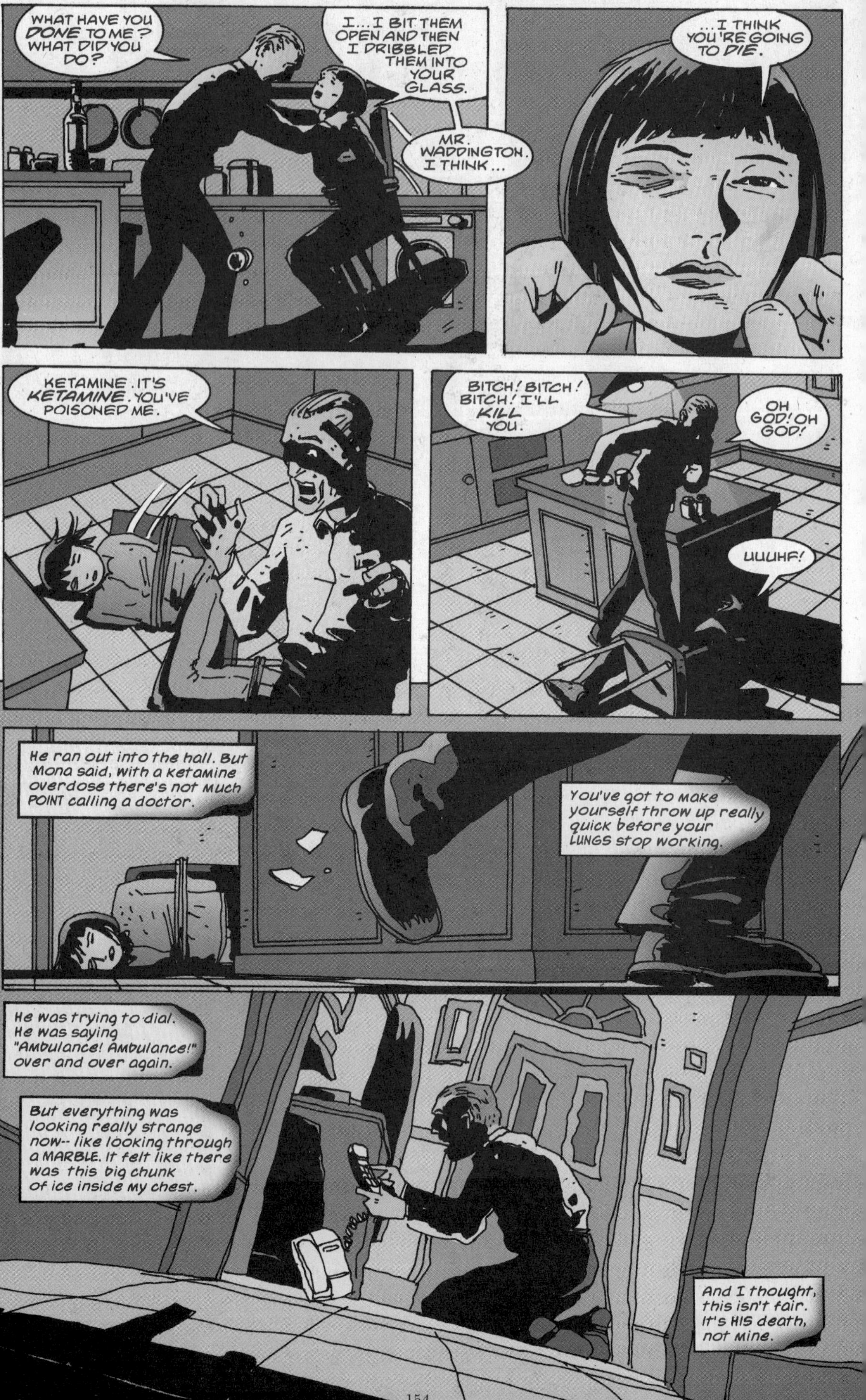

WHAT HAVE YOU DONE TO ME? WHAT DID YOU DO?
I... I BIT THEM OPEN AND THEN I DRIBBLED THEM INTO YOUR GLASS.
MR. WADDINGTON. I THINK...
...I THINK YOU'RE GOING TO DIE.
KETAMINE. IT'S KETAMINE. YOU'VE POISONED ME.
BITCH! BITCH! BITCH! I'LL KILL YOU.
OH GOD! OH GOD!
UUUHF!
He ran out into the hall. But Mona said, with a ketamine overdose there's not much POINT calling a doctor.
You've got to make yourself throw up really quick before your LUNGS stop working.
He was trying to dial. He was saying "Ambulance! Ambulance!" over and over again.
But everything was looking really strange now-- like looking through a MARBLE. It felt like there was this big chunk of ice inside my chest.
And I thought, this isn't fair. It's HIS death, not mine.

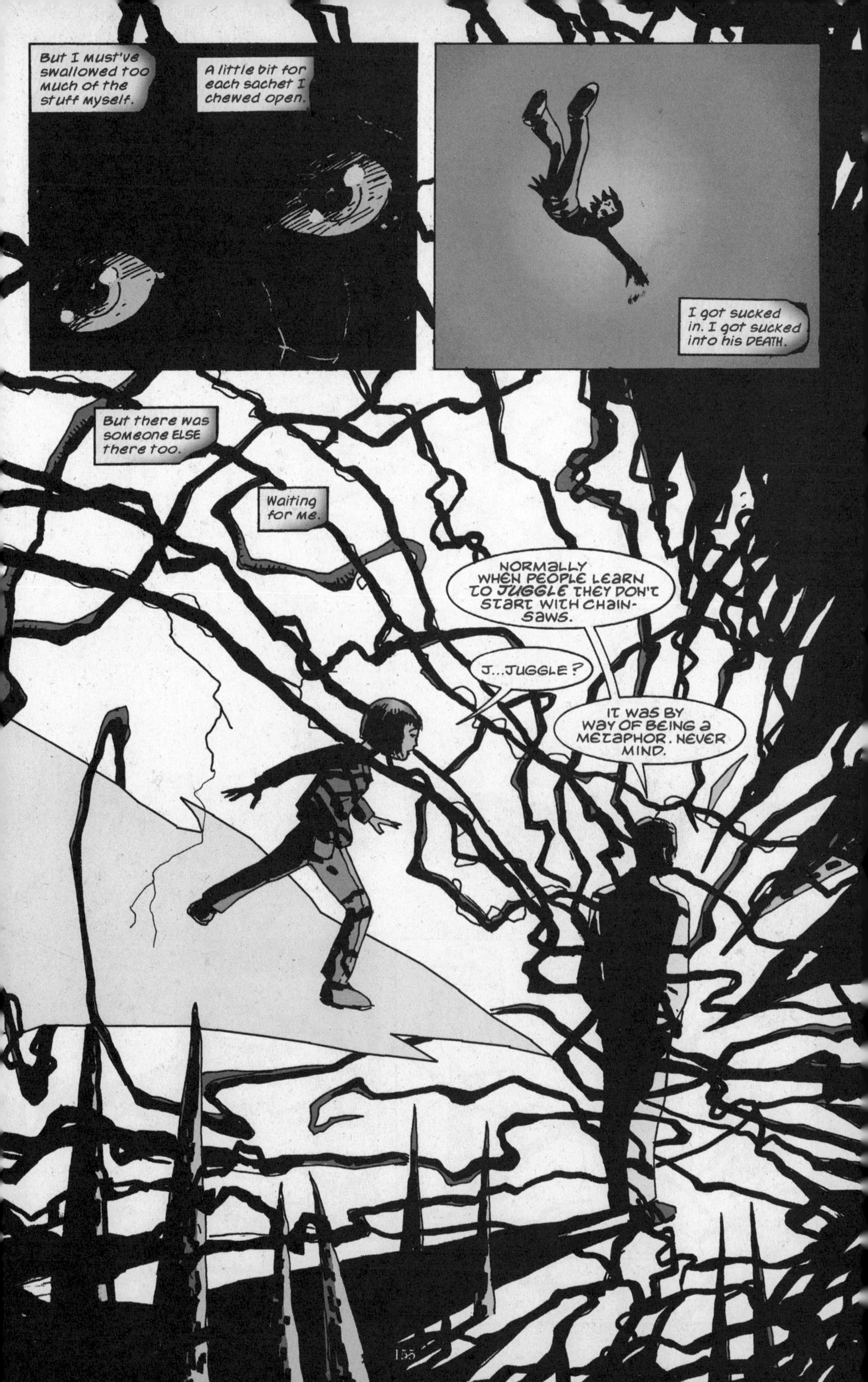
But I must've swallowed too much of the stuff myself.
A little bit for each sachet I chewed open.
I got sucked in. I got sucked into his DEATH.
But there was someone ELSE there too.
Waiting for me.
NORMALLY WHEN PEOPLE LEARN TO JUGGLE THEY DON'T START WITH CHAIN-SAWS.
J...JUGGLE?
IT WAS BY WAY OF BEING A METAPHOR. NEVER MIND.

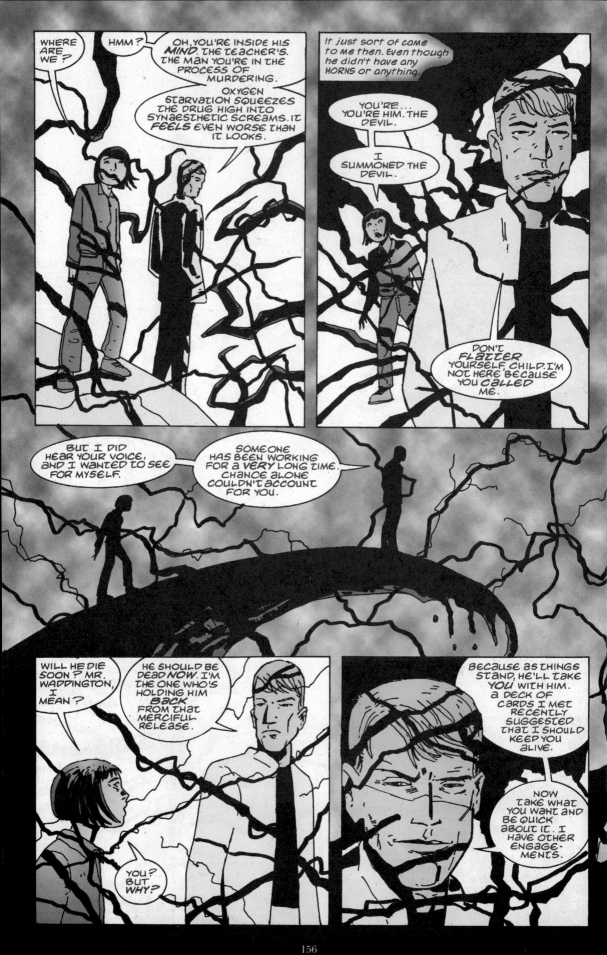

WHERE ARE WE?

HMM?

OH, YOU'RE INSIDE HIS *MIND*. THE TEACHER'S. THE MAN YOU'RE IN THE PROCESS OF MURDERING.

OXYGEN STARVATION SQUEEZES THE DRUG HIGH INTO SYNAESTHETIC SCREAMS. IT *FEELS* EVEN WORSE THAN IT LOOKS.

It just sort of came to me then. Even though he didn't have any HORNS or anything.

YOU'RE... YOU'RE *HIM*. THE DEVIL.

I SUMMONED THE DEVIL.

DON'T *FLATTER* YOURSELF, CHILD. I'M NOT HERE BECAUSE YOU *CALLED* ME.

BUT I DID HEAR YOUR VOICE, AND I WANTED TO SEE FOR MYSELF.

SOMEONE HAS BEEN WORKING FOR A *VERY* LONG TIME. CHANCE ALONE COULDN'T ACCOUNT FOR YOU.

WILL HE DIE SOON? MR. WADDINGTON, I MEAN?

HE SHOULD BE DEAD *NOW*. I'M THE ONE WHO'S HOLDING HIM *BACK* FROM THAT MERCIFUL RELEASE.

BECAUSE AS THINGS STAND, HE'LL TAKE *YOU* WITH HIM. A DECK OF CARDS I MET RECENTLY SUGGESTED THAT I SHOULD KEEP YOU ALIVE.

NOW TAKE WHAT YOU WANT AND BE QUICK ABOUT IT. I HAVE OTHER ENGAGEMENTS.

YOU? BUT *WHY*?

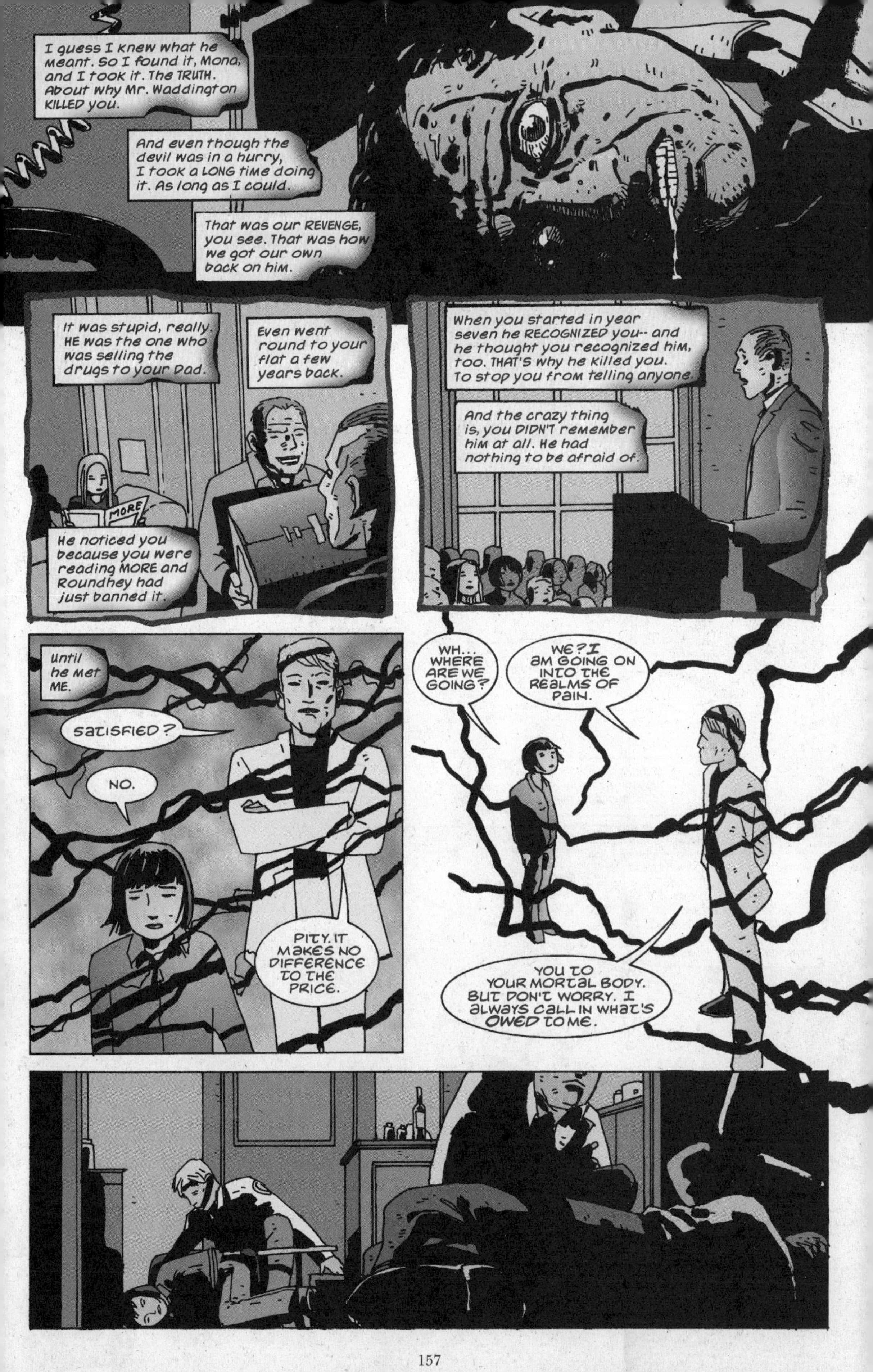
I guess I knew what he meant. So I found it, Mona, and I took it. The TRUTH. About why Mr. Waddington KILLED you.
And even though the devil was in a hurry, I took a LONG time doing it. As long as I could.
That was our REVENGE, you see. That was how we got our own back on him.
It was stupid, really. HE was the one who was selling the drugs to your Dad.
Even went round to your flat a few years back.
MORE
He noticed you because you were reading MORE and Roundhey had just banned it.
When you started in year seven he RECOGNIZED you-- and he thought you recognized him, too. THAT'S why he killed you. To stop you from telling anyone.
And the crazy thing is, you DIDN'T remember him at all. He had nothing to be afraid of.
Until he met ME.
SATISFIED?
NO.
PITY. IT MAKES NO DIFFERENCE TO THE PRICE.
WH... WHERE ARE WE GOING?
WE? I AM GOING ON INTO THE REALMS OF PAIN.
YOU TO YOUR MORTAL BODY. BUT DON'T WORRY. I ALWAYS CALL IN WHAT'S OWED TO ME.

THE LUCIFER LIBRARY

Lucifer
Devil in the Gateway
BOOK ONE: DEVIL IN THE GATEWAY

Lucifer
Children and Monsters
Mike Carey
Peter Gross
Ryan Kelly
Dean Ormston
BOOK TWO: CHILDREN AND MONSTERS

Lucifer
A Dalliance with the Damned
Mike Carey
Peter Gross
Ryan Kelly
Dean Ormston
BOOK THREE: A DALLIANCE WITH THE DAMNED

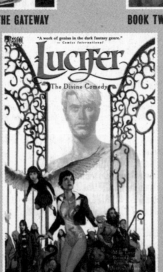

"A work of genius in the dark fantasy genre."
— Comics International
Lucifer
The Divine Comedy
BOOK FOUR: THE DIVINE COMEDY

"Not merely a good comic, but one of the best." — The Fourth Rail
Lucifer
Inferno
Mike Carey
Peter Gross
Ryan Kelly
Dean Ormston
Craig Hamilton
BOOK FIVE: INFERNO

OTHER TITLES FROM THE WORLD OF THE SANDMAN:

THE SANDMAN LIBRARY
Neil Gaiman/various
One of the most acclaimed and celebrated comics titles ever published — a rich blend of modern myth and dark fantasy in which contemporary fiction, historical drama, and legend are seamlessly interwoven.

Volume 1: PRELUDES & NOCTURNES
Volume 2: THE DOLL'S HOUSE
Volume 3: DREAM COUNTRY
Volume 4: SEASON OF MISTS
Volume 5: A GAME OF YOU
Volume 6: FABLES & REFLECTIONS
Volume 7: BRIEF LIVES
Volume 8: WORLDS' END
Volume 9: THE KINDLY ONES
Volume 10: THE WAKE
Volume 11: ENDLESS NIGHTS

DEATH: THE HIGH COST OF LIVING
Neil Gaiman/Chris Bachalo/Mark Buckingham
One day every century, Death assumes mortal form to learn more about the lives she must take.

DEATH: THE TIME OF YOUR LIFE
Neil Gaiman/Chris Bachalo/Mark Buckingham/ Mark Pennington
A young lesbian mother strikes a deal with Death for the life of her son in a story about fame, relationships, and rock and roll.

DEATH: AT DEATH'S DOOR
Jill Thompson
Part fanciful manga retelling of the acclaimed THE SANDMAN: SEASON OF MISTS, part original story of the party from Hell.

DESTINY: A CHRONICLE OF DEATHS FORETOLD
Alisa Kwitney/various

THE LITTLE ENDLESS STORYBOOK
Jill Thompson

THE SANDMAN: THE DREAM HUNTERS
Neil Gaiman/Yoshitaka Amano

THE SANDMAN: DUST COVERS — THE COLLECTED SANDMAN COVERS
Neil Gaiman/Dave McKean

THE SANDMAN PRESENTS: THE FURIES
Mike Carey/John Bolton

THE SANDMAN PRESENTS: TALLER TALES
Bill Willingham/various

THE SANDMAN COMPANION
Hy Bender

THE QUOTABLE SANDMAN
Neil Gaiman/various

OTHER GREAT COLLECTIONS FROM VERTIGO

ALL TITLES ARE SUGGESTED FOR MATURE READERS

100 BULLETS
Brian Azzarello/Eduardo Risso
With one special briefcase, Agent Graves gives you the chance to kill without retribution. But what's the real price for this chance — and who's setting it?
Volume 1: FIRST SHOT, LAST CALL
Volume 2: SPLIT SECOND CHANCE
Volume 3: HANG UP ON THE HANG LOW
Volume 4: A FOREGONE TOMORROW
Volume 5: THE COUNTERFIFTH DETECTIVE
Volume 6: SIX FEET UNDER THE GUN

ANIMAL MAN
Grant Morrison/Chas Truog/ Doug Hazlewood/various
A minor super-hero's consciousness is raised higher and higher until he becomes aware of his own fictitious nature in this revolutionary and existential series.
Volume 1: ANIMAL MAN
Volume 2: ORIGIN OF THE SPECIES
Volume 3: DEUS EX MACHINA

THE BOOKS OF MAGIC
Neil Gaiman/various
A quartet of fallen mystics introduce the world of magic to young Tim Hunter, who is destined to become the world's most powerful magician.

THE BOOKS OF MAGIC
John Ney Rieber/Peter Gross/various
The continuing trials and adventures of Tim Hunter, whose magical talents bring extra trouble and confusion to his adolescence.
Volume 1: BINDINGS
Volume 2: SUMMONINGS
Volume 3: RECKONINGS
Volume 4: TRANSFORMATIONS
Volume 5: GIRL IN THE BOX
Volume 6: THE BURNING GIRL
Volume 7: DEATH AFTER DEATH

FABLES
Bill Willingham/Lan Medina/ Mark Buckingham/Steve Leialoha
The immortal characters of popular fairy tales have been driven from their homelands, and now live hidden among us, trying to cope with life in 21st-century Manhattan.
Volume 1: LEGENDS IN EXILE
Volume 2: ANIMAL FARM
Volume 3: STORYBOOK LOVE

HELLBLAZER
Jamie Delano/Garth Ennis/Warren Ellis/ Brian Azzarello/Steve Dillon/ Marcelo Frusin/various
Where horror, dark magic and bad luck meet, John Constantine is never far away.
Volume 1: ORIGINAL SINS
Volume 2: DANGEROUS HABITS
Volume 3: FEAR AND LOATHING
Volume 4: TAINTED LOVE
Volume 5: DAMNATION'S FLAME
Volume 6: RAKE AT THE GATES OF HELL
Volume 7: HAUNTED
Volume 8: HARD TIME
Volume 9: GOOD INTENTIONS
Volume 10: FREEZES OVER

THE INVISIBLES
Grant Morrison/various
The saga of a terrifying conspiracy and the resistance movement combating it — a secret underground of ultra-cool guerrilla cells trained in ontological and physical anarchy.
Volume 1: SAY YOU WANT A REVOLUTION
Volume 2: APOCALIPSTICK
Volume 3: ENTROPY IN THE U.K.
Volume 4: BLOODY HELL IN AMERICA
Volume 5: COUNTING TO NONE
Volume 6: KISSING MR. QUIMPER
Volume 7: THE INVISIBLE KINGDOM

PREACHER
Garth Ennis/Steve Dillon/various
A modern American epic of life, death, God, love, and redemption — filled with sex, booze and blood.
Volume 1: GONE TO TEXAS
Volume 2: UNTIL THE END OF THE WORLD
Volume 3: PROUD AMERICANS
Volume 4: ANCIENT HISTORY
Volume 5: DIXIE FRIED
Volume 6: WAR IN THE SUN
Volume 7: SALVATION
Volume 8: ALL HELL'S A-COMING
Volume 9: ALAMO

SWAMP THING: DARK GENESIS
Len Wein/Berni Wrightson
A gothic nightmare is brought to life with this horrifying yet poignant story of a man transformed into a monster.

SWAMP THING
Alan Moore/Stephen Bissette/ John Totleben/Rick Veitch/various
The writer and the series that revolutionized comics — a masterpiece of lyrical fantasy.
Volume 1: SAGA OF THE SWAMP THING
Volume 2: LOVE & DEATH
Volume 3: THE CURSE
Volume 4: A MURDER OF CROWS
Volume 5: EARTH TO EARTH
Volume 6: REUNION

TRANSMETROPOLITAN
Warren Ellis/Darick Robertson/various
An exuberant trip into a frenetic future, where outlaw journalist Spider Jerusalem battles hypocrisy, corruption, and sobriety.
Volume 1: BACK ON THE STREET
Volume 2: LUST FOR LIFE
Volume 3: YEAR OF THE BASTARD
Volume 4: THE NEW SCUM
Volume 5: LONELY CITY
Volume 6: GOUGE AWAY
Volume 7: SPIDER'S THRASH
Volume 8: DIRGE
Volume 9: THE CURE

Y: THE LAST MAN
Brian K. Vaughan/Pia Guerra/José Marzán, Jr.
An unexplained plague kills every male mammal on Earth — all except Yorick Brown and his pet monkey. Will he survive this new, emasculated world to discover what killed his fellow men?
Volume 1: UNMANNED
Volume 2: CYCLES
Volume 3: ONE SMALL STEP

BARNUM!
Howard Chaykin/David Tischman/ Niko Henrichon

BLACK ORCHID
Neil Gaiman/Dave McKean

COWBOY WALLY
Kyle Baker

GODDESS
Garth Ennis/Phil Winslade

HEAVY LIQUID
Paul Pope

HUMAN TARGET
Peter Milligan/Edvin Biukovic

HUMAN TARGET: FINAL CUT
Peter Milligan/Javier Pulido

I DIE AT MIDNIGHT
Kyle Baker

IN THE SHADOW OF EDGAR ALLAN POE
Jonathon Scott Fuqua/ Stephen John Phillips/Steven Parke

JONNY DOUBLE
Brian Azzarello/Eduardo Risso

KING DAVID
Kyle Baker

MR. PUNCH
Neil Gaiman/Dave McKean

THE MYSTERY PLAY
Grant Morrison/Jon J Muth

THE NAMES OF MAGIC
Dylan Horrocks/Richard Case

NEIL GAIMAN & CHARLES VESS' STARDUST
Neil Gaiman/Charles Vess

NEIL GAIMAN'S MIDNIGHT DAYS
Neil Gaiman/Matt Wagner/various

ORBITER
Warren Ellis/Colleen Doran

PREACHER: DEAD OR ALIVE (THE COLLECTED COVERS)
Glenn Fabry

PROPOSITION PLAYER
Bill Willingham/Paul Guinan/ Ron Randall

SHADE, THE CHANGING MAN: THE AMERICAN SCREAM
Peter Milligan/Chris Bachalo

TRUE FAITH
Garth Ennis/Warren Pleece

UNCLE SAM
Steve Darnall/Alex Ross

UNDERCOVER GENIE
Kyle Baker

UNKNOWN SOLDIER
Garth Ennis/Kilian Plunkett

V FOR VENDETTA
Alan Moore/David Lloyd

VEILS
Pat McGreal/Stephen John Phillips/José Villarrubia

WHY I HATE SATURN
Kyle Baker

THE WITCHING HOUR
Jeph Loeb/Chris Bachalo/ Art Thibert

YOU ARE HERE
Kyle Baker

VISIT US AT WWW.VERTIGOCOMICS.COM FOR MORE INFORMATION ON THESE AND MANY OTHER TITLES FROM VERTIGO AND DC COMICS.
CALL 1-888-COMIC BOOK FOR THE COMICS SHOP NEAREST YOU, OR GO TO YOUR LOCAL BOOK STORE.